THE

MAKING

OF

Social Psychology

D1319331

THE
MAKING
OF
Social Psychology

Discussions with Creative Contributors

By Richard I. Evans

Gardner Press Inc., New York
Distributed by the Halsted Press
Division of John Wiley & Sons, Inc.
New York ● London ● Sydney ● Toronto

Library of Congress Cataloging in Publication Data
Main entry under title:

The Making of Social Psychology.

   Includes bibliographical references.
   1. Social psychology—United States. 2. Psychologists—United States
—Interviews. I. Evans, Richard Isadore, 1922-
HM251.M2816   301.1   79-16034
ISBN 0-470-26811-5
ISBN 0-470-26812-3 pbk.

First Edition
Copyright © 1980 by Richard I. Evans
All rights reserved

No part of this book may be reproduced
in any form or by any means, electronic or mechanical,
including photocopying,
without permission in writing from the author and the publisher.
All inquiries should be addressed to
Gardner Press, Inc., 19 Union Square West, New York, N.Y. 10003.
Published in the United States by Gardner Press, Inc., New York.

Grateful acknowledgement is made to the following
for permission to reprint previously copyrighted material:

Discussions with Gordon Allport, David McClelland, Milton Rokeach,
Stanley Schachter, Albert Bandura, Stanley Milgram, and Philip Zimbardo
published previously in *The Making of Psychology,* by Richard I. Evans, Ph.D.
Copyright © 1976 by Alfred A. Knopf, Inc., New York.
Reprinted with permission of the contributors and Alfred A. Knopf, Inc.

*To my lovely wife, Zena,
and children and theirs*

CONTENTS

PREFACE

For the help received during the long process of planning and completing the discussions presented in this volume, I am indebted to a great many individuals. Though space prohibits mentioning everyone who so kindly assisted me in this venture, I wish to express my appreciation to at least some of these persons.

I am grateful for the support of the National Science Foundation, without which this project could not have been implemented.

Thanks also to Bettye Earle Raines, Ann Rushing, Kathy Boynton, Larry Hanselka, and Carlla Stewart who assisted me with this volume.

Special thanks go to Gary Walls, who made valuable contributions in every phase of this book, providing extensive editorial assistance, checking relevant bibliographical sources, and collating the final manuscript.

For permission to utilize sections of previously published discussions, thanks are accorded Alfred A. Knopf, Inc. and E. P. Dutton and Company, Inc.

The willingness of Theodore M. Newcomb to prepare a Foreword to this volume is particularly appreciated. Finally, the wonderful cooperation of the various participants cannot be emphasized enough. They were not only willing to participate in the taping sessions involved in this project but were willing to make a number of excellent suggestions in their reactions to the final form of the manuscript, which reflect my discussions with them.

Richard I. Evans

FOREWORD
By Theodore M. Newcomb[1]

Nineteen creative social psychologists between two covers! All spent most of their professional lives in America. Eighteen men and one woman, whose years of birth range from 1895 to 1938. They are a divergent lot, viewed from within the population of psychologically trained social psychologists.

Insofar as the discussions published in this book seem to be varied, I suspect that is exactly what Dr. Evans, the interviewer, intended. He has a knack for drawing out his interviewees, and pursuing those special and varying interests that are dear to the hearts of the nineteen subjects he chose for this initial volume.

A full half of the persons interviewed were born in 1918 or before. This is hardly surprising in a book titled *The Making of Social Psychology*. The primeval "makers" were of course born long before 1895, the earliest birth-year of those who were interviewed. The earlier makers— e.g., James, McDougall, Ross, G. H. Mead, F. H. Allport (some of whom were sociologists)—could not, of course, be interviewed. Perhaps, therefore, the title of this collection might well have been followed by some such phrase as "Second Stage".

Since I am more or less well acquainted with all of the nineteen interviewees, both personally and through their publications, I jotted down my own notions of their important contributions *before* reading the interviews. Not surprisingly, I identified each of them with a single, social-psychological problem, or perhaps two or three. In most cases I had un-

[1]Theodore Newcomb (born in 1903) is a major figure in the development of social psychology, as an influential researcher, integrator of the field, and trainer of social psychologists. Presently he is a Professor Emeritus at the University of Michigan. A 1929 Ph. D. from Columbia University, he has held many distinguished academic positions. He has received significant recognition, including, in 1976, being the recipient of the American Psychological Association's Distinguished Scientific Contribution Award, having been elected as their president in 1955–56 and, since 1974, to membership in the National Academy of Sciences.

derestimated their ranges of interest. Perhaps other readers will also be surprised.

I note an interesting difference between the three oldest interviewees, two now deceased, and the three youngest ones. Heider, Murphy and Allport tend to deal with broad psychological principles, whereas the youngest three (Milgram, Zimbardo, Darley) are more concerned with experiments in "natural" settings, and with institutions and society at large. Murphy and Allport were, of course, deeply involved in public issues (both were active in the Society for Psychological Study of Social Issues), but this concern tended to be, for them, more a matter of good citizenship than of research. At any rate, this is what emerges from a perusal of their lists of their own publications. While it would be folly to generalize from these few cases, I suspect that this "generation gap" (an approximately forty-year difference in age) does represent a generational change on the part of social psychologists. Another age difference is that none of the thirteen interviewees born after 1914 refers to Freud. Three of the six born in 1914 or before do refer to him.

For those who have been concerned about "the crisis in social psychology," it may be significant that only Janis has directly referred to it. (How many species and subspecies of this crisis are there?) His brief treatment of the subject seems to me wise and convincing.

Finally, my congratulations to the interviewer-editor-author Richard Evans for providing a segment of oral history of special interest to social psychologists, particularly those trained in psychology, and to students in social psychology classes.

INTRODUCTION
A Perspective on the
Discussion Style and Content

This book is the twelfth in a series based on discussions with outstanding contributors to the field of psychology, and the second to include discussions with a number of contributors. While the first collection represented a diverse range of areas in psychology, the present volume focuses specifically on the area of social psychology. To assist in understanding the goals of the discussion style used here, as well as its content, some perspective may be of value. This series was launched in 1957 with completion of the recorded conversations with the late Carl Jung and the late Ernest Jones (Evans 1964, 1976), supported by a grant from the Fund for the Advancement of Education. Continued support for the series has been provided under a grant from the National Science Foundation. The basic purpose of the project is to produce, for teaching purposes, a series of films and books that introduce the student to significant contributors in the field of psychology. It is hoped that these films and books may also serve as documents of increasing value in the history of the behavioral sciences.*

The interviews presented in this book are designed to introduce the reader to the contributors' major ideas and points of view, hopefully conveying through extemporaneous discussion a feeling of the personality of each contributor. The contributors included in this volume were selected to represent some of the major areas in social psychology. However, no effort was made to provide a complete coverage of the field. Many of the individuals included here have produced significant ideas in more than one area of psychology. One of the characteristics of creative contributors may be that their work cannot be easily pigeonholed into any one field in psychology.

The sample of contributors included in this volume, although not exhaustive, is at least representative. In looking over the field, it is obvious that there are many other contributors who might just as easily have

*The films are distributed by Macmillan Films, Inc., 34 MacQuesten Parkway South, Mt. Vernon, New York 10550.

been included here. And, in fact, they may be included in a second volume.

When I completed the first book in the series based on discussions with Jung and Jones (Evans 1964) I thought the word "conversation" best described the process and content of the material. I soon learned that this implied to some potential readers something a bit more casual and superficial than we had intended. Even though I emphasize spontaneity in the discussions with our participants, this should not detract from the significance of the content. A relatively informal discussion with an outstanding contributor to a discipline, as he or she seriously examines his or her own work, should not be less significant by virtue of its informality. A more detailed description of the philosophy and techniques of this project is reported elsewhere (Evans 1969c).

A few additional points bearing on the contents of this particular volume should be made. The questions I use are intended to generate discussion of the ideas found in many of the published writings of the interviewees, but it is not expected that a comprehensive summary of their work could be evoked. For one thing, the selectivity necessary in completing the discussion within a limited time interval made such an inclusive summary impossible. But I hope that I have produced material that offers a pleasant alternative to those students today who have become increasingly dependent upon and satisfied with only secondary sources to learn about the major contributors to psychology. The content developed through these discussions provides "original source" exposure to the ideas of creative psychologists, which in turn may ecourage the reader to go back to the original writings that develop these ideas more fully. I would hope that such original statements by significant contributors would be more stimulating to the student than many of the books of "readings" appear to be.

It might be in order to explain my role in these discussions. As codiscussant or interviewer, I saw my role as that of a medium through which the interviewees could express their views. Extensive critical examination of the views of the participants must be left to another type of project. In a limited space it would be impossible both to introduce the contributors' views and to criticize them as well. Also, I expect that some people who worked with us on this project would not have done so if they had sensed primarily a critical attack on their work.

It should also be pointed out that in their writings, these individuals can rewrite and polish until they deem the product satisfactory. In the spontaneity of our discussions, they are often called upon to develop ideas extemporaneously. As mentioned earlier, I hope that this element of spontaneity presents a feel for the "men and women behind the ideas" as well as the ideas themselves. Because preservation of this naturalness of communication is essential, few liberties have been taken with the basic content of the responses to my questions, although some editorial license by both our interviewees and myself was exercised in the interest of readability and clarity. So the discussions presented here duplicate, insofar as possible, the tenor of the exchange between the interviewees and myself.

Let me outline the overall format of the questions that I posed in the discussions. In almost all the discussions, I attempted to evoke a statement of the most important work of the participant, and also to elicit information on the research leading to this work. The interviewees were also provided an opportunity to react to some criticism.

Although many of these discussions were completed in the past year, some were extracted from earlier books or transcriptions of films, and they were not updated. References are made to the published dates of the books or films from which such discussions were extracted.

It has been exciting for me, as a social psychologist, to have had an opportunity to interview such a unique sample of creative colleagues. Even in those instances when the persons were previously known to me only through their published works, their genuine interest in communicating their work to students in this less didactic manner, and their willingness to trust me in mediating this process, is greatly appreciated.

REFERENCES

Evans, R. I. 1964. *Conversations with Carl Jung and reactions from Ernest Jones.* New York: Van Nostrand.

1966. *Dialogue with Erich Fromm.* New York: Harper.

1968. *B. F. Skinner: The man and his ideas.* New York: Dutton.

1969a. *Dialogue with Erik Erikson.* New York: Dutton.

1969b. *Psychology and Arthur Miller.* New York: Dutton.

1969c. Contributions to the history of psychology: Ten filmed dialogues with notable contributors to psychology. *Psychol. Reports* 25: 159–164.

1971. *Gordon Allport: The man and his ideas.* New York: Dutton.

1973. *Jean Piaget: The man and his ideas.* New York: Dutton.

1975a. *Carl Rogers: The man and his ideas.* New York: Dutton.

1975b. *Konrad Lorenz: The man and his ideas.* New York: Harcourt.

1976a. *R. D. Laing: The man and his ideas.* New York: Dutton.

1976b. *Jung on elementary psychology.* New York: Dutton.

1976c. *The making of psychology.* New York: Alfred A. Knopf.

1

GARDNER MURPHY
(1895–1979)

Gardner Murphy has influenced the careers of several generations
of social and personality psychologists through his publications
and inspired teaching. He did his undergraduate work at Yale,
and pursued graduate studies at Harvard and at Columbia,
where he received his doctorate in 1923. He taught at Columbia
from 1920 until 1940, then moved to the City College of New
York, where he remained until 1952. From 1952 until 1967 he
was the director of research at the Menninger Foundation, and in
1967 he accepted a faculty position at George Washington
University. The range of his interests was apparently boundless,
including social psychology, personality psychology, perception, learning, attitude measurement, and parapsychology. His
book Experimental Social Psychology, first published in 1931,
was a comprehensive pioneer effort to take social psychology
out of the armchair and put it on an empirical, scientific basis.
His commitment to solving important social problems is
reflected in his work for UNESCO during which he studied the
tensions between Muslims and Hindus in India. Dr. Murphy was
one of the founders of the Society for the Psychological Study
of Social Issues. He was elected president of the American
Psychological Association in 1944, and received the American
Psychological Association's Gold Medal Award in 1972, in
recognition of a distinguished and long–continued record of
scientific and scholarly achievement. With the recent death of
Gardner Murphy, we lost perhaps one of the most sophisticated
and intellectually profound contributors to not only the making
of social psychology but to the social and behavioral sciences in
general.

Eclecticism/ Motivation/ Socio-Cultural Reciprocities/ Biocentric Theo-
    ry/Homeostatic Model/Personality: A Biosocial Approach//The
    Operant Concept/ Ego and Self/ Determinism/Sigmund Freud/
    Three types of Human Nature// Creativity/ Cosmic Roots/ Ex-

1

trasensory Perception/ Clairvoyance/ Mental Telepathy// Cross-Cultural Research/ UNESCO Project in India// The Units of Observation/ Perfect Research// Progressive Education/ Discipline// Personality/ Understanding the Individual// The Variety of Methods in a Young Science//

Dr. Murphy and I begin by discussing critics who contend that eclecticism is synonymous with loose and inconsistent ideas, and he offers two separate meanings of eclecticism, the uncritical acceptance of "a patchwork of ideas which have no basic relation to each other." We discuss motivation, and Dr. Murphy urges a socio-cultural approach to motivation which examines the nature of the reciprocal relationship between the external environment and the individual. Criticizing traditional homeostatic conceptions of motivation, he states, "I think homeostasis is useful as a step in the understanding of scientific history, but as a formal principle to teach students, it is very misleading." In discussing Freud, Dr. Murphy cites two of his enduring contributions to psychology: the concept of unconscious dynamics, and the "ego psychology" of Freud's later years. He describes the cross-cultural research he did in India, studying the tensions between Muslims and Hindus. Dr. Murphy then defines his three types of human nature, and relates them to his ideas on creativity. We examine his interest in extrasensory phenomena, and he asserts that this is an issue with which a mature psychology will have to come to terms. Dr. Murphy discusses some popular misinterpretations of the psychological theories of Dewey and Freud which are used to support arguments for permissive education. Commenting upon the use of discipline in education, he states, "The issue is whether the discipline is one which is arbitrarily imposed, or whether it meets the child's needs at a particular time." He discusses the role of the personality concept in psychology, and states, "I think we need a word to describe the integrated totality in which one person differs from another." As we close, Dr. Murphy urges greater attention to clarifying and defining psychological concepts.

Evans: Dr. Murphy, as we look over your particular approach to personality, it would appear to be one that was integrative or eclectic. I think some philosophers have argued that the eclectic position is loose and inconsistent, and I was wondering if you will accept this description of your particular approach to personality, and secondly, if so, how we can justify eclecticism.

Murphy: I think that the term "eclectic" is used in two very different senses. One has to do with the method which has to be pursued. The other has to do with the concepts which have to be fitted into a meaningful whole. You might perhaps use the analogy from physics. A scientist who is studying magnetic fields should use different methods than another person who is interested in measuring decibel level. The integrity of physics does not depend in any way upon the uniformity of method except with regard to some very general principles.

Evans: In other words, an eclectic could use different methods and not necessarily be consistent as you see it.

Murphy: Yes, I think the most highly unified conceptual systems use very diverse procedures. The experimental, clinical, and social psychologists are frequently working, as the physicist would be, by different methods, but attempting to achieve a well-structured, integrated conceptual scheme. I would reject eclecticism in the sense of the patchwork of ideas which have no basic relation to each other, but I would firmly support great tolerance and openness regarding the admissibility of many methods for modern psychology.

Evans: As we look at some of the classical areas in personality and psychology in general, one area that we look at is motivation. Are there any particular observations that might be helpful in understanding motivation?

Murphy: I feel very strongly that motivation is a relational concept in which the environment and the person require equal attention. I think it has been a great mistake to say that these things are inside the skin and to look for loci. It doesn't even help very much if you recognize that the central nervous system is just as important as the viscera. We have come a long way from considering motive spots and visceral tensions as the basis of motivation. I think that we have forgotten that in the evolutionary system, life arose in reciprocity with a particular ecology. Man has invented, over the years, an extraordinarily complicated external supporting environment. A socio-cultural analysis requires that we look constantly for reciprocities. You can't find a relation between one thing; you must have a relation between two things that are acting (or more than two). So, I don't think that the quest for motives inside the skin of the individual has been very helpful.

Evans: In a sense you are addressing yourself to what we sometimes call the biocentric theory that many of our introductory textbooks seem to emphasize. According to that view, you have a number of primary motives that are unlearned, and then with learning, these primary drives are modified into secondary and social drives. What you are saying is that this orientation fails to recognize what Murray (1938) calls the press, or the social influence on motivation.

Murphy: Murray's idea was very much in the right direction. Of course, that was some years ago, and I think that somewhat more sophis-

ticated ideas have developed regarding the structure of the environmental situation. It's a lure and an invitation as much as it's press.

Evans: Much of our motivation theory, certainly in Freud's system
and in behavioristic drive reduction, is what has been called a homeostatic model. This is the model that we borrowed from physiology, the
idea that all motivation is a process of reducing tension in the direction of
balance. Some have argued that the homeostatic model needs some
investigation, that it doesn't seem to be a certainty that we can look at
motivation in this sense. How do you feel about this?

Murphy: Well, I think the concept is badly dated. I think that as the
organism becomes more complex, more is borrowed from future relationships and anticipated events. I think that for every return to the homeostatic state there has to be a big departure from it. And which is more
real? Is it more real to come back or to go out?

Evans: You are saying that we could hypothesize that the organism is
seeking tension rather than reducing it.

Murphy: Yes, it's got to be moving away from the homeostatic state
just as much as coming back to it. One often accumulates great tension at
a higher purposive level as well as at an unconscious level. I think
homeostasis is useful as a step in the understanding of scientific history,
but as a formal principle to teach students it is very misleading.

Evans: One of the things that you emphasize throughout your
writings, and especially in your book, *Personality: A Biosocial Approach* (1947), is the interaction of biological and social factors in personality. What exactly do you mean by a biosocial approach?

Murphy: With the development of the social sciences, and the impact
of cultural anthropology, there has been a tendency to divide attributes
into biological attributes and social attributes. One often hears of the
original biological tendencies and then the superimposed social tendency. I don't believe anything like that happens at all. I think that the
biological phenomena undergo a certain amount of molding in particular
directions, but I don't think you tack on new attributes the way you put
postage stamps on an envelope. It would be more nearly correct to say
that the reciprocity of one organism responding to another, or to a pattern of organismic responses, remains both biological and social.

Evans: I know from your work you seem to be willing to see the value
of conditioning theory and social learning theory. How does conditioning enter into developing the personality?

Murphy: We are beginning to understand the enormous importance
of the operant concept. I think that whatever anyone may think about
Thorndike's (1931) or particularly Skinner's (1953) overall theories, the
principles of shaping and of schedules of reinforcement are absolutely
imperative to any systematic personality theory. I think a great deal that
in the earlier years was stated rather mechanically in terms of association
we now see as the expression of functional necessities, motives. Even if
Skinner doesn't use those terms, I think it is quite plain that a purposive

psychology in the classical sense is being realized as we understand more fully the nature of these operants.

Evans: It might be interesting to have you address the problem of ego and self as a means of looking at the conscious, rational, organizational side of the personality. There have been a lot of different terms used. How do you think we can resolve this problem of language here?

Murphy: Well, I would suggest following an article of Isador Chein (1944), in which the term "ego" relates to the dynamic processes organized around one's own individuality. Awareness of one's own body would be one of the things involved, but there is a great deal of unconscious adjustment, as in protecting one's self from falling, or self-enhancement of many sorts. I would use the term "self" to describe the perceptual response to one's own individuality. I would put it in the perception-cognition aspect of life. We get into some difficulty because in everyday life these terms are used in several senses.

Evans: Related to this issue of self and ego has been a problem of autonomy of the self and ego. The question of self-determinism goes back to the old philosophical free will–determinism problem, but today personality theorists seem to be reexamining the problem of self-determinism. How meaningfully can we deal with this so-called free will–determinism problem?

Murphy: Well, I like the phrase "self-determinism" as contrasted with "hard determinism" as used by William James (1890/1950). There is just as much determinism in being the cause of your own behavior as in being acted on by other forces. I think what typically happens is that the individual realizes himself through doing what he really wants, in terms of the most comprehensive value system he can define. I think the word "freedom" has been awfully misleading here. What would it mean to be free of one's own wants? Some people speak as if this kind of uncaused behavior (what James called "arbitrary spontaneity") has some sort of intrinsic value. Not all determinism is external; it is sometimes determinism by one's own nature.

Evans: How do you regard Freud in the history of psychology? Would you consider him the outstanding genius, or perhaps something less than genius?

Murphy: I think from our perspective on history, he probably is the greatest figure that we have had in psychology. I've tried at times to work out comparisons of William James with Sigmund Freud. I love James very much, but James is often unperceptive regarding issues in which there is at least subtlety and profundity in Freud, particularly regarding unconscious dynamics. This doesn't mean that I think one should follow Freud. I think one should use Freud as a tool, as a guide in looking.

Evans: What specific contributions has Freud made which you think will endure?

Murphy: Well, I think the conception of unconscious dynamics

(Freud 1915/1949), the idea that a very large part goes on out of the area of which we are aware, will be enduring. And the ego psychology of Freud's last years (1961) was of enormous importance in outgrowing instinct theory.

Evans: It would be interesting to hear your thoughts on creativity. I know throughout your book *Human Potentialities* (1958), in which you talk about three types of human nature, you seem to be addressing yourself to this problem. How do your ideas on human nature bear on the idea of creativity?

Murphy: Well, I think that the biology of human nature with all of its variations is a limiting condition. Creativity is highly limited by the cognitive-affective potential of the individual and of the human stock in general. The first human nature represents the positive assets and the inherent limitations in the human stuff. With the invention of culture and its almost infinite elaboration, we have created a transfigured human nature in which symbolic life plays an enormous part. This second human nature is the product of an over-arching system of socially real events which precondition and limit the biological. The extraordinary conservatism of most human societies is broken by individual or collective pressures coming from the interaction between the first and the second human natures, essentially defining a third kind of human nature which is the protest or creative kind of human nature.

Evans: Hasn't it been one of the most difficult problems for the personality theorists to construct a meaningful picture of creativity that would lend itself to research?

Murphy: I think there are two different difficulties. If you contrast what we do as psychologists with what Lowes (1927) did in his studies of Coleridge (which were enormously detailed, sensitive studies of twenty-five years of one man's life), you can see the shallowness of short-range studies compared to the tremendous power of a multi-dimensional study of an individual. I think the other difficulty is that we are, as a rule, rather afraid of being accused of being complicated or even mystical with regard to the physical resources that we use in creativity. I tried to bring out in *Human Potentialities* (1958) that the rhythms of heavenly bodies may be related to seasonal and diurnal events of living things. Man is much closer to his cosmic roots than he realizes. For instance, consider the extraordinary new use of rhythms Beethoven created in the Fifth Symphony. I think that respiratory, cardiac, sexual, and many other types of rhythms are directly related to artistic achievement, but we haven't been very sophisticated in looking for the many kinds of rhythms which I think go into most creative work. I think that art and creativity are pretty complex, and derive from many things not explained by the psychology that we have today.

Evans: One study looked at the early life history of creative people (e.g., Barron 1961) and found that they seem to be suffering from quite a bit of rejection, very much like most of our studies show that many schizophrenics had an early life history of rejection. Do you think these kinds of analyses that try to tie in early life histories with creative effort have validity? Could we say that a person who is creative had to rise above certain kinds of problems in early life?

Murphy: No, I think the individual factor is tremendous. We all think of cases like Lord Byron, whose early experiences with rejection certainly played an important part in his later creativity (see Mayne 1969); but on the other hand we can also think of young people who were born with silver spoons in their mouths who early achieved some recognition and went on to greater and greater honors. I don't think we can prove that being rejected is a cardinal feature in all creativity.

Evans: Another difficult area that you, among others in psychology, have tackled is described by Rhine's term "extrasensory perception" (Rhine 1934/1964). You have been among the forerunners studying this particular phenomenon. Perhaps we might start out by asking how you became interested in so-called extrasensory phenomena?

Murphy: Well, I grew interested when, at the age of sixteen, I read a book in my grandfather's library called *Psychical Research* (1911), by Sir William Barrett, and I was very responsive when Rhine's first publications appeared in the thirties.

Evans: In those days, did you feel some reservations on the part of many psychologists toward the fact that you were beginning this kind of thing?

Murphy: Oh, there was not only great reserve, but there was a fair amount of hostility; you just expect that as part of the game. We haven't achieved anything that is firmly replicable, but I have felt all along that there was massive evidence that this was an issue with which mature psychology would simply have to come to terms.

Evans: I think there is quite a bit of confusion about the terms used here. We have such terms as "clairvoyance" and "mental telepathy." How are these terms defined?

Murphy: Various definitions come from Frederick Meyers (1903/ 1961). Telepathy is defined in terms of intercommunication from one person to another or mind to mind. Clairvoyance is defined in terms of direct perception of an object or event, not necessarily entailing another person. If one accepts evidence for water-devining, one would say that's clairvoyance, but it does not involve telepathy. Now what Rhine did in his 1934 book (Rhine 1934/1964) was to bring the two concepts together and use the term "extrasensory perception" to describe both telepathy and clairvoyance. What he called general extrasensory perception in test situations allowed both functions. If you look, for example, at a card, under proper experimental controls a person at a distance can sometimes devine which card of a series you are looking at. He may be able to get this from your mind or he may directly see the card. It could be a clairvoyant process, and would not depend on telepathy, or vice versa. The term "extrasensory perception" as used today comprises telepathy, clairvoyance, and general extrasensory perception.

Evans: Moving to another phase of your career, you did some extremely interesting cross-cultural work when you traveled to India. Could you tell us a little bit about what brought you to India in the first place?

Murphy: Yes. My wife and I had already been interested in India. She had taught courses in comparative religion at Sarah Lawrence College, and I had read a good deal in this field and about the problems of modern India. When Otto Klineberg was with UNESCO, he learned about an invitation of the government of India to initiate a study of social tensions among the Indian people. As you know, the separation of India and Pakistan in 1947 had precipitated much violence, and although the government of India had things pretty well in hand in 1950, they very much wanted to understand what was going on. This was the first time that a nation had ever invited outsiders to come and study its own local difficulties. Lois, at the same time, was asked by another group in India to help start a child development institute. So we went together, each with a professional assignment, in August of 1950, and stayed for six months. We both reported our observations in the book that finally was brought out, called *In the Minds of Men* (1953).

Evans: How did you approach the task of doing research in India, where the social structure is very different from our own?

Murphy: We did not offer ourselves as experts on India, but we were able to find strong personnel—psychologists, sociologists, economists, and political scientists—at the Indian universities who were eager to work on this problem using their limited funds from UNESCO. We traveled around from one university to another. During the six months, we were helping in every way we could to introduce Western social science techniques. At the same time, we made such contact with village and urban life as would give us some perspective on the problems. We learned to work with the university people and see through their eyes, while helping them to be able to see through our eyes, but the job was mainly done by Indian social scientists.

Evans: What were some of the results of this study?

Murphy: The report is an attempt to communicate the results of our efforts to combine fairly exact instruments with very free observation. We isolated one source of social tensions in the communication systems of Muslims and Indians. We found that there was almost no interchange from one to the other at the level of mass communication. The Muslim group was reading a Muslim newspaper, getting no idea what the Hindu group was thinking, and vice versa. Each newspaper got credit with its own people by playing up its adversities and injustices. The people would read and discuss the content of the paper, and reinforce their own hostility to the other group. Of course in the U.S. we do the same thing, but to a less dramatic extent.

Evans: Your study in India has been regarded by some as a prototypical model of cross-cultural studies. What would you regard as the significant value of cross-cultural research in psychology?

Murphy: Well, it bears on the question of whether there is a common core of human nature: What degree of variability is possible through genetic differences between people, and how these genetic factors interact with cultural differences in family and community life? I think, also, that seeing human nature in this relativistic way will raise the question of how far in the coming centuries man can adapt to an environment other than the green mother earth that he has lived on before, especially with respect to the high pressures of modern living. This mix of biology and psychology is highly relevant to our planning the human future. I think anthropology and cross-cultural research in the social sciences can provide information to improve the quality of our future life.

Evans: Many social psychologists who are going into cross-cultural research have sometimes appeared to be rather naive to cultural anthropologists, and at the same time they have been accused by the so-called hard-nosed psychologists of being rather loose. They seem to have a role that is acceptable neither to the anthropologist nor to the more "rigorous" orientations in psychology. Do you see any possibilities that this will change? By definition, is this kind of research not as rigorous, but an approximation rather than a definite kind of thing?

Murphy: I think that there are many problems in breaking down complex events into very simple little units to be observed with the severe rigor used in microscopic studies of field biology. It's primarily a question of how big and complex the units of observation are. If you could carry motion pictures and sound recordings into the anthropological field situation, it might make possible quick observation and perhaps computerizing of large numbers of objectively observed minute facts. Maybe that will meet the same standard as the most severe biological and psychological research in laboratories, but I rather suspect that in the hierarchy of observation there will remain events at such a level of complexity that the interdependence of many events are involved. Perhaps the isolation-fractionalization method just won't work with these, and I would suspect that we'll be in the same boat with general biology. It seems to me that psychology needs to be capable of a high level of integrative conceptualization, at least at a level at which medical and biological research frequently works.

Evans: I think one of the real problems in research is evaluation of social change. We try to come up with research designs that are not the simple bivariate kind, but are multivariate in the most complex sense. At best, we can only control certain conditions, and sometimes we end up doing research that may be more of an approximation than we would like. In spite of the inherent weaknesses in these kinds of designs, would you say that we should still plug away and be satisfied with something less than the most rigorous research, or should we conclude that we can't really research certain areas at all?

Murphy: I think in general it's worthwhile to do less than perfect research as long as you do the best you can do. I don't know quite where we would get in the history of science if we insisted always that the researcher do only 100 percent perfect work. Certainly a large part of what

Darwin did was a very long way from perfect research, but would he have accomplished very much if he had set that kind of standard?

Evans: One of our problems in getting some of our experimentalists interested in these larger social problems is that one doesn't have enough control over all of the variables. There isn't a simple independent variable that they can manipulate.

Murphy: Oh, there's room for all kinds of people. Let the experimentalists do what they can do, and let the rest of us do what we can do.

Evans: One stigma that has been attached to psychological insight, through no fault of competent psychologists, is the result of an incorrect interpretation of Dewey and Freud. The idea is that we have suggested to society that permissiveness is the answer, that we shouldn't stifle the individual growth of the child. There's a suspicion that the "psychological approach" is creating a monster, an individual who cannot adjust to the limits and controls of the society.

Murphy: I think it's quite plain that kids need and want quite a good deal of order and planfulness, and I think it's quite clear that the idea that the child will automatically flow into the kind of activity that is best for him or for society is very naive. As I understand progressive education, the issue is to ask whether the discipline is one that is arbitrarily imposed, or whether it meets the child's needs at a particular time. Take, for example, the discipline of school subject matter. You can't learn math or English grammar except with a certain amount of order and discipline. That's intrinsic to the subject matter, but it's entirely different from being coerced step by step throughout the multiplication table, and so forth. Human coercion is often added in vastly greater amounts than are required. I would say that if the child is once interested in the school task, and is supported by his peers who are also interested, the intrinsic discipline of the subject matter carries quite a lot of weight. I don't suggest that there doesn't have to be any external discipline, but this is very different from classical Puritan coercion, or the feeling that human nature is bad and has to be licked into shape. I recommend some sort of moderation, with the emphasis upon the intrinsic appeal of the subject matter and getting the child interested.

Evans: The concept of personality has historically been the focus of much interest in social psychology. There are behaviorists who would say that the term is a wastebasket concept, rather useless. On the other hand, some psychologists, such as Allport (1937), tried to conceptualize personality as very useful for psychology. Do you feel that their term "personality" continues to be a useful term in psychology?

Murphy: Yes, in two senses. I tried to bring out in my book on personality (Murphy 1947) that personality is something which all human beings possess. Just as a body, teeth, and eyes go with the package of being human, so having a personality goes with the package of being human. I don't think we can go without it. And second, it is a focus for the study of variations from person to person. Even identical twins who are very much alike in almost everything nevertheless have an individuality that can be conceived qualitatively and quantitatively. When it comes to the broader biosocial realities of how we differ from one another, I think we need a word to describe the integrated totality in which one person differs from another. I don't know any other word than "personality" to describe this.

Evans: Doing justice to the uniqueness of the person makes sense. A distinction between nomothetic and idiographic approaches has been made, contrasting the search for general laws to apply to all people and studying the ultimate uniqueness of personality, or the way in which each person differs from every other person. Do you think that because experimental psychology is looking for general laws, experimentalists aren't making many contributions to the understanding of personality?

Murphy: Yes, I'm inclined to say that. I would say in matters of growth, of what we can expect of a child (because he happens to be six years or ten years of age), that to forget the highly individual character of growing up is a serious error. Different curves of learning and different motives influence the learning process differently in different people. I think perception and thought processes and so on are understood only when the interaction of broad biological dynamics with specific individual genetic and environmental components is emphasized. I would go along completely with B. F. Skinner and his classical study (Skinner 1956) of one individual case. He said that we often don't need a lot of statistical garbage if we have the clear specification of what's involved. A single individual man or pigeon may give us quite fundamental and beautiful general laws. Often the complexity of the situation requires that we go beyond, but the idea of understanding the individual in the full sense remains. In that connection, I don't really believe that idiographic and nomothetic are two kinds of studies, but are poles on a continuum. Individual psychology is not unrelated to the law-setting principles of general psychology.

Evans: Characteristic of your work is a willingness not to leave out any possibilities, to have an open system, as contrasted with some of the very definite closed systems that we have had in the study of personality. In our discussion here, there has not been one idea that we have entertained that you have necessarily ruled out. You are open to some of the Skinnerian ideas, some of the conceptions of experimental psychology, and you have not ruled out multidisciplinary orientations. Do you pay a price for being so willing to look at different areas of focus?

Murphy: Well, I feel that methods that have attracted any serious amount of attention will probably always be valuable, and the number and variety of methods should be increased in a young science. There is a place for the constant inventive elaboration of better and richer methods. I would not apply at all the same logic to psychological concepts. I think there are often too many concepts, a great many of them poorly defined. They're confused, and they interlace and interact in various ways which require disentangling, ordering, and clarification. I'd have to say that I think tolerance for ways of looking at psychological problems should be as great as we can make it, but I think attention needs to be given to defining and clarifying concepts.

REFERENCES

Allport, G. W. 1937. *Personality: A psychological interpretation.* New York: Henry Holt & Co.

Barrett, W. F. 1911.*Psychical research.* New York: Henry Holt & Co.

Barron, F. 1961. Psychotherapy and creativity. Paper presented at the XIV International Congress of Applied Psychology in Copenhagen, Denmark, August, 1961.

Chein, I. 1944. The awareness of self and the structure of the ego. *Psychol. Rev.* 51: 304–314.

Freud, S. 1949. The unconscious. In *Collected Papers* (Vol. IV), ed. J. Strachey. London: The Hogarth Press & the Institute of Psycho-analysis.

———. 1961. (Originally published, 1927.) *The ego and the id,* ed. and trans. J. Strachey. New York: Norton.

James, W. 1950. (Originally published, 1890.) *Principles of psychology.* New York: Dover.

Lowes, J. L. 1927. *The road to Xanadu: A study in the ways of the imagination.* Boston: Houghton Mifflin Co.

Mayne, E. C. 1969. *Byron.* 2nd ed. New York: Barnes & Noble.

Meyers, F. W. H. 1961. (Originally published, 1903.) *Human personality and its survival of bodily death,* ed. S. Smith. New Hyde Park: University Books Inc.

Murphy, G. 1947. *Personality: A biosocial approach to origins and structure.* New York: Harper & Brothers.

———. 1953. *In the minds of men.* New York: Basic Books.

———. 1958. *Human potentialities.* New York: Basic Books.

———, and Murphy, L. B. 1931. *Experimental social psychology.* New York: Harper.

Murray, H. A. 1938. *Explorations in personality: A clinical and experimental study of fifty men of college age.* New York: Oxford University Press.

Rhine, J. B. 1964. (Originally published, 1934.) *Extra-sensory perception.* Boston: B. Humphries.

Skinner, B. F. 1956. A case history in scientific method. *Amer. Psychol.* 11: 221–33.

Thorndike, E. L. 1931. *Human learning.* New York: The Century Co.

SELECTED READINGS

Murphy, G. 1947. *Personality: A biosocial approach to origins and structure.* New York: Harper & Brothers.

Murphy, G. 1958. *Human potentialities.* New York: Basic Books.

Murphy, G. 1961. *Challenge of psychical research.* New York: Harper & Row.

Murphy, G. 1969. Psychology in the year 2000. *Amer. Psychol.* 24: 523–30.

Murphy, G. and Kovach, J. K. 1972. *Historical introduction to modern psychology.* 3rd ed. New York: Harcourt, Brace.

Murphy, G., Murphy, L. B., and Newcomb, T. M. 1937. *Experimental social psychology.* Rev. ed. New York: Harper & Row.

2
FRITZ HEIDER
(1896–   )

Fritz Heider was born in Vienna, Austria, and first studied psychology
under Meinong at the University of Graz, where he received a
Ph. D. in philosophy in 1920. He later attended lectures by Wertheimer, Kohler, and Lewin in Berlin. He became an assistant to
William Stern at the University of Hamburg in 1927, before coming to Northampton, Massachusetts, to work in the Research
Department of the Clarke School for the Deaf under the direction of Koffka, who then held a special professorship at Smith
College in the same city. His book The Psychology of Interpersonal Relations, published in 1958, had a tremendous impact on
social psychology, providing the theoretical foundations of
balance theory and attribution theory, as well as stimulating vast
amounts of research and theoretical extensions of his original
ideas. In 1959 he received the Kurt Lewin Memorial Award and
in 1965 won the Distinguished Scientific Contribution Award of
the American Psychological Association. From 1947 until his
retirement he was a member of the faculty of the University of
Kansas.

Lewin/Field Theory/Analysis of Concepts//William Stern/The Person//
B. F. Skinner/ Habits//Balance Theory/Unit Formation/The Enemy
of My Enemy Is My Friend/ Festinger's Cognitive Dissonance The-
ory//New Look in Perception//Attribution Theory/Causes and Reasons, Persons and Things/Interpersonal Relations/Perceptions//
Questionnaires//The Import of Life Experiences//Criticisms//

Begining with a description of his early experiences in Berlin, Dr. Heider
and I discuss some of the work of Kurt Lewin, with whom he had
contact at that time. Dr. Heider comments on Lewin's field
theory, and suggests that Lewin's emphasis on establishing clearly formulated concepts was perhaps his most important contri-

13

bution to psychology. We then discuss William Stern, whose concept of "the person" strongly influenced Heider's later conceptualizations. Dr. Heider criticizes Skinner's treatment of the person as a machine, stating that although, in part, people are creatures of habit, they are more importantly creatures of reason and thinking. He describes the genesis of balance theory, which began with his study of Spinoza's conceptual representations of interpersonal relations and coalesced when he applied to it Wertheimer's concept of unit-forming factors. Balance depends on two factors, the unit relations (to be in a unit or not), and the sentiment that connects them (love-hate). Dr. Heider then gives an illustration of balance in the Arab proverb "the enemy of my enemy is my friend." We discuss Festinger's theory of cognitive dissonance, which Dr. Heider views as having some validity but as being inadequately defined conceptually. Dr. Heider and I discuss the New Look in perception, and he comments that the subjective factors in perception often aid in perceiving reality accurately rather than distorting it, just as scientific theories increase our understanding of facts. We then move into attribution theory, which states that people do not respond to stimuli directly but usually respond to what they think is the cause of the stimulus. Dr. Heider clarifies the distinction between reasons and causes by defining their referents, persons and things. We discuss an example of attribution as it operates in an interpersonal situation with a husband and wife. Dr. Heider reacts to some of the other work in the field of attribution, including that of Harold Kelly and Bernard Weiner. He then criticizes the unreflective use of questionnaires in psychological research, and also the tendency for psychologists to use only the psychological research literature for their empirical base. Finally, Dr. Heider considers the criticisms of his work, and comments, "I think the main one was that my theories were just common sense."

Evans: Dr. Heider, your ideas have been critically important in the current development of social psychology, especially in the area of attribution theory, and in the theories of interpersonal relations relevant to your balance theory. Earlier in your career you had extensive contact with two extremely important figures in psychology, Kurt Lewin and William Stern. Where did you first meet Dr. Lewin?

Heider: That was in Berlin. I had gotten my Ph.D. in Graz with the philosopher Meinong in 1920, and in 1921 I went to Berlin. I just wanted to gain more experience. I had not realized that there would be very important things going on in Berlin.

Evans: This was during the period when many of the major Gestalt psychologists were there?

Heider: Especially Köhler and Wertheimer.

Evans: And Lewin was also on the scene at the time?

Heider: Yes, that is right. And I very soon got into contact with Lewin. We had some common interests and we had many discussions about all sorts of different things. At that time he had not yet developed his method of representing action by topology, his mathematical system.

Evans: Of course, he went on to make some major contributions with his so-called "field theory" (Lewin 1951). One of the major positions that he stated was that a historical analysis might be more profitable for psychology than a preoccupation with the past, such as is characteristic of Freudian theory. He emphasized studying all factors in the present psychological field, the life span of a person. How do you feel about that?

Heider: I suppose one has to consider both, but certainly I found Lewin's insistence upon the present field and the present forces affecting the person to be of obvious importance. He considered the past as part of the present, as far as the person's awareness of something that happened yesterday was part of his present thinking.

Evans: Yes, exactly. The individual brings his past with him to the present situation.

Heider: But the past that isn't part of the present situation was not important.

Evans: Which of Lewin's ideas do you consider to be the most important?

Heider: One thing that was especially important for me was an idea Lewin really got partially from the philosopher Ernst Cassirer. That is the idea of analyzing and establishing the concepts that one uses in theories in such a way that their relation is really clear. It is not very fruitful to make empirical studies without having cleared up one's concepts, which are the tools, so to speak, with which we think about things. There are many cases in the history, not especially of psychology, but of physics and chemistry, in which the important breakthroughs came about not through empirical investigation but through an analysis of concepts. For instance, our life is now very much dependent on what's going on in nuclear physics, on atomic energy and atom bombs and so on. That did not come from empirical investigations. Einstein sat down and thought through Newton's concepts and found some logical incompatibilities. He sat there in his study and came to conclusions that became terribly important for our understanding of the physical environment. Einstein's theories did not come from experimenting.

Evans: So you think that Lewin's most important contribution was giving us an understanding of the importance of developing conceptual frameworks.

Heider: Yes, and he made an important contribution with applying topology to the action space, defining all the different factors that influence action. I myself did not use that because it was not especially helpful in the analysis of interpersonal relations, and that was what concerned me most.

Evans: Another important figure with whom you had some contact was William Stern (e.g., 1938). Stern received considerable recognition in the United States partly because of his influence on Gordon Allport. He seemed to be preoccupied, perhaps more than most psychologists, with the uniqueness of the individual. Where did you meet Stern?

Heider: I was in Berlin and I was looking for a job at that time. Lewin came to me and said that Stern was looking for someone to teach education at the University of Hamburg. So, I became an assistant professor there.

Evans: I might ask you the same question about Stern as I asked you about Lewin. Which of Stern's ideas would seem to you to be the most important to contemporary social psychology?

Heider: With Stern one has to consider that he was only half a psychologist. He was also half a philosopher. And he considered his findings in philosophy more important than in psychology. His basic concept was the person. The concept of a person is something that is different from the concept of a thing. In America, of course, there are tendencies to treat the person as a thing.

Evans: A major figure in contemporary American psychology is B. F. Skinner (Evans 1968), who does emphasize the importance of empiricism, and who has been accused of looking at the individual more as a machine. If Lewin and Stern were alive today, do you think that they would find themselves quite sharply in disagreement with Skinner?

Heider: Yes, certainly. I don't quite know what they would think, but thinking of man as a thing would be very offensive to them. My own opinion is that Skinner treats human beings as guided and determined by habit. I think that in part humans are creatures of habit, but there is another part that may be even more important. Humans are also creatures of reason and thinking, and maybe in an example I can oppose the two. At the entrance of the Psychology Department at the University of Kansas there used to be a door that had to be opened by a handle on the left side. When some remodeling was done, the handle was placed on the right. After this change, when I went there without thinking very much, busy with other things, my action was determined by the habit that I had had for years and years. So I would reach again to the left side of the door. But when I was fully aware, I knew right away that I had to reach to the right. In some ways we are creatures of habit, but in some ways we follow what we know about the past to reach the present goal. If, for instance, you have gone for years to visit a restaurant on a certain street (you have developed a habit of going there), you were, you might say, conditioned to go there in a certain way. But now somebody tells you that this restaurant burned down yesterday. It isn't there anymore, you have to go to this other restaurant. Does it take you a long time to extinguish your habit? No, you right away go to a very different place and contradict your habits, so to speak.

Evans: Some of the Skinnerians would argue that some of the contingencies had changed and that this, therefore, has altered the behavior. In other words, the person is simply appropriately responding to changes in the contingencies of the environment.

Heider: They consider the contingencies of the environment only insofar as the stimulus conditions the behavior. That is, they can train an animal to do one thing or another thing by the arrangement of contingencies. But they do not contend that the contingencies of the environment can quickly extinguish a well-established habit. To extinguish a habit, you need a long time.

Evans: Another very important force in contemporary social psychology has been a whole range of theories sometimes called "balance theories." For example, Festinger's (1957) theory of cognitive dissonance and Osgood's theory of attitude congruency (Osgood and Tannenbaum 1955) all seem to go back to the notion of balance.

Heider: Osgood developed his ideas independently, although his work did not come out until after I had published mine, it was his own idea. He did not take it from me.

Evans: I see.

Heider: But with Festinger I am not sure. I think Festinger was influenced by my ideas.

Evans: I wonder if you could trace through a little bit of what balance theory was all about. How did you develop this notion?

Heider: I was always attracted by Spinoza's thoughts because I was very interested in interpersonal relations and in some kind of conceptual representation of these interpersonal relations. Spinoza has both. Spinoza was one of the philosophers who talked about love and hate, and he had a very finely worked out system of thinking about these things. He took his logical system from Euclid. So I studied Spinoza (1910), especially the third book of his ethics. I tried in many different ways to juggle it around. I wasn't satisfied with Spinoza's geometrical logical derivation of these things. I even tried topology, but it didn't work. I finally brought in Wertheimer's (1945) unit-forming factors, and from then on it was clear sailing. So that was the origin.

Evans: Could you explain what you mean by "balance theory"?

Heider: Buddha had already glimpsed a part of balance theory around 500 B.C. He talked about the misfortunes that a person could experience. He had seven different misfortunes, but two of them were the following: First, to be tied to something one hates; and second, not to be able to get to something one loves. In balance situations two kinds of relations are usually involved. One is a unit relation that tells whether the person is or is not connected with something else, and the other is an attitude relation, e.g., love or hate. Both of these relations can be either positive or negative, and if they are both positive or both negative the situation is in balance. If one relation is positive and the other negative, as for instance in Buddha's example of being tied to something one hates, the situation is unstable. One can apply these considerations to a triad and get similar results, only then the story is a little more complicated.

Evans: Could you clarify what you mean by "unit formation"?

Heider: Wertheimer talked about unit formation using abstract forms to illustrate what he meant. He showed that two spots on a sheet of paper are more likely to be seen as belonging together if they are similar in color or in form, or if they are placed close together. Thus, he spoke of *similarity* and *proximity* as two factors that make for the appearance of belonging or *unit formation,* and also described several others. These factors are of great importance in our perception of the world about us.

I may add something that I have thought about a good deal during the last years. In the past when we have talked about balance, we have considered configurations that contained only attitude relations or configurations that contained both attitude and unit relations. I am now convinced that balanced configurations with only unit relations are important for our cognitive makeup, and that we tend to favor them in our thinking. For instance, we often assume that when two things are similar in one way they are also similar in another way. This is one form of our tendency to think in terms of analogy. When we make order in our bookcase, we try to make the factor of proximity coincide with similarity of content. We put together the books that are similar in content. As long as these two unit-forming factors are not in agreement, there is disorder in the bookcase.

Evans: As you describe your own views of balance theory then, at the time that you were formulating it, were you attempting to develop a theory that would account for all human behavior or were you just looking at one facet of behavior?

Heider: I would think that it accounts for many aspects of behavior. For instance, if you would go through most of the tragedies in world literature, the situations are mostly ones of imbalance.

Evans: In your balance theory were you arguing that the organism was seeking balance or, since almost all individuals are in some state of imbalance, maybe that the individual is seeking imbalance?

Heider: Well, that is an old question. Certainly, too much balance is boring.

Evans: So you wouldn't be necessarily making a simple statement that perhaps the organism always seeks balance at the psychological level. Physiologically, the organism appears to seek some form of homeostasis, equilibrium or balance, but this would not necessarily be true in terms of human decision-making and judgment. Sometimes the person almost appears to be seeking imbalance.

Heider: In many cases it is true that we seek balance, but there are borderline cases in which the organism also seeks some kind of imbalance, to be stimulated. But, for instance, people would not pour out their gas in order to be able to wait for a long time at the gas station. If they were to seek imbalance, that would be a certain way to get into an imbalanced situation.

Evans: Could you give me an example of how "balance" operates?

Heider: Well, the typical case of balance is illustrated by an old Arab proverb: the enemy of my enemy is my friend. See, for a triad to be in balance it has to have either all three positive connections, or two negative and one positive. If there is between me and this person a negative connection, and if between this person and the third person there is a negative connection, that makes for a plus connection between me and that third person: the enemy of my enemy is my friend. That is a typical case of balance.

Evans: In terms of your balance theory, getting back to Festinger, do you feel that Festinger's (1957) book *A Theory of Cognitive Dissonance* presented a conceptual framework that was consistent with what you were talking about in your earlier work?

Heider: Well, that's a difficult question. I have the feeling that his system lacks a definition of dissonance, and of a dissonant situation and a consonant situation. If you look carefully through his book, there is no definition. Now with balance, whether the original situation is agreeable or disagreeable is defined mathematically using pluses and minuses. With dissonance one has a general feeling it fits together, but it is not really defined. There is a case with purchasing a car, for instance. One has bought a car and one likes to read advertisements that agree with the purchase one has already made.

Evans: So suppose you're considering the purchase of a Chevrolet, Plymouth, or Ford. If you end up buying a Chevrolet, the question is: Would you be reading the Chevrolet advertisement more intensely before or after you made the purchase? In such situations Festinger suggests that the person would tend to be more likely to read the advertisements more intensely after the decision, to resolve post-decision dissonance.

Heider: Yes, and I have the feeling that conceptually it is not brought out clearly why that is a case of dissonance. He has some other cases of dissonance that one has the feelings are dissonant because Festinger *says* they are, but he has not really defined it. I don't think that anyone has touched on the essence of the definition of dissonance in such situations.

Evans: The late Robert MacLeod (1947) wrote a very important paper on the phenomenological approach in psychology, bringing the philosophical notion of phenomenology, such as Husserl's (1967), to psychology. This was reflected in the so-called New Look in perception, which partly arose from Bruner and Goodman's (1947) rather important paper, "Value and Need as Organizing Factors in Perception." There was a tendency to move away from the more structural determinants of perception to functionally selective perception; that is, perception based on our needs, moods, values, past experiences, etc. This brought the more naive phenomenological view to the field. Would you like to comment about this trend toward emphasizing the functional nature of perception?

Heider: Besides Meinong, one of my teachers at Graz was an Italian, Benussi, who dealt with perception. He had done experiments in Gestalt perception before Wertheimer. In these experiments, Benussi very often dealt with how the set of the person, or the intention and attention of the

person, influences the percept. When I later read the experiments on the
New Look in perception, I felt that I had learned this already from Benussi.

Evans: Some of these experiments tried to prove that the state of the
person at any given moment influences how he or she perceives the
world, and raises a question about the absolute nature of reality. Isn't
this in a way restating Kant, that there is no reality without man's perception of it?

Heider: Although I think this Kantian idea is very important, one
must not forget that the "set" a person has doesn't always lead to a falsifi-
cation of perception. We are always in contact with important features of
the environment, and to a surprising degree we see them correctly. We
do not react to the stimulus pattern or gradual understanding of the stimulus pattern. It is not that this subjective factor distorts; actually it often
gets us closer to reality. Just as we make theories in science, these "perceptual sets" or naive theories may give us a better picture of the environment than the mere perception without theories.

Evans: On the other hand, this line of research would suggest that we
sometimes do distort our perceptions because of some particularly strong
emotion or need at the moment.

Heider: That's right, it is possible.

Evans: Your 1958 book, *The Psychology of Interpersonal Relations,*
and your earlier papers on social perception and phenomenal causality
(1944) led to a whole trend of research that today we sometimes call "attribution theory." It's become the center of research activities of, for instance, Harold Kelly (e.g., Kelley 1971, 1972; Thibaut and Kelley 1959),
Ned Jones (e.g., Jones and Nisbett 1971; Jones, Rock, Shaver, Goethals,
and Ward 1968) and many other investigators in social psychology. Almost all of this work points back to your early ideas of the nature of interpersonal relationships. What, as you see it, is "attribution theory?"

Heider: I really don't know whether one could call it a theory. It was
just pointing out that we are usually not responding to the stimulus but
are responding to what we think is the cause of the stimulus. When I see a
red spot here on my arm, I do not respond to red as such. I think, "Now
what is it? Did I bump myself? Or is it a sign that I have here some underlying process going on which is a disease?" and so on. If this red spot appears on the wall, I do not respond in the same way. I try to find out
what caused it.

Evans: So you attribute causality of some sort.

Heider: Yes, I attribute the superficial process, which I see directly, to
some underlying cause. And then I respond to the cause, not to the
superficial thing.

Evans: There was a recent review of this by Allan Buss (1978). He
makes a very interesting point. He says that most attribution research
fails to define the concept of cause. In other words, if you ask a person
for the "cause" of his or her behavior, the person will always give you the
"reason" for his or her behavior. What he was trying to say is that the

term "cause" is ambiguous because if you are going to do research in this field, then you're trying to study what people see as a cause. Buss was really saying that researchers may be confusing the "cause" of behavior . . . with the "reason" for behavior. Do you agree with his criticism?

Heider: I would like to have first a definition of the difference between cause and reason. That is difficult.

Evans: In Buss's (1978) article reason pertains to the purposes of the person's behavior. A cause has more to do with the mechanics of cause and effect.

Heider: That goes into the difference between person and thing. Animate objects differ from things in important ways. We assume they are real solid objects having functional properties, making them fit with or interfere with our purposes. Persons are also objects that occupy a certain position in the environment. However, they are usually perceived as action centers, and as such can do something to us. People can have wishes and sentiments, and can act purposefully. Our naive understanding of this difference would of course affect out attributions. A person will attribute reasons, or purposes, to his or her own behavior and to that of other persons. I am not sure how this has caused a confusion in the literature.

Evans: Could you give an illustration of this principle in interpersonal relations? For instance, suppose in a relationship between a husband and wife in a marital situation the wife is trying to irritate her husband by not talking to him. How will attribution come into play here?

Heider: The husband would be likely to think, "Now, why doesn't she talk to me? Did I do something? Does she have some great worry now or did I really do something that offended her?" According to how he interprets it, and to what he attributes her behavior, will he respond to her differently.

Evans: In other words, it's not the fact that she's giving him "the silent treatment" that's the important issue. The husband tries to formulate a theory about what's causing his wife to behave toward him this way. That is "attribution."

Heider: That's right.

Evans: On the surface you'd think that people would react to things, and the idea that people instead are reacting to what they believe are the *causes* of things is both obvious and yet, in a sense, subtle. How did you arrive at this very interesting theory of perceived causality?

Heider: I really don't know, but partly it goes back to my dissertation. Meinong wrote about perception and causal theories of perception. He said, "Why is it that when we look at this house we do not say that we see the sun?" since our vision of the house is caused by the sun. That was a question that puzzled me and led me to go beyond the retina to study the ecology of perception. Gestalt theory, for instance, ended with the retina, and most people studied only what was immediately affecting perception. I tried to elaborate on the process by considering as distinct the proximal stimulus, which was the image on the retina, and the distal stimulus, which was the object out in the world. The object, such as a house, and the medium, such as light (which conveys the stimulus), have different structures which make one of them an object of our perception. All of these things affect the way we perceive the world. Brunswik (1934), of course, who was influenced by the ideas in my 1927 paper, "Thing and Medium" (1959), contributed much to the theory in this area.

Evans: There are now many researchers actively studying this attribution dimension. What research in this field do you think is most interesting?

Heider: I always like Harold Kelley's (e.g., Thibaut and Kelley 1959) schema of different factors. For example, his notion of co-variations is interesting.

Evans: In other words, X attributes causality to behavior of Y and Y does to X and so on. Of course, Ned Jones, (e.g., Jones and Nisbett 1971; Jones, Rock, Shaver, Goethals, and Ward 1968) work in this area is also important. But there are many researchers in this field I could mention.

Heider: That's right. I also like what Weiner (e.g., Weiner, Frieze, Kukla, Reed, Rest, and Rosenbaum 1971) has done. I found very interesting his work about judging the production of schoolchildren, whether it is attributed to their ability or to their effort.

Evans: And the way they are often judged is in terms of the attribution of the person doing the judging.

Heider: Yes. Overall I have the feeling that the more different people who work on something from different points of view, the better it is.

Evans: To move to another area, I know you have reservations concerning the use of questionnaires in psychological research.

Heider: When I see a questionnaire, I right away read one question and have to analyze it. What does it mean? I sometimes feel that with the roughshod statistical procedures that are used, they are burying very interesting problems. It is as if instead of colors mixed like in a fine painting, they just mixed all the colors up without any structure. I have tried several questionnaires during my life. I went question by question and asked the individual to talk about this and that. They say yes or no and so on. I tried to figure out what is behind these different questions. I would say questionnaires are often very naive and not very fruitful attempts at quantification. However, there may be other attempts that are very good and very profitable, and I would never state any absolutes about what one should do. Try to go ahead with quantification, but do it in a sensible way and do not think that because it's quantified, it's good.

Evans: I'm rather intrigued that many of your ideas seem to be based on information outside of the formal field of psychology. One of the points I believe you've made is that psychologists should make use of that common store of knowledge about human psychology that is contained in literature and fables.

Heider: Yes, I feel that many psychologists develop a kind of encapsulated system. They read other psychologists' work and use their results as the empirical background for their theories. Now, for me the empirical background is not from reading psychological papers, but it is first of all from one's own experiences, in talking with other people and so on, and from reading literature. The empirical background should not be just the latest psychological experiments. That's kind of an incestual and very restricted way to develop knowledge. At least the same importance should be given to life experiences. You should keep going back to life and not to the laboratory for fresh insights in psychology.

Evans: Does some of the research in attribution get so abstract and schematic that it no longer truly reflects human experience?

Heider: Sometimes. Of course, maybe there is some mathematical foundation. Lewin (1936) has shown that for action his topological theory, which is very abstract and mathematical, nevertheless can show a lot about action, and it makes one look for things for which one would not have looked without the system.

Evans: So abstract theory and laboratory science can be a helpful way of looking at the world. At the same time real life should be a guide. Neither should be the only basis for our store of information and knowledge in psychology.

Heider: Yes.

Evans: Like most pioneers in our field, you probably have been subjected to criticism by others. What are some of the criticisms of your work that trouble you the most?

Heider: I think the main one was that my theories were often described as simply being "common sense," but I can't say that it troubled me.

Evans: Erik Erikson (Evans 1968), in the discussion I had with him, said, "Why do people make so much fuss about my ideas. They really are kind of simple."

Heider: I guess I feel the same way. If they want to call my ideas "common sense," so be it.

REFERENCES

Bruner, J. S., and Goodman, C. C. 1947. Value and need as organizing factors in perception. *J. Abnorm. Soc. Psychol.* 42: 33–44.

Brunswik, E. 1934. *Wahrnehmung und Gegenstandswelt.* Vienna: Deuticke.

Buss, A. 1978. Causes and reasons in attribution theory: A conceptual critique. *J. Pers. Soc. Psychol.* 36: 1311–21.

Byrne, D. 1971. *The attraction paradigm.* New York: Academic Press.

Evans, R. I. 1968. *B. F. Skinner: The man and his ideas.* New York: Dutton.

———. 1969. *Dialogue with Erik Erikson.* New York: Dutton.

Festinger, L. 1970. (Originally published, 1957). *A theory of cognitive dissonance.* Stanford, Calif.: Stanford University Press.

Heider, F. 1944. Social perception and phenomenal causality. *Psychol. Rev.* 51: 358–74.

―――. 1958. *The psychology of interpersonal relations.* New York: Wiley.

―――. 1959. Thing and medium. *Psychol. Issues* 1: 1–123.

Husserl, E. 1967. *Ideas: General introduction to pure phenomenology,* trans. W. R. Boyce Gibson. New York: Humanities Press.

Jones, E. E., and Nisbett, R. E. 1971. *The actor and the observer: Divergent perceptions of the causes of behavior.* Morristown, N.J.: General Learning Press.

―――, Rock, L., Shaver, K. G., Goethals, G. R., and Ward, L. M. 1968. Pattern of performance and ability attribution: An unexpected primacy effect. *J. Pers. Soc. Psychol.* 10: 317–40.

Kelley, H. H. 1971. *Attribution in social interaction.* Morristown, N.J.: General Learning Press.

―――. 1972. *Causal schemata and the attribution process.* Morristown, N.J.: General Learning Press.

―――, and Thibaut, J. 1978. *Interpersonal relations: A theory of interdependence.* New York: Wiley.

Lewin, K. 1936. *Principles of topographical psychology,* trans. F. Heider and G. M. Heider. New York: McGraw-Hill.

Lewin, K. 1951. *Field theory in social science,* ed. D. Carlwright. New York: Harper.

MacLeod, R. B. 1947. The phenomenological approach to social psychology. *Psychol. Rev.* 54: 193–210.

Osgood, C. E., and Tannenbaum, P. H. 1955. The principle of congruency in the prediction of attitude change. *Psychol. Rev.* 62: 42–55.

Spinoza, B. 1910. *Ethic.* 4th ed., trans. A. H. Sterling. New York: H. Frowde.

Stern, W. 1938. *General psychology from the personalistic standpoint,* trans. H. D. Spoerl. New York: The Macmillan Co.

Weiner, B., Frieze, I., Kukla, A., Reed, L., Rest, S., and Rosenbaum, R. M. 1971. *Perceiving the causes of success and failure.* Morristown, N.J.: General Learning Press.

Wertheimer, M. 1945. *Productive thinking.* New York: Harper.

SELECTED READINGS

Heider, F. 1944. Social perception and phenomenal causality. *Psychol. Rev.* 51: 358–374.

Heider, F. 1946. Attitudes and cognitive organization. *J. Psychol.* 21:107–112.

Heider, F. 1958. *The psychology of interpersonal relations.* New York: Wiley.

Heider, F. 1959. Thing and medium. *Psychol. Issues* 1:1–123.

Heider, F. 1960. The other person: How we perceive it. Proceedings of the *Sixteenth International Congress of Psychology.* Amsterdam: North-Holland. 564-565.

Heider, F., and Heider, G. M. 1961. A comparison of sentence structure of deaf and hearing children. *Volta Rev.* 43:364–67; 406; 536–40; 564; 599–604; 628–30.

3

GORDON ALLPORT
(1897–1967)

The contributions of Gordon Allport to psychology represent perhaps
the most integrated approach to personality theory of any contemporary psychologist. Educated at Harvard University, Professor Allport took his A.B. in 1919, spent a year teaching in Turkey,
and then returned to Harvard to complete his Ph.D. in 1922. This
was followed by two post-doctoral years in Europe. Except for a
two year period at Dartmouth College, his entire career was
spent at Harvard where he was the first Richard Cabot Professor
of Social Ethics and was instrumental in the formation of the department of social relations. Involved in all areas of personality,
Professor Allport's most significant contributions included the
measurement, organization, and social determinants of personality, his classic work in prejudice and communication, and his
approach to a systematic study of values. He was president of
the American Psychological Association in 1939 and received
the Gold Medal of the American Psychological Foundation and
the Distinguished Scientific Contribution Award of the American Psychological Association.

S-O-R/The Nature of the O/Stimulus-Response versus Individual-Cen-
tered Psychology//A Frame of Reference/Traits//A Sense of Self/
The Functional Autonomy of Motives//Who Am I?/A Sign of
Growing Maturity/Existentialism//An Element of Ignorance/The
Nature of Prejudice//Extrinsic or Intrinsic Values/The Religious
Dimension of Personality//How Are You Going to Know?/Person-
ality Testing//

We begin the discussion as Dr. Allport reacts to the stimulus-response
(S-R) versus the stimulus-organism-response (S-O-R) model, relating his answers to such areas as determinism and personal re-

sponsibility. "Man has a great deal more freedom than he ever uses," Dr. Allport explains, "because he operates out of habits, prejudices and stereotypes." He reevaluates his concept of traits in personality theory, distinguishing between nomothetic and morphogenic, as well as central, cardinal, and secondary traits. Our discussion of motivation leads to the concept of functional autonomy, and Dr. Allport clarifies self, ego, and proprium. We explore existentialism and the nature of man and the thinking that led to the study of prejudice. After defining prejudice and discrimination, Dr. Allport makes some suggestions about dealing with both areas, and the direction he feels is most productive of change. We discuss the religious dimension of personality, and he connects it with the extrinsic and intrinsic values of the individual. In conclusion, Dr. Allport explains why he thinks personality testing is a valuable tool for the psychologist and the way in which he believes it should be done.

This discussion is an excerpt from the book *Gordon Allport: The Man and His Ideas* by Richard I. Evans. Copyright © 1971 by Richard I. Evans. Reprinted by permission of the publishers, E. P. Dutton & Co., Inc. Awarded the 1971 American Psychological Foundation Media Award in the Book Category.

Evans: Dr. Allport, your writing and thinking has transversed an important shift in theoretical orientation in psychology, where the stimulus-response (SR) paradigm which de-emphasizes the organism has been increasingly challenged by the stimulus-organism-response (SOR) paradigm which attributes more importance to the organism and its characteristics. Do you feel that it would be possible for the young scholar to accept the validity of these two diverging streams of thought and still make some sense out of psychology?

Allport: I think that he should first of all realize that the simple SR model is extremely attractive because it is based on a very healthy desire to know exactly what is going on, and both stimuli and responses can be measured quite accurately. On the other hand, it seems to me that with some nine trillion brain cells, what's going on inside the organism simply cannot be adequately depicted in terms of SR. I would argue for a small "s" and a small "r," but a very large "O," because it seems to me that all the interesting things in personality lie in the inferences we must make about what's going on in these intervening variables in terms of motivation, interests, attitudes, values, and so on. On the other hand, I may add one warning about the nature of "O." You could also consider the "O" as a being trying to establish an equilibrium of contradictory forces impinging on itself, and that "O" represents this homeostatic mechanism at work. If you consider the O as having tension-reducing propensities, or as establishing homeostasis or equilibrium, that is one view of O. Actually, however, I take a more proactive view of the nature of O. As I see it, it not only tries to establish equilibrium under some circumstances, but also attempts to maintain disequilibrium. It even goes out to seek disequilibrium in order to maintain tension. So your conception of the nature of the O forms the basis for your notion of what personality really is.

Evans: Does this not also embrace the notion of personal responsibility or self-determinism? We might ask how much emphasis should the organism be given in the self-deterministic model of human behavior.

Allport: You have leapt into the most difficult question of all—the problem that the philosophers call human freedom. Speaking as a psychologist and a scientist, I have to say that I think man has a great deal more freedom than he ever uses, simply because he operates out of habits, prejudices, and stereotypes, often going off, as it were, half-cocked. If he reflected and kept uppermost the selective set to ask himself, "Is this my style of life or isn't it?" he would have a lot more self-determinism than is reflected in the traditional materialistic, mechanistic view of man as a reactive being. Of course, our behavior is to some extent determined by society, heredity, and our organic nature, and we must acknowledge that; but beyond that it revolves around whether we consider "O" a proactive or just a reactive organism. I am inclined to think that the answer lies in the direction of proaction, thereby admitting into psychology the importance of such concepts as goals, purposes, intentions, plans, values, and the like. I would not, however, argue for the absolute untrammeled freedom espoused by some of the existentialists. The answer lies somewhere in the middle course.

Evans: Dr. Allport, you have, of course, been identified with the personality trait and the way in which it can be used in assessing personality. It would be very interesting to know a little more about how you happened to develop this focus and how you feel about the label "trait psychologist" which some psychologists have given you.

Allport: When I was a student just beginning to be interested in differential psychology, this field was most clearly represented by William Stern, who held that it is just merely a matter of measuring degrees of intelligence. Stern invented the I.Q. concept, which was a rating of degrees of intelligence or degrees of dominance, anxiety, and what not. That's been going on ever since. When I studied with Stern later in Hamburg, we developed the ascendence-submission dimension as an early personality test of the same sort. I liked to get at the dimensional aspects of values, and used the six values of Spranger (1928) as a base. I called these variables traits; there was nothing original about that. But to put a label of "trait psychology" on my work since then is to misrepresent it. I've been troubled by misinterpretation of the distinction between common traits and individual traits. At first I thought I could make clear the distinction between comon traits, which are the abstracted trait categories we use for measuring personality, and the individual traits, which represent the way a given individual is actually organized. I found, however, that people merely doubled the use of the word "trait" and heard me to be suggesting traits again. Recently I've tried to change the terminology so that common traits would still be a valid field for research, but personal dispositions would focus on the morphogenic study of the individual in order to find out how he is organized. We have morphogenic and molecular biology, and I think the parallel represents the distinction I'm trying to make in psychology. It seems to me that to adequately distinguish these frames of reference, one could use nomothetic to mean general laws, principles, and dimensions, as opposed to morphogenic to mean the unique individual organism.

Evans: You've made the point here that we should not become confused between common traits and the unique characteristics of the individual. You have, however, also written about central traits, cardinal traits, and secondary traits, and I wonder if you might distinguish among these for us.

Allport: I didn't intend for these to become fixed classificatory schemes at all. It is simply a means to call attention to the fact that if you know one thing about a person's trait system, you could predict his attitude toward a great many other things. Most people have some important foci of development, but we can usually distinguish six or eight, and these would be more central traits. There would likely be secondary ones which are not as well integrated as the others, as well as reflecting situational and opportunistic expression. The trait categories I postulated are meant to be a sort of continuum between the very central, central, and more peripheral or accidental developments in the personality.

Evans: The distinctive feature of organizing character on the basis of your system would be that you emphasize the uniqueness of the individual rather than his conformity to a set pattern of characteristics. You emphasize the uniqueness of the individual also in your concept of motivation. Many theorists still emphasize a biocentric theory of motivation which ascribes maintenance of the organism to physiological drives such as hunger, thirst, and so on, but allows for the development of various drives derived over time from these fundamental physiological drives. These would include the various social motives. It is about this point where your rather controversial concept of the functional autonomy of motives comes in. In your writings you have tried to explain that there are many drives, motives, or needs influencing our day-to-day behavior which are not clearly derived from the primary drives; that they are for the individual functionally autonomous, and become self-sustaining. To illustrate this point, you had a generation of students rather seasick as they read your description of the sailor who went out to sea and remained there long after his early *original* needs for going out to sea were outgrown. his continuing urge to go out to sea you suggest is an illustration of functional autonomy. Would you care to elaborate on this notion?

Allport: To me it was simply a way of stating what was perfectly obvious to me, that motives change and grow in the course of one's life. I still can't understand why a person would challenge that basic proposition unless he were a die-hard believer in reactivity instead of proactivity, of homeostasis instead of transcendence, of balance or equilibrium instead of growth. To me it is more or less self-evident. I realized that it wasn't self-evident to others when I had to defend it and try to answer the very difficult question of how functional autonomy comes about. Most theories stress the importance of events which occur early in life through conditioning, and the analytical theory requires that the life be traced backward in time. But people are busily living their lives forward; they are oriented toward the future, and therefore, the psychologist cannot be correct if he's oriented entirely to the past, simply because his subject is not so oriented. One must have some proactive view of human motivation to explain plans and intentions, and self-image and long–range goals, which are not like those of childhood, and are not just conditioned reactions. They are proactions and plans, and it seems to me to be basic to a valid theory of personality that they be accounted for.

Evans: Just to illustrate how functional autonomy works, could you give us an example of autonomous motivation in operation?

Allport: Let's take, for example, the phenomenon of the son following in the father's profession, such as politics. I don't question that they might have had a father identification when they were six years old; most boys do. If daddy made a speech, the son would play that he made a speech; if daddy went to work, he would go out to work, and so on. But is that what sends senators to the Senate to work hard for what they believe in? Does their committee work represent an attempt to be daddy at age fifty? It seems perfectly ridiculous to me to believe that a normal person can be so motivated. But, giving Freud due credit, I can conceive of a neurotic who is still trying to step into daddy's shoes, or still trying to win mother's approval by making like daddy. But we would be able to distinguish this kind of neurotic motivation by its compulsive, inappropriate, and not age-related character.

When people ask how functional autonomy comes about, I have to say there are two different levels. There is first a perseverated mechanism in the nervous system which is evident in repeated observations, that what has started tends to continue. This kind of mechanism is well known even in lower animals, where you can establish a rhythm by training and then take away the training or the food or the reward, and the rhythm continues for a very long time. At the human level, we see that children are enormously repetitive. This kind of perseverated functional autonomy is a mechanism which feeds itself. But this does not fully satisfy me as a basis for behavior. I labeled another kind of functional autonomy "propriate functional autonomy," which refers to oneself.

Perseverated functional autonomy is still within the sphere of reactivity; sometimes stimulates, feeds back, and stimulates again—the person is reacting to himself, his own circuits, and not to outside stimuli. But we are, after all, also proactive, and given to a kind of functional autonomy that responds to interests, goals, purposes, and relates warmly to one's sense of self. This is what I call propriate functional autonomy. If you ask me how it comes about, I would have to say merely that it is the nature of the human organism.

Evans: Your discussion of functional autonomy suggests that you would agree with the late Professor Kurt Lewin's (1936) emphasis on a contemporaneous, ahistorical view of personality and motivation. Is this correct?

Allport: Yes. I think Lewin and I both stress contemporaneity of motives. What drives the individual must drive him now, and if the past is at all relevant it has to be incorporated into the present. We do have memories and skills that we call on under specific motivational conditions, and so the past can be active in the present. I think that Lewin and I would agree that in normal behavior, the regions of the personality under tension at a given moment are the motives, and they are affected very much by the field or the situation that one is in.

Evans: The same growth factor that you postulate as necessary for functional autonomy would be needed to describe the concepts of self and ego, and in fact, focusing on ego autonomy is one important contemporary approach to understanding personality. Your concept of propriate, which relates to self and ego, while it implies this growth factor, doesn't appear to be exactly the same as ego or exactly the same as self. It seems to have a unique quality. I wonder if you would elaborate on this.

Allport: To explain why I have coined the term "proprium," and especially the adjectival form, "propriate," I would say that in the literature I found at least eight different uses or definitions of ego and self. Both terms are practically interchangeable by different authors, so I don't think we can make a systematic distinction, even though all the meanings were acceptable. To avoid the question-begging approach involved in the usage of the words self or ego, I felt that we might take a word that is fresh so that every time it was used it wouldn't have to be defined, nor would it be cluttered with the baggage of former connotations of self or ego. But in my books, I do use self, especially in relation to the development of the self or sense of self evolving from childhood, and I feel it is an important construct.

Evans: The developmental approach to the concept of self is not as broad in perspective as the notion of proprium as you have proposed it. What often happens when someone proposes a term that has growth connotations in psychology is that some individuals accuse him of being transcendental or even metaphysical, and while I'm certain you had no intention of proposing a metaphysical concept, I wonder how you would defend the concept of proprium against this kind of criticism.

Allport: Anyone who says it's transcendental or mystical just hasn't read what I've written. I stated very carefully that the idea of an agent, a separate agent, whether metaphysical or mystical, is not what I intended. I've often said that proprium is an entirely operational construct which is necessary and can't be avoided in a systematic personality theory. I would define proprium in terms which might be considered phenomenological by saying it's that part of the personality which seems to be warm and central to the person, involving matters that are of importance in this life over and above the mere matters of fact in it. If you begin from the phenomenological core it can be demonstrated that this sense of proprium, when it is present, makes an operationally demonstrable difference in behavior.

Evans: As soon as we discuss terms such as proprium, self, or ego we begin to relate to the existentialist or phenomenological points of view introduced into psychology by individuals such as Robert McCleod and Rollo May. The notions of phenomenology or existentialism cause us to ask to what degree must a psychologist be concerned with "under the skin" facets of the individual. Might we, for instance, go too far in introducing such nonoperational frames of reference into the science of psychology?

Allport: To say that we go too far is a matter of subjective judgment. I think we can go a good deal farther than we have before we've exhausted the value that comes from reports of experience when they're done thoroughly. We've neglected subjective reports in psychology so long that I'm not immediately worried about being too phenomenological.

Evans: When we examine a developmental model such as Freud's which postulated that the child at first is irrationally nondiscriminating and emerges slowly to a point where its own rationality begins to govern its behavior, we encounter the same problem of determinism. Even though the child has evolved what Adler called a style of life, he still seems to have introjected a great deal from his period of development when he was essentially dominated by irrational behavior. Can we accept such notions of the effects of early influences on present behavior? Certainly, virtually all contemporary developmental models, with the possible exception of Paiget's (Evans 1973) (which views the child as being in a sense rational from the beginning), stress the importance of these chaotic early influences.

Allport: We must look for truth somewhere in the middle. We sometimes, I think, much overdo the emphasis on early life. A factor important to the socialization process which has not yet been mentioned is the self-image of the individual. One's conception of what one is, one's proper style of life, must fit into the present style of being, and is an important factor in making or breaking habits and in forming attitudes, and so on. Individuals are in a constant process of becoming. Many factors enter into the process, including some mechanical learning out of habits from the past, but all these factors must be accounted for when we attempt to determine how personality becomes what it is. We may learn to keep to the right in traffic or how to run a machine or some skill which might be explained by traditional theory, but the concept of becoming includes also the self-image, maturation, identification, and all forms of cognitive learning. They must all be accounted for in an adequate theory of personality.

Evans: You would be inclined to agree, then, with Jung's (Evans 1976a) discussion of the individuation process. He felt that individuation is an important process even into middle age, and his ideas are consistent with the emergence of the existential movement in that the individual begins to raise the questions of "who am I," "what am I here for" and so on. Do you feel that it is a healthy thing for the individual to become more and more preoccupied with thoughts of his own existence?

Allport: When you raise questions about aging, you almost invite me to speak introspectively, but I realize that you are getting at the increased length of life which allows a man more time for such questions. I would say that there are probably as many ways of aging as there are individuals because I argue for uniqueness at every stage of being. The Hindu psychologists tell us that it is very characteristic of older people to seek a fourth stage of life which is called meaning or liberation, but represents a disengagement from the activities of the first stages that are more pleasure—and success—seeking and doing one's duty. The fourth stage is the one you referred to which brings up the questions, "who am I," "what's it all about," "what next," and so on. It's a natural concern as one grows older, but not peculiar to old age alone. Perhaps it's characteristic of our times that the question will have a more subjective, personal tone to it. The Aristotelians asked the question, "what is man" and that led to all the sciences of man, but we today are asking it more personally, as "who am I." This shift of emphasis is part of the so-called existential trend of our times, and I don't think it's either good or bad, though it's probably good because we have a right to know the answer to both the questions, "what is man" and "who am I."

My one criticism of the existential movement is that it tends to be rather egghead and philosophical and ascribes to all human beings the same existential vacuum. The eggheads and the elite would give to all men their own anxiety, nausea, and alienation. I just don't think it's true that every man goes through this anxiety and anguish and alienation in his effort to find meaning. However, as the educational level increases, more people read more books, and ponder more the questions they encounter, and I suppose it's natural to have more and more of this type of concern.

Evans: It's interesting that you suggest that this whole existential question could be the product of an intellectual culture. Though the question of existence is dealt with differently by different religions, another problem with existentialism is that it is very loosely defined. Each writer defines it differently and it may be that its only definition comes from within the individual and can't really be intellectualized at all.

Allport: The movement is a broad one, of course, and solutions have been offered from both the atheistic and the theistic points of view. Some stress alienation and some stress the need for commitment and responsibility; some search for meaning, and others for different things. It's rather lately come to America, but the American version has a little less of the pessimistic or fatalistic flavor than the European existentialism. America has produced her own existentialists, but they are generally more hopeful that in confronting the mysteries of life, even when starting with anguish and despair, one can work out a commitment and a solution adequate to himself.

Evans: Do you feel that man will arrive at a stage in development where he will become increasingly less concerned with this existential question?

Allport: The history of ideas has always been a reflection of historical conditions: plagues, wars, etc. The danger of the atomic bomb and the terrible tragedies which it implies has thrown this century into a kind of reflective mood. I am inclined to think it's a sign of growing maturity to ask the question "Who am I," to ask whence and whither, without being overcome by the need to adjust to the realities of technological advances. It puts more strain on the personality to do the adapting and the socializing and to continue to meet the economic problems of life while at the same time going on as a human being to think about one's own nature and destiny.

Evans: Dr. Allport, you've contributed a great deal over the years to the understanding of prejudice. Perhaps we might begin by asking you to define prejudice.

Allport: Oddly enough, the best definition for prejudice is a slang one: "Prejudice is being down on something you're not up on." We can be down on something that we are up on, too. We can be against criminals, assassins, Hitler's gang, and so forth; and for good reasons—because they violate our values—we are up on them. But in prejudice there is always an element of ignorance—unwarranted hostility—or else it's not prejudice. Prejudice must be defined as having two variables—one is hostility, and one is ignorance or erroneous judgment. Let me add, of course, that there can be prejudice in favor of others.

When I wrote *The Nature of Prejudice* (1954), the problem of causation was so large that it took several years for me to figure out the table of contents for the book. There is no single, simple thing that causes people to be prejudiced. I've divided the causes into rough levels for the purpose of analysis: historical, sociocultural, character and personality factors, perceptual factors, and the qualities of the victim himself. For example, if you don't know anything about the history of slavery in this country, you wouldn't know much about the nature of current prejudice. And on the sociocultural level, factors including a way of life that gets established must be included with some of the distal factors which are actually translated into behavior. Psychologically, elements which entered into the character, structure of personality, attitude, and training of the individual must be considered, while perceptual elements such as the way individualism in the minority group is perceived are important.

Finally, you must take into account the qualities of the victim himself because sometimes his behavior is perceived more or less corruptly and it puts an element of factuality into the judgment which may or may not support his prejudice. It's a very complicated question which would have to include perhaps eighteen to twenty distinguishable causal factors.

Evans: And you see that these factors originate both from within the individual, his psychological makeup, and from the environment or culture in which the individual operates, resulting in a wide variety of interactive effects.

Allport: Yes, but I would emphasize that the historical and sociocultural factors have to be translated into the nervous system of the individual. They don't act automatically. The term that is missing here to describe the interaction is conformity. We have never answered why people pick up the historical and sociocultural traditions and translate them into attitudes and behavior.

Evans: Another question integrally related to prejudice is the concept of discrimination, toward the elimination of which we are spending a great deal of energy in our country. Would you, with your orientation toward the individual, be satisfied that merely changing the environment through legal means would be an effective means to cut down prejudices and/or discrimination?

Allport: I would concede here a little to my sociological colleagues. If it's a matter of attitudes and prejudices, will we not have to effect changes in the education and exhortation of children to make long-range changes in the prejudice? It does not seem to follow from what I have previously said because when an external situation is changed by fiat or through law, you may have eliminated discrimination but you have not necessarily also eliminated prejudice. After discrimination has been eliminated and people come into equal-status contact with one another, then their attitudes may be affected away from prejudice. I would not, of course, rule out intercultural education, or exhortation, or working with individuals, but I really feel it's more efficient to begin with a large-scale change in the social structure.

Evans: Could we consider now the question of religion and the part it plays in the personality structure. There are some who feel that psychologists are not sympathetic to religion, but you have given the subject a great deal of thought and exposition.

Allport: The study of religious values is an outgrowth of my interest in personality theory, which is the basic concern out of which all my professional work has come. In 1937, I postulated a general theoretical approach in my book, *Personality: A Psychological Interpretation* (1937), but since then a lot of special problems have arisen that must be dealt with: What is the nature of attitudes in personality structure; what can you do with personal documents; what is the formation of prejudice that makes it so central to personality structure; what about some of the major values, etc. The work I did on the Study of Values Test is an aspect of the interest in more complex levels of personality. Religion, obviously, belongs in the same category as one of the complex sentiments that many, if not most, people develop. It represents a problem of personality—perhaps a specialized part of personality—and I think it's ridiculous for a psychologist to neglect it or overlook its importance in the structure of personality. In order to bring religion into line with a comprehensive study of personality, I presented six lectures on the subject which were later published in the book *The Individual and His Religion* (1950).

Evans: Would you summarize some of the main ideas you presented in those lectures to give us an insight into how you feel about the religious dimensions of personality?

Allport: I think it is helpful to take the developmental approach in this study. A child is totally incapable of understanding the abstraction of theology, and so he takes on the family religion simply as a matter of course, just as he takes to brushing his teeth or speaking the English language or taking on political sentiments. This is particularly true during the period of his close family identification between ages eight and eleven or so. Ordinarily the normal child begins after a while to question the family pattern simply because the statements are obviously abstract, and some of them sound rather outrageous to his literal-minded ears. Usually he goes through a period of questioning, but it's not that he's questioning religion as such. He's questioning what he thought his parents taught; he's questioning the dogmas as he understood them, not as the parents understood them. He's questioning his own childish approach, and that is the essential element for any personality if it is eventually to grow up. There are some, of course, in whom the childish formations and beliefs don't change; they go through life with essentially a juvenile, undeveloped religion. But about sixty percent, I should say, of the college students report having a very acute adolescent rebellion. What happens to them after that is subject to a wide variety of differential influences, and the personality develops in an individual style.

Evans: The adolescent rebellion you refer to here is rebellion against what they believe to be some of the basic dogmas of religion?

Allport: Yes, I'm glad you made that point clear. The adolescent thinks it's the parents' fault, so it takes its place among other emotional upheavals or rebellions he undergoes in his attempt to get away from parental domination. Then later he attempts to resolve this turmoil by a variety of means, such as adopting the same attitude his parents had when he has children of his own. This phenomenon often occurs around the age of thirty or so. The twenties are perhaps the least religious age of man.

Evans: Several early studies investigating the effects of religion in the individual personality found a high correlation between religiosity and prejudice, which would seem to indicate that religion was narrowing the individual. Still our later study (Evans 1952) has suggested that there might be two aspects of religion which operate differentially on the individual; the one reflected in more humanitarian concerns while the other is reflected in more selfish aspects of religion. Do you feel that this notion, opening the possibility of a differential impact of religion, is consistent with your experience?

Allport: We are presently engaged in a research project which deals with this very question. All research indicates that churchgoers on the average are much more prejudiced than nonchurchgoers, and that's a fact. It would seem to be a curious finding in view of the fact that most of the people who have devoted themselves to brotherhood are religiously motivated, and some good examples of this are Albert Schewitzer, Mahatma Gandi, and Martin Luther King. There must be some kind of contradiction going on here and so reviewing the research makes it obvious that we must distinguish between two kinds of religious orientation, the extrinsic value and the intrinsic value. When we tested for these dimensions using a scale for extrinsicness and one for intrinsicness, lo and behold, we found that the extrinsic attitude is correlated with prejudice, and the intrinsic is correlated with very low prejudice. I have to define extrinsic here as something that the person uses for his own purposes: to make friends, influence people, sell insurance, good times, prestige in the community, comfort, or wish fulfillment. He uses his religion in the same way that he uses his social groups and memberships. It's an exclusionistic point of view that can lead to prejudice because it is part of the fact that religion is solely for his benefit, and other people are not for his benefit. It's a very self-centered orientation and you would have to say a majority of people take their religion that way because the majority of churchgoers show this bigotry. On the other hand, there is a sizable minority whose attitude toward religion is quite the opposite; it plays an entirely different function for them because they serve it, it doesn't serve them. They have decided that the creeds and doctrines, including the doctrine of human brotherhood, are necessary for their value system, and they adopt for themselves the entire religious system, then live by it.

Evans: Another area of current and continuing interest in psychology is the area of personality testing and measurement in that it seems to imply a nomothetic approach where the tester looks for common traits, as you call them. In order adequately to understand the individual, one must use phenotypical (descriptive) information, and yet at the same time know that it doesn't do adequate justice to the individual. Is there a means by which we can handle this dilemma?

Allport: Yes, I've worked on that problem, and I think that I have the proper direction to look for an answer. We've simply neglected the study of personal dispositions which I think can be done purely quantitatively. For example, when Cantril asks people to define the best possible way for themselves and the worst possible way, then he puts these on a ladder of ten rungs. Then he asks the people where they stand now, where five years ago, and where they expect to stand two years from now. This gives him a morphogenic anchorage point, and indicates their best possible way of life. It's more than just a common trait. Another example is the case of personal documents which represents strictly morphogenic material. I have some very fascinating material called *Letters from Jenny*

(1965) which one of my former students, Professor Al Baldwin, used in a course to count the relationship of ideas in Jenny's mind.

The approaches used by people like Dr. Magda Arnold with the Thematic Apperception Test try to get at personal characteristics through a fairy-story sequence which serves as a diagnostic indicator, but is not scored routinely according to an established pattern of responses. These are problems which have not yet been adequately resolved.

Evans: Some people have suggested that this projective testing emphasizes the unconscious unduly, making it difficult to validate them properly. Do you feel there is a legitimate place for them in psychological research?

Allport: Yes, I certainly do feel they have a place. What I've said about them is that they should never be used without also using direct methods. If a person, for example, is consciously and unconsciously anxious, it means something very different from when he's only unconsciously anxious. How are you going to know that you're tapping the unconscious unless you know also what is conscious? I think I would be dogmatic and say that we should never use projective tests unless we also use direct methods of interview or pencil-and-paper tests in order to make comparisons between them.

Evans: Would you feel this way also about the use of dream interpretations?

Allport: Yes, I think so.

Evans: Incidentally, we couldn't engage in a discussion of personality measurement without pursuing further the significant personality measure which you yourself have developed along with Professors Vernon and Lindzey, the Study of Values. It's another example of the use of ostensibly nomothetic measurement designed to get at individuality, is it not?

Allport; That particular instrument is a curious hybrid. Actually, that instrument stands halfway between dimensional and morphogenic methods in a curious respect. There are, at the outset, six common traits: the theoretical, aesthetic, social, political, religious, and economic. These were defined by Spranger (1928) originally, and our test invites you to indicate the relative strength of these six values in your own personality. Consequently, your score cannot be compared with anyone else's because the test reflects relative strengths of those values within your own personality. We begin with an instrument which measures six common traits, but end with a profile that is strictly personal and individual.

Evans: In a different vein, Dr. Allport, would you share with us your feelings concerning the contributions you have made to psychology that you feel to be the most important?

Allport: It seems odd, perhaps, but I have never thought about this matter at all. All my work has focused on personality theory, particularly on the structure and the motivation of the personality. Everything has been focused around the central question of the nature of the human being. I have attempted to get reasoned empirical answers that shed some light on the issue, and they have come from different directions.

REFERENCES

Allport, G. W. 1937. *Personality: A psychological interpretation.* New York: Holt.

———. 1942. *The use of personal documents in psychological science.* New York: Social Science Research Council Bulletin 49.

———. 1943. The ego in contemporary psychology. *Psychol. Rev.* 50: 451–78.

———. 1950. *The individual and his religion.* New York: Macmillan.

———. 1954. *The nature of prejudice.* Cambridge: Addison-Wesley.

———. 1955. *Becoming: Basic considerations for a psychology of personality.* New Haven, Conn.: Yale University Press.

———. 1961. *Pattern and growth in personality.* New York: Holt.

———. 1965. *Letters from Jenny.* New York: Harcourt.

Allport, G. W., and Vernon, P. E. 1933. *Studies in expressive movement.* New York: Macmillan.

Evans, R. I. 1952. Personal values as factors in anti-Semitism. *J. Abnorm. Soc. Psychol.* 47: 749–56.

———. 1976a. *Jung on elementary psychology.* New York: Dutton.

———. 1973. *Jean Piaget: The man and his ideas.* New York: Dutton.

Lewin, K. A. 1936. *Principles of topological psychology,* trans. F. Heider and G. M. Heider. New York: McGraw-Hill.

Spranger, E. 1928. *Types of men.* New York: Stechert.

SELECTED READINGS

Allport, G. W. 1931. What is a trait of personality? *J. Abnorm. Soc. Psychol.* 25: 368–372.

Allport, G. W. 1954. *The nature of prejudice.* Cambridge: Addison-Wesley.

Allport, G. W. 1955. *Becoming: Basic considerations for a psychology of personality.* New Haven, Conn.: Yale University Press.

Allport, G. W. 1960. The open system in personality theory. *J. Abnorm. Soc. Psychol.* 61: 301–310.

Allport, G. W. 1961. *Pattern and growth in personality.* New York: Holt.

Allport, G. W. 1965. *Letters from Jenny.* New York: Harcourt.

4

MUZAFER SHERIF
(1906–   )

CAROLYN WOOD SHERIF
(1922–   )

Muzafer Sherif earned his B. A. at Izmin International College, and an M. A. at the University of Istanbul before coming to the United States, where he received an M. A. at Harvard University in 1932, and his Ph. D. at Columbia University in 1935. A prolific researcher, his work includes the important early study of the autokinetic phenomenon, a prototypical application of psychophysics to the study of social judgments and attitudes. He has contributed fundamental concepts to social psychology through his studies of norm formation, group relations, attitude and attitude change, conformity and deviance, and the measurement of attitudes. Dr. Sherif has held distinguished professorships at the Gaza Institute, Turkey (1937–1944), the University of Oklahoma (1949–1966), and until his retirement was a professor and director of the Psychosocial Studies Program in the Department of Sociology at Pennsylvania State University. he was awarded a Guggenheim Fellowship in 1967, and the Distinguished Scientific Contribution Award by the American Psychological Association in 1969.

Carolyn Wood Sherif took her B. S. at Purdue University, received her M. A. at The State University of Iowa, and earned her Ph. D. at the University of Texas in 1961. Since 1945 she has been co-author and collaborator with Muzafer Sherif in numerous studies of intergroup relations, group behavior, attitudes, attitude change, and adolescent psychology. Outside of this prodigious collaboration, she has published important studies in adolescence and the psychology of women. Dr. Carolyn Sherif has held posts at the University of Oklahoma, the University of Texas, and visiting professorships at Cornell University and Smith

39

College. She is a Fellow in Division 8 (Personality and Social), and Division 35 (Psychology of Women) of the American Psychological Association, and is listed in Who's Who in America (1978) and American Men and Women in Science. Currently she is professor of psychology at Pennsylvania State University.

Bringing Psycho-Physics to Measuring Attitudes/ Thurstone's Early Attitude Toward War Scale// When the Situation Is Sharply Defined, the Stimulus Overcomes Affective Differences/ Selective Perception// The Semantic-Differential Scale/ Measuring Attitudes// Adaptation Level/ An "Own Categories" Scale/ Assimilation and Contrast/ Latitude of Acceptance, Latitude of Rejection, and Latitude of Noncommitment// Involvement of the Self// Autokinetic Effect/ Conformity Behavior// The "Robbers' Cave" Experiment/ The Formation of Intergroup Conflict// Negative Stereotypes// Superordinate Goals// Some Criticism/ We Profited from our Colleagues' Feedback// Significant Social Problems/ Women's Opportunity in Social Psychology//

The Sherifs and I begin with a discussion of the development of various attitude scales, including Thurstone's Attitude Toward War Scale and Osgood's Semantic Differential. Based on the idea that cognitive and affective processes influence one another in attitude measurements, the Sherifs developed a projective technique called an "own categories" scale, which in principle is an unstructured stimulus allowing the subject to express his attitude in his own terms. The Sherifs then define several of their important concepts, including assimilation, contrast, and latitudes of acceptance, rejection, and noncommitment. Muzafer Sherif describes his famous studies of the autokinetic phenomenon, in which he induced individuals, alone and in groups, to create "norms" under laboratory conditions. Carolyn Sherif compares these studies of behavior in unstructured situations to later work by Solomon Asch and Stanley Milgram on behavior in situations where the stimulus is structured in other specific ways, highlighting the underlying themes of conformity and deviance. Next, we discuss the Robbers' Cave study, a natural experiment on the formation of groups and intergoup conflict and cooperation, which was conducted in a summer camp for young boys. Carolyn Sherif reacts to the criticism that their work has received, and comments on the scientific "crisis" in social psychology: "If they think it's a crisis, for them it's a crisis. I see the present time as one in which there is more opportunity to explore creatively than there was ten or fifteen years ago." Finally, Carolyn Sherif responds to my question about the future for

women in psychology, suggesting that not only would the inclu-
sion of more women serve the interest of fairness, but it would
also "diversify the academic community and insure a broader,
more comprehensive social psychology."

Evans: Muzafer, I know that you were involved in two very important psychological centers, Harvard and Columbia, during your training. Which individuals do you feel influenced your thinking and career?

M. Sherif: My thinking was influenced by various people, mostly by
authors on anthropology and sociology as well as psychology whose
works I read. At Columbia, Gardner Murphy was very encouraging of
my career. As editor of the Harper psychology series, he asked me to
write my first book, *The Psychology of Social Norms* (1936/1966). At
Harvard I was influenced by J. G. Beebe-Center (1932). He translated
psychophysical ideas to the field of affectivity. Later, I applied such ideas
to social psychology in the study of attitudes and social judgment.

Evans: It is interesting that Thurstone, in developing his classic attitude scale, was employing psychophysics in measuring attitudes as
well.

M. Sherif: Yes, but Thurstone made a very important assumption
which was not true. When judging his attitude statements he assumed
that people are not influenced by their own attitudes. In building his
scale he thought that intellectual things and affective or motivational
things are separate or independent of one another. We started our work
on social judgment by challenging this assumption that cognitive and
motivational processes are independent. Our idea was that they influence one another.

Evans: To be more specific, let's consider Thurstone's early Attitude
Toward War Scale (Thurstone and Chave 1929). This scale had a number of different statements about war which had been calibrated in terms
of median scale values along an eleven point scale of favorability or
unfavorability toward war, and subjects were asked to check those items
with which they agreed. Calibrated to be among the strongest pro-
statements on the eleven point scale was, "There can be no progress without war." How would you react to scaling of such an item in this manner?

M. Sherif: If it were as clear-cut as this example, we'd look at it in
much the same way. But, in general, we'd be interested in how the person
categorizes a statement as well as whether it is accepted or rejected. Most
people would categorize that one as an extremely pro-war statement.

Evans: OK. Let's take another, less clear-cut statement, "War is only
effective some of the time."

M. Sherif: That would allow for displacement one way or another, depending on a person's attitude. A person who is pro-war will consider it anti-war, and a person who is anti-war will consider it as very pro-war.

Evans: In other words, two people may read what is exactly the same statement and because they are perceiving it quite differently in terms of their own frames of reference and their agreement or disagreement with the statement, it may have entirely different implications for each of them.

M. Sherif: Yes. Still our hypothesis was that when the situation is sharply defined, the stimulus overcomes affective differences. If the environment is too strong, like a car coming toward you, your behavior is dominated by the stimulus. When the situation is more unstructured it allows displacement one way or the opposite, depending on the attitude of the person.

Evans: So in your early work on attitude measurement you were already introducing the idea of selective perception, and beginning to develop a scaling method that anticipated the so-called new look in perceptual theory (e.g., Bruner and Goodman 1947), which was to become a rather important focus in psychology.

M. Sherif: Yes. Thurstone eliminated equivocal statements, but we used a good many ambiguous statements so that internal factors—that is, attitudes—could come into the picture.

C. Sherif: I want to add that Muzafer and Carl Hovland (Sherif and Hovland 1953) used the replication of the Thurstone procedure with demonstrators for desegregation in the early civil rights movement; and they did, indeed, displace a lot of statements both toward their own position on the issue and away from it.

Evans: Sometime after your work, Charles Osgood and his colleagues (Osgood, Suci, and Tannenbaum 1957) began to move in a far more phenomenological direction in scaling with their semantic differential. They developed several adjective bipolarities of meaning: good/bad, valuable/worthless, etc., which they believed would apply to any concept. How do you feel about the semantic-differential scale as an answer to this problem?

C. Sherif: Certainly it is a different technique, and it can be very useful. We're not hammering away at every attitude technique. The problem here is two-fold as I see it. One is that they do make the same assumption that most of the other scales do. In the ratings made between the bipolar adjectives, numbers are assigned as though these are invariant scales. There is evidence that they are not invariant. An additional problem is that both in the Likert format and in the semantic differential, intermediate ratings don't have any meaning psychologically. Our work over the years has led us to be fascinated by what intermediate or moderate attitudes mean.

Evans: Festinger (1957) discussed the relationship between attitudes and behavior, and painted a very grim picture. He pointed out that rarely do attitudes correlate with behavior. Of course, this continues to be an issue in contemporary social psychology. Do you think that one of the problems in establishing this relationship between attitudes and behavior is partly the way we are measuring attitudes?

C. Sherif: Oh, yes. We live in a society that prizes measurement tremendously. When the early social psychologists began to devise scales for attitude measurement, they provided a justification for survey research, the polls, and measuring attitudes in a variety of social contexts. I think that these techniques became popular and were widely used without ever asking the question, "What are the psychological and social meanings of these measurements in different social contexts?" We know that in some contexts when you give a person an attitude scale, you get a response that means the person thinks this is how they *should* behave in that situation. You can't say you're measuring the person's attitude.

Evans: I notice an interesting kinship between your ideas, and Harry Helson's (e.g., Helson 1948) work on adaptation level. I think he drew his ideas pretty heavily from your work on the autokinetic effect. You could attend a Ku Klux Klan meeting and say that "black people are almost as nice a white people" and the members would be outraged. On the other hand, if you attend a meeting of the NAACP, and make the same statement, these members would also be outraged.

M. Sherif: That's why we call our attitude measure an "own categories" scale. We leave the subjects free to choose as many or as few categories as they wish. We developed a projective technique in terms of the number of categories and number of items in each category. When a person has an attitude, these categorizations reflect it even when agreement or disagreement with each attitude statement is not requested. To be precise, the more involved the person is in an attitude position, the fewer the number of categories he uses and the larger the number of items within those few categories, particularly in those objectionable to the person. The milder one gets in attitude, the more shadings one uses.

Evans: You use the terms "assimilation" and "contrast." Could you define specifically what you meant by these two terms?

M. Sherif: In order to do that we have to introduce three concepts: latitude of acceptance, latitude of rejection, and latitude of noncommitment.

C. Sherif: Latitude of acceptance refers to all of the items or people (whatever it is we're looking at) that are acceptable to the person. Latitude of rejection comprises all those items that are objectionable; and latitude of noncommitment comprises those of which there isn't any clear acceptance or rejection. The person is noncommittal toward them. We were talking earlier about psychophysics and affective judgments. When people are dealing with stimuli that are personally meaningful to them, they can't help implicating themselves in the process. If during their life history they have developed a set of categories for dealing with the objects in that domain, their affective judgments are expressed by that set of categories. By "assimilation" we simply mean a displacement in a judgment or perception that is toward one's own position. "Contrast" is affective and cognitive exaggeration of the difference between one's own position and what one is against.

Evans: It is clear that in your work you focus on the individual level of social analysis even though you do look at group dynamics and social institutions. Your earlier term "ego involvement" seems to suggest this.

M. Sherif: We now prefer to say "involvement of the self" instead of "ego involvement." We learned that when we say ego involvement people think of Freudian ego. Our concept comes more from sociology and from George Herbert Mead (1934) and William James (1890/1950).

Evans: Perhaps you'd like to expand on that a little bit.

M. Sherif: Attitudes and self are closely related. Attitudes that have greatest weight are self-involving, describing or delimiting the boundaries of the self, as an individual sees himself. I came to the idea of self because I thought it is essential for the study of attitudes. When the person himself is involved, the attitude is "personalized" and so are events related to it.

Evans: So you're saying that the mechanism to socialization, or development of self, is attitude development, and you have to interpret attitudes in terms of involvement of the self.

C. Sherif: Yes. This is one of the reasons that the issues of gender are so fascinating. In every society children encounter very early and in a very compelling way the fact that they are identified by gender. In contrast, not all attitudes are equally implicating of the self. We all carry around a lot of baggage in which we do find attitudes, but they're not very central to us. The person's reactions to efforts to change their attitudes are different depending on how much the self is implicated.

Evans: There's a consistency in your thinking that carries over to the experimental work that Muzafer (Sherif, M. 1935) did on autokinetic effect. Your experiments with autokinetic effect, based on the perception of apparent movement of a specific source of light, have influenced a whole body of theory. How did you happen to develop this line of research?

M. Sherif: In 1932–33 the literature I read on attitudes was patchwork, and I wanted to tie that together. I wanted to find a neutral term first. "Norm" was not used at that time in connection with cultural or social norms. I defined "norm" as the criterion of conduct that's standardized in a given culture; marriage, traditions, or short-lived fashions are all examples of norms.

Evans: The behavioral aspect of a norm is that which most people in that society will actually do?

M. Sherif: Yes. A great many people abide by a norm. You can point at it. "Attitude" is personal and psychological. "Norm" is a sociological term that exists independently of a particular person. An attitude corresponding to it is psychological, personalized. Its strength may vary from person to person. I wanted to find something to study norms, which exist independently of individuals.

Evans: Where did you get the idea that to study the formation of norms you should look for an unstructured stimulus situation?

M. Sherif: The idea was that what is not structured is also open to individual interpretation. I got the idea from Emile Durkheim (1915), whose word for "norm" was "collective representation." According to

Durkheim, "norms" arise in fluid situations far away from the established way of doing things. So I wanted to find an unstructured, fluid situation. I learned from the Gestalt psychologists of one's tendency to structure his perception, even when there is little to go on.

C. Sherif: I would like to interject that I don't think Muzafer was sure that individuals would structure the autokinetic situation when he started. He was interested in asking if an individual who faced an unstructured input would create, over time, some framework within which to view it. Next, he was interested in what would happen when individuals with different frameworks came together in an unstructured stimulus condition. Would they each stick to their own framework or would they create together some common one? Would some common perspective emerge that would carry over to a single individual alone?

Evans: In your experiment, if I remember, the subject's task was to estimate the distance a tiny light moved in a completely darkened room. Actually, the light never moves, but is always experienced as having some motion. Some subjects made these estimates alone, and some made them in groups. Your interest was in finding if individuals formed "norms" when they were alone, and when they were in groups; and if so, how established norms affected later judgments when previously alone subjects were placed in groups, and vice versa.

M. Sherif: That's right.

Evans: So you were trying to create norms in the laboratory to study the genesis of norms and how they influence human judgments.

M. Sherif: Exactly. Individuals, even without the influence of others, will have their own "norms." I started with the individual subjects, got 400 judgments from each, 100 per session in four sessions, and established that individuals establish their own "norms." In groups, there is a convergence of individual judgments, which creates a "group norm." This "group norm" will later continue to operate when an individual is placed in the dark room alone.

Evans: Suppose you brought a person who presumedly was an expert in measurement, like an engineer, who was going to measure that length of movement. How would you predict that he would affect the individual's "norm"?

C. Sherif: The relationship between the individuals is all important. In the original studies they were strangers who just came to the laboratory. Research since (Mausner 1953; Graham 1962; Croner and Willis 1961) shows that if somebody is presented as an expert or if he has a personal relationship, he will exert much more influence on the other. On the other hand, if there's antagonism between the people, they'll diverge and never reach a "norm."

Evans: Going a little further, in the work of Asch (1952), Milgram (1963), and others there is a tremendous amount of interest in conformity behavior which seems to have sprung from your work.

C. Sherif: I think that Muzafer's norm formation experiments, coming very early in the history of experimental social psychology, did have a tremendous impact. Dr. Asch was probably influenced on these issues; however, his problem was quite different. He was really interested in what happens when the individual faces not an unstructured situation, but a highly structured situation. In Asch's experiments the stimulus is very clear, but other people are telling the subject that they see something entirely different. If you then look at Stanley Milgram's studies of obedience, he takes leads from both of these studies to essentially ask the question: How is the environment structured maximally in order to get people to comply to what may seem an absurd request from authority? We sometimes forget that these studies show that when you start introducing ambiguity in the environment, people don't obey at all.

Evans: Have some people misunderstood your work, or thought that Muzafer was merely studying conformity, when both deviance and conformity are involved?

C. Sherif: Muzafer has been dubbed in some people's minds a conformity man. Those who consider him that often refer to a study (Sherif, M. 1937) in which he introduced a confederate giving autokinetic judgments in a certain pattern and found that the naive uninstructed subject was following along. But this study was just one part of the overall work in autokinetic judgment. The real social parallel for the autokinetic experience would not be conformity, but a situation when people are very uncertain about things and they're facing problems in which there are alternatives. How do they come to view this situation in a common framework? Is it a creative act on both the individual and group level. And, as you know, we've been interested in social change, which always involves deviation from something.

Evans: The "Robbers' Cave" experiment was one of your most famous studies (Sherif, M. and Sherif, C. 1953). It was a naturalistic experiment involving a group of boys in a summer camp. The focus, I believe, was the study of intergroup relations, the formation of in-groups and out-groups, and the generation and reduction of intergroup conflict. I wonder if you'd like to describe this study?

M. Sherif: First of all that experiment was one in which the natural environment becomes very important. Secondly the structure of the activities that were going on among the boys becomes very important. Thirdly, the individual boy's relationships to those activities and the environment are absolutely crucial. We started with unacquainted boys, with a hypothesis about when groups would form, with a pattern to the relationships among them and a little culture of norms. The development of status differentiation, reciprocal roles, and group norms regulating behavior were our criteria for group formation.

C. Sherif: Our hypothesis was that this takes time, but not time alone. It involves interactions among them over time and activities that to each individual are highly appealing and that require some interdependence. Interdependence occurs at the task level where cooperation is required to achieve goals that benefit all the members of the group. We also predicted that something more than interdependence arises. This is a power relation among the individuals, such that some words, some actions count more than others. A new social environment was created, and the focus of that study was on the formation of intergroup conflict. Our interest was in attitudes toward one's own group and toward another group with whom one was in conflict, as well as in the process of change.

Evans: What kind of boys participated in the experiment?

M. Sherif: There were twenty-two boys about eleven years of age. They all came from middle-class, stable, Prostestant families. They were purposely selected to be healthy and well adjusted so that the conflicts generated could not be attributed to previous frustration or maladjustment.

C. Sherif: Our hypothesis was that although the preexisting differences between groups (religious differences and gender differences and so on) do contribute to the conflict, that for individuals to develop these nasty ways, it was not necessary that they have a long history. To have a realistic confrontation between those groups was a sufficient condition.

M. Sherif: And within groups they were as harmonious as they come.

Evans: As I understand it, no imposed experimental manipulations were used to generate conflict. Is that correct?

C. Sherif: Yes, that's correct. We didn't have to impose anything to create the conflict. In the Robbers' Cave experiment, at first they didn't even know there was another group in the camp. As soon as they knew there was another group there, they said, "Oh, goody, we'll challenge them and we'll win."

Evans: So generation of conflict arose spontaneously and was not really planned.

C. Sherif: That's right. Of course, it wasn't entirely unplanned, but it wasn't manipulation. The plan had something to do with the selection of the boys, who were very active, healthy boys. If you pick a bunch of quieter boys, they might not have challenged each other right away. All we had to do was systematize the competition. Instead of just a one-shot game with each other, we organized a tournament. We told them, "Tell us what you want included in the tournament and there will even be prizes." That seemed natural to them, but that was what had been planned.

M. Sherif: We had to develop a theory of conflict: What will be conducive to conflict and what might reduce it. We predicted that repeated competition between groups in which only one could win the series and the other must lose would be sufficient to produce conflict.

C. Sherif: We had two hypotheses about reduction of conflict. Once you get two groups fighting each other, individuals in each group begin forming negative stereotypes of the members of the other group, finally not wanting to have anything to do with each other. What do you do? One well-known hypothesis in psychology was that, first of all, you've got to get them together as equals. There has to be contact as equals, because if they are unequal they're going to magnify any differentiation.

And so, what kind of contact? One hypothesis would say, let it be contact in which both groups are doing something they want to do very much and their pleasure at these activities will spread to their relationships with one another. For about three days this hypothesis was tested, and in a total of thirteen different situations in which the groups were together, they continued to fight and call each other nasty names. In short, those sorts of situations just served as occasions for the conflicts to come out. Our final hypothesis was that the contact between equals, in order to cause change, had to involve interdependence of a kind that required the resources and energies of all the members of both groups. There had to be some goal to be achieved in the environment that they couldn't ignore, but that everyone was needed to do. We called those "superordinate goals."

Evans: Groups in harmony must have superordinate goals.

M. Sherif: That's right. They really had to learn to deal with each other on other than hostile terms. They had to learn how to cooperate in these situations. It was in the process of learning and cooperation that they began to change their images of each other. They decided that they had been wrong in their appraisals of one another, that there were some good guys on the other side.

Evans: So you were able to use this as a study for looking at several major areas—for example, sociometry, norms, and stereotypes—in a context of a naturalistic situation. It seems to me that the bottom line of all of this was that you were able to demonstrate that although it's difficult, you can move out of the laboratory and test some very important hypotheses in social psychology.

C. Sherif: Yes. I understand young social psychologists are getting very discouraged when we think how much work is involved in carrying out such research. But we really believe that social psychology has got to move forward through the cooperative efforts of many people. We spend a lot of the time plugging away, but the the real question is: Are we plugging along in a fruitful direction?

M. Sherif: That's why we spent a great deal of effort for about ten years on the study of natural groups of adolescents in their own environments, on a project reported first in our book *Reference Groups* (Sherif, M. and Sherif, C. 1964). Ideas have to be tested in actual life. And to do so, one has to do sociological and anthropological work as well as psychological work. Of course, studies in the field are also productive of worthwhile new ideas for experimental study.

Evans: As innovators in research in natural settings, a field that at that time and even today is perhaps overly dominated by laboratory work, you have undoubtedly been subjected to some criticism. How do you react to some of that criticism?

C. Sherif: It must be said in all honesty that when people make criticisms and you feel that they have not tried to understand you, it is very frustrating. But when somebody comes along and has read your work and sees something that you haven't seen, it can be most rewarding and constructive. Unfortunately, you don't usually go out and thank that person, but you really should. I think we profited from our colleagues' feedback, and it would be fun to go through some of our work and see which things were in response to such criticisms, because I know they've made a difference.

Evans: One final question. Where do you think the field of social psychology is going? We have a tremendous battle still going on between the need to maintain the experimental rigor of laboratory experiments and the need to address ourselves to significant social problems by doing work in applied settings. Some individuals even say there is a crisis in our field. How can we resolve this? Do we know enough now to take on some of the pressing societal problems?

C. Sherif: You're right! Social psychology is in what some people like to call a crisis. If they think it's a crisis, for them it's a crisis. I think it's a changing picture. I see what's going on as a very hopeful sort of thing. I think it's not hopeful only under two conditions. One is if it makes some people feel very discouraged so that they quit too early. And another one is if some people feel the need to defend what they are doing so strongly that they can't change. I see the present time as one in which there is more opportunity to explore creatively than there was ten or fifteen years ago. Now, as to your question: Are social psychologists ready to go out and tackle major problems of society? I have to be a little cautious and say that if that's going to happen you have to allow two things to occur. First, in our graduate training we have to go different ways than we have been, and train people not only in scientific methodology and classical psychology but in related disciplines like sociology, antropology, or political science. We can be better social psychologists if we'd go out into medicine, for example, or courts of law or the workplace and find out what the problems are and see how we can study them. Second, I think that ultimately it can have a beneficial effect provided that we don't promise too much and we admit our relative ignorance from the start.

Evans: Carolyn, do you have some feeling that there will be increasing numbers of women who will have an opportunity to make contributions to social psychology?

C. Sherif: Well, I certainly hope so. The statistics are that there are more young women coming into social psychology than there were. But this is happening at a time in which academia is getting more crowded with white middle-aged males who are going to occupy their jobs for a long time. And so, both women and young men are faced with the fact that the opportunities in academia are going to be tighter for them, at least for a while. Maybe that will be a good thing; perhaps they will find roles in society that we didn't even dream of. But I'd like to have more women colleagues, and I think that a great deal of effort is needed to diversify the academic community by including more women and more social psychologists from diverse ethnic and racial backgrounds. The effort will serve the interest of fairness, of course, but it is also needed to insure a broader, more comprehensive social psychology.

REFERENCES

Asch, S. E. 1952. *Social psychology*. New York: Prentice-Hall.

Beebe-Center, J. G. 1932. *Pleasantness and unpleasantness*. Princeton, New Jersey: Van Nostrand.

Bruner, J. S., and Goodman, C. C. 1947. Value and need as organizing factors in perception. *J. Abnorm. Soc. Psychol*. 42: 33–44.

Croner, M. D., and Willis, R. H. 1961. Perceived differences in task competence and asymmetry of dyadic influence. *J. Abnorm. Soc. Psychol*. 62: 705–708.

Durkheim, E. 1916. *Elementary forms of religious life*. New York: Macmillan.

Festinger, L. 1957. The relation between behavior and cognition. In *Contemporary approaches to cognition*. Cambridge: Harvard University Press.

Graham, D. 1962. Experimental studies of social influence in simple judgment situations. *J. Soc. Psychol*. 56: 245–69.

Helson, H. 1948. Adaptation-level as a basis for a quantitative theory of frames of reference. *Psychol. Rev*. 55: 297–313.

James, W. 1950. (Originally published, 1890.) *Principles of psychology*. New York: Dover.

Mausner, B. 1953. Studies in social interaction: III. Effect of variation in one partner's prestige on the interaction of observed pairs. *J. Appl. Psychol*. 37: 391–94.

Mead, G. H. 1934. *Mind, self, and society*, ed. C. W. Morris. Chicago: University of Chicago Press.

Milgram, S. 1963. Behavioral study of obedience to authority. *J. Abnorm. Soc. Psychol* 67: 371–78.

Osgood, C. E., Suci, G. J., and Tannenbaum, P. H. 1957. *The measurement of meaning*. Urbana, Illinois: University of Illinois Press.

Sherif, M. 1935. A study of some social factors in perception. *Archives of Psychology*. 187: 5–60.

———. 1937. An experimental approach to the study of attitudes. *Sociometry* 1: 90–98.

———. 1966. (Originally published, 1966.) *The psychology of social norms*. New York: Harper & Row.

———, and Sherif, C. W. 1964. *Reference groups*. New York: Harper & Row.

———, and Sherif, C. W. 1953. *Groups in harmony and tension*. New York: Harper & Brothers.

———, and Hovland, C. I. 1953. Judgmental phenomenon and scales of attitude measurement: Placement of items with individual choice of number of categories. *J. Abnorm. Soc. Psychol*. 48: 135–41.

Thurstone, L. L. and Chave, E. J. 1929. *The measurement of attitude*. Chicago: University of Chicago Press.

SELECTED READINGS

Sherif, C. W. 1976. *Orientation in social psychology*. New York: Harper & Row.
Sherif, C. W. 1979. What every intelligent woman should know about psychol-

ogy and women. In *Women: Study toward understanding*, ed. E. Snyder. New York: Harper & Row.

Sherif, M., and Sherif, C. W. 1953. *Groups in harmony and tension*. New York: Harper & Brothers.

Sherif, M., and Hovland, C. I. 1953. Judgmental phenomenon and scales of attitude measurement: Placement of items with individual choice of number of categories. *J. Abnorm. Soc. Psychol.* 48: 135–41.

Sherif, M., and Sherif, C. W. 1964. *Reference groups*. New York: Harper & Row.

Sherif, M., and Sherif, C. W. 1969. *Social psychology*. New York: Harper & Row.

5

NEVITT SANFORD

(1909–   )

Nevitt Sanford took his undergraduate degree at the University of Richmond and his master's at Columbia University. He received his doctorate from Harvard in 1934. He has held posts at Massachusetts Institute of Technology, the University of California, and Stanford University. He is now president of The Wright Institute, which he founded in 1968. Dr. Sanford has made extensive contributions to the areas of social psychology, higher education, personality development, and clinical psychology. He was the leader of the "California Group," which did the classic research on the authoritarian personality. His work reflects his concern for the maintenance of human dignity and his dedication to the solution of social problems. He is a past president of both the American Psychological Association's Division of Personality and Social Psychology and the Society for the Psychological Study of Social Issues. He organized and directed the Institute for the Study of Human Problems at Stanford from 1961 to 1969. His numerous honors include the Kurt Lewin Memorial Award in 1969, the Award for Distinguished Contributions to Clinical Psychology in 1970, and the Nevitt Sanford Award of the International Society of Political Psychology.

The "California Group"/The Authoritarian Personality/The Usefulness of Freudian Concepts/A Scale for Measuring Anti-Semitism/The Ethnocentrism Scale/Fromm's Escape from Freedom/The Meaning of Behavior/Types of People Who Score Low on Authoritarianism//The Values of the Investigator/Scientific Method//Education for Human Potentiality//Complex Phenomena in Real Life Situations/The Laboratory Experiment Was for Demonstration/ Studies of Alcoholism/Interdisciplinary Inquiry/Teenage Drinking//Students Should Bring to Graduate School a Demand for Relevance to the Problems in Society//

In response to my initial question concerning the famous authoritarian personality studies, Dr. Sanford states that the research demonstrated the usefulness of the Freudian approach to studying ordinary phenomena of life. He narrates a brief chronology of the study's beginnings and the gathering together of the research group, including Adorno, Frenkel-Brunswik, and Levinson, since known as the "California Group," who produced the monumental report The Authoritarian Personality. *He then defines the syndrome called the authoritarian personality, which the authors emphasize is an underlying personality structure and not a particular behavior pattern. Dr. Sanford also discusses the various ways a person can be low on authoritarianism. He then reacts to some of the criticism directed at the study, in particular the charge that its results were merely a confirmation of the values of the investigators. Dr. Sanford argues that one must work on problems that reflect human values and concerns, and that this need not necessarily interfere with objective science: "If people suspect that we had wishes in the matter and that these are expressed in our work, then they have to point to the precise instances in which the method went wrong. I would say to our critics, 'Go ahead and repeat our work, and see what you discover.' " As we continue, Dr. Sanford evaluates the limited success of modern liberal arts education to further personality development of college students. Although many college catalogs still pay lip service to liberal arts ideals, Dr. Sanford points to a disturbing neglect of education directed toward expanding human potential, in the interest of increasing specialization and professionalization. He then discusses his own efforts to be a problem-oriented psychologist, which often necessitates multidisciplinary collaboration. Dr. Sanford comments on the problems attendant to multidisciplinary cooperation, and insists that we need to recognize our universities to facilitate such cooperation. Finally, he urges that students "bring to graduate school a demand for relevance" and insist that their professors show them the relationship of their courses to genuine societal problems.*

Evans: Dr. Sanford, during the 1940s, in a creative integration of your background in psychoanalysis with your interests in social psychology, you became part of a group, which came to be referred to as the "California Group," that embarked on one of the most significant breakthroughs in social psychology. This was the work (Adorno, Frenkel-Brunswik, Levinson, and Sanford 1950) done on the authoritarian personality at the University of California. How did you get involved in the study of authoritarianism?

Sanford: This should probably be called a study in the psychopathology of everyday life. It is often said by some writers that Freud's ideas are all right for explaining neurosis or neurotic behavior, but not normal behavior. I would say that the study we conducted would not have been possible had we not believed that everybody has remnants of their childhood fixations and maladaptive resolutions of their conflicts, and that this childishness expresses itself particularly in critical situations or in situations of great controversy or conflict. I believe that, in general, our studies of the authoritarian personality show the great usefulness of Freudian concepts. It is not that we proved the validity of this or that Freudian proposition, but I think that we did show that this kind of psychology can be quite useful in studying ordinary phenomena of life.

Evans: How did this group get together? Was this a reaction to the totalitarianism in Germany?

Sanford: Well, that story is worth telling. People's present-day conceptions of how research is done are so different from the way it was actually done in those days that it will be interesting to report. As a matter of fact, some reviewers of our book assume that we had put together a proposal and sought to raise funds to do a study of the authoritarian personality and that some beneficent foundation came forward with loads of money so that we were able to carry out this project. Nothing could be farther from the truth. I was approached one day by the provost of the University of California, who said that he had $500 from an unknown donor to be used for the study of anti-Semitism and could I make use of it. I remembered a student named Daniel Levinson who needed the money and who probably would be interested in this problem, so we undertook to carry out a study of anti-Semitism (Levinson and Sanford 1944). We tried it with a number of classes of University of California students and found that, as a matter of fact, this scale very nicely separated people who in interviews were diagnosed as anti-Semitic from people who were not. We presented this to our unknown donor and, lo and behold, he came through with another $500. This made it possible for us to continue. I do not remember the precise history there, but we noticed that in our anti-Semitism scale the items not only made reference to Jews, but there were various *kinds* of accusations that were being made against Jews. Some people held it against Jews that they were too weak. Others complained that Jews were too strong. Some complained about their violation of conventional moral standards, and so on. In other words, we began to conceive the notion that what was really important here was the inclination on the part of our subjects to insist that people conform to conventional moral standards, and the need to find people who were weaker than themselves. In other words, the deeper underlying psychological functions were expressed in anti-Semitism. This led us to ask ourselves whether these human tendencies were not also expressed in prejudice and discrimination against various other kinds of people, and we began working on what we later called the ethnocentrism scale (Adorno, et al. 1950). I think that began quite early in the game, perhaps with that second $500. Then Dr. Else Frenkel-Brunswik, who was at the University of California at the time, became interested in this, and pretty soon we were able to enlist her in our project.

The crucial stage of our work came when we began carrying out rather intensive interviews with subjects to whom we had earlier given our scales. We would give the anti-Semitism and ethnocentrism scales to groups of people, and then interview the subjects who had scored at the extremes on these scales. We thought the best way to learn something would be to start with the extremes where these phenomena were rather vividly expressed. It became clear to us that people who were against Jews and against minorities had quite characteristic ways of talking about child training, their parents, work, and so on. So this began giving us the idea that there was a general way of looking at people, at the world, at group relations, and so on, that was rather characteristic of some people and could be distinguished from ways found in other people. It was about that time that we were joined by Dr. Adorno.

Evans: Since Dr. Adorno had contact in Europe with Erich Fromm, did he bring any of Fromm's ideas to your group?

Sanford: I think Dr. Adorno brought many ideas of a Frommian sort to us. Of course, we were reading Fromm's *Escape from Freedom* (1941) also, and I think it is fair to say that there was an interaction between his ideas of the authoritarian character described in *Escape from Freedom* and our own observations from our interviews and scales. I think it is fair to say, as a matter of fact, that most of the basic ideas about the structure of authoritarianism were actually put forward by Eric Fromm in *Escape from Freedom.* In a way, what we were doing was bringing to bear upon this problem the techniques of American social psychology, and by publishing a big book that described numerous ways in which this hypothetical structure was being expressed in belief, in attitude, and in behavior, we were able to have somewhat of an impact.

Evans: Moving from the ethnocentrism, or E scale, you then developed an instrument called the F scale (Adorno, et al. 1950), which was a measure of a pre-fascist propensity. Would it be correct to describe a high-scorer on this instrument as being an "authoritarian personality"?

Sanford: I would rather not say "authoritarian personality" when speaking of any one individual. It would not be appropriate to say "he" or "she" is an authoritarian personality. You see, this would be to assume that everything of any significance about him or her is somewhat embodied by this concept. It is *so* easy to stereotype people in this fashion, which, ironically, is something that we thought was a main mark of authoritarianism, or that authoritarianism "looms relatively large" in his or her scheme of things. We thought of it as a syndrome, or a structure of some importance in the personality that manifested itself in a diversity of ways, but we always recognized that any two people who were high on authoritarianism nonetheless differed in other significant ways. One person's authoritarianism played itself out in this way and another person's in that way.

A lot of trouble has come, also, from the fact that many people would like to define authoritarianism strictly in terms of behavior. You can't do that, you see, not if you have some Freudianism in your makeup. The concept of authoritarianism stands for a hypothetical structure in the personality that may manifest itself in this way, but may manifest itself in another way. The essence of Freudianism consists of paying attention to the meaning of behavior, in allowing for the possibility that behavior patterns that are very similar may have different sources in a personality and that different kinds of behavior may be referred to the same source. If you can't think of it that way, you can't really get close to our meaning of authoritarianism. In the study of authoritarianism, once you have come to the notion that this kind of structure underlies several patterns of behavior, you then ask yourself whether it might not be true that another quite remote or quite different kind of behavior might also be referred to this underlying structure. This, in fact, is the way we proceeded in describing authoritarianism.

Evans: Doesn't authoritarianism correlate with other characteristics?

Sanford: Yes. We not only made reference to ethnocentrism and anti-Semitism and so on, but to the fact that people high on authoritarianism also tended to be submissive to authority, to be uncritical of authority, and wanted to have an authority in the immediate environment. Students of this frame of mind would want to be told just what to do and how to go about it. There would also be characteristic ways of thinking, such as the inclination to think in rigid categories or to make categorical distinctions among things that actually were separated only quantitatively, and so on. What I would like to stress is that when you speak of authoritarianism you are speaking of an inner structure and not of certain particular patterns of observable behavior. You can't diagnose authoritarianism just by looking at short sections of behavior, which may be ascribed to quite different structures in the personality. You have to observe the person long enough so that you can reasonably infer the existence of this structure that is called authoritarianism. The question of what underlies authoritarianism—that is another question, you see, which we actually attack with the use of more theory.

Evans: The other side of the coin is the nature of the individual who is low on authoritarianism. *The Authoritarian Personality* (1950) deals with this as well, of course.

Sanford; Our general view of the matter was that there are various ways of being low on authoritarianism. You may recall that in *The Authoritarian Personality,* in a chapter by Dr. Adorno, there is a description of types of people who score low on authoritarianism. You could be very low on authoritarianism, for example, if you could not bring yourself to be aggressive toward other people. You might have something in your conscious that makes it impossible for you to make accusations against people. If this were true, you would be bound to come out fairly low on authoritarianism. Also, there are people who are distrustful of our big systems of thought. They don't like any kind of ideology and are immediately suspicious of big generalizations and the like. They don't go for stereotyping and great generalizations that organize the world for them; they like to concentrate on concrete reality. You can be low on authoritarianism in that fashion. But we are far from having described all types of people. The sad thing is that more psychologists have not undertaken to discover other syndromes that relate personality and ideology, many of which might very well exist and be of as much importance as authoritarianism.

Evans: One of the problems that I think we all recognize is that scientific inquiry should limit the intrusion of the values of the investigator as much as possible. Let's consider the work on authoritarianism; without any question this work, although acclaimed, has been the subject of some criticism on that very point. For example, Edward Shils (1954) implies that the high authoritarian turns out to be a bad guy, the low authoritarian turns out to be a good guy, and for some reason or another the good guy reflects the kind of values that the investigators may have had. He also suggests that a "self-fulfilling prophecy" may have been involved, that your research group found what you believed you would find. How would you handle this criticism of the research on the authoritarian personality?

Sanford: I would ignore much of it, as I have tried to do. I would say that were you not working on problems of some genuine human concern, problems that arouse feelings in people and that people care about, you would hardly need science. A major function of scientific method is to make sure that your wishes do not distort your observations. If people suspect that we had wishes in the matter and that these are expressed in our work, then they have to point to the precise instances in which the method went wrong. If you want to talk about values and social science or psychological science, I believe that psychologists and other social scientists who think they have no values are somewhat lacking in self-insight. If you do work in the social sciences that has no obvious value implications, it will always turn out to be a support for those values that are already most prevalent in our society. Of course, we were concerned about anti-Semitism and fascism, and we still are. In the climate of the war years, many people desperately felt the need to understand Nazism. I would say that unless we can understand it, we won't be able to prevent its happening again. And it could happen again, because the general level of understanding, I think, is rather low. Surely, we can investigate significant problems of this kind without being open to the accusation that we merely find out what we want to find out. I would say to our critics, "Go ahead and repeat our work, and see what you discover."

Evans: So you do not deny that value judgments were a part of your study, but maintain that your measurements were still, in a scientific sense, unbiased. Some critics object, I think, to what they perceive as a negative judgment of people who strongly believe in the value of authority.

Sanford: A lot of writing in *The Authoritarian Personality* (1950) tends to discredit the person who is high on authoritarianism, but our view of him is really compassionate. I think we speak of his deficiencies as we would those of a child. The fact that a child needs to get over this, that, and the other is not exactly against him; it is no basis for rejecting him or regarding him as beyond the pale. As a matter of fact, Jane Loevinger (1975) suggested that authoritarianism should be regarded as a stage of development, and I think that is a very good conception. Probably most of us go through a stage in adolescence in which the authoritarian orientation is pretty strong. Many people, unfortunately, seem to get stuck there. But to say that this is something that should be modified is not the same thing at all as saying, "These people are really bad and they ought to be punished," or something of that kind.

Evans: An area in which you have also pioneered has been the study of the personality development of the student in college. In your book *Where Colleges Fail* (1967), you suggest that colleges fail by not paying enough attention to individual student development. Why do they seem to be ignoring the personality development of the student during the formative years?

Sanford: Perhaps the first thing to do is to call attention to the Cold War and to the heavy accent at that time on training in the sciences, in using education to build a strong society, and so forth. At that time the federal government was pouring money into education at all levels, hurrying the process by which we could build our strength as a nation to defend us against aggression. We might as well confess that after World War II and again in the fifties, when funds became so readily available, we psychologists in graduate schools devoted ourselves to building psychology as a discipline. We were much more interested in getting good graduate students, getting handsome research grants, and so on, than we were in teaching undergraduates. But if you go back to the thirties or twenties, you would find that the idea of college education as a means for developing the potentialities of individuals was almost taken for granted. In college catalogs there is still much talk of opening the student to new worlds of experience, developing his self-insight, making him increasingly capable of participating fully in our culture and thereby leading a rich life, and so on. This educational aim is quite traditional with us, but after World War II, particularly after 1950, this kind of education was seriously neglected in the interest of graduate education. This, I think, is the main reason why we came to a time a few years ago when students in huge numbers began to feel that they were really being neglected in the interest of these various other concerns that faculty members had. It is also fair to say, I think, that even those educators, such as John Dewey, who were interested in an education for human potentiality, didn't have the psychological theory that could further that kind of aim very effectively. You might say that what my colleagues and I have been up to has been to try to build a kind of theory of personality development and to accumulate facts about personality development that are really relevant to these great educational aims of undergraduate education.

Evans: In your career you have been among those at the forefront of perhaps one of the most crucial movements in American psychology, the study of human problems. I think that you have carried this through in a very dramatic fashion by organizing an institute at Stanford University for the study of human problems. Your idea was to bring together many other disciplines that could focus on significant youth problems, such as alcoholism, drug adiction, and so on. The laboratory traditionally has been the focus for research in psychology because it allows control, but that kind of control will presumably not be possible when we start delving into real human problems.

Sanford: I am glad you referred to a movement. I am really quite glad to hear that, because I hadn't heretofore been impressed by how many psychologists were moving on this front. I would say that the antecedents of this actually would be primarily Kurt Lewin and his action research, particularly his work during the war years (Lewin 1946). You remember, when he actually undertook to deal with very genuine problems that were of a very great concern. For example, he undertook to change food habits in a very practical way (Lewin 1947). The other main antecedent, of course, has been the Travistock Institute in London, whose mode of consultation in industry has supplied much of the model for the kind of thing that I am interested in. However, concerning the last part of your question, I would actually turn that around and say that unless you observe complex phenomena directly in real life situations, you are not really going to find out much about psychology. And, after all, the laboratory experiment was never intended for discovery in science. It was intended, rather, for demonstration; and you demonstrate things in the laboratory that everybody knows already. In fact, many people are fond of saying about the work of psychologists: "That's just great. It demonstrates what everybody knew already." But psychologists still have the task of making discoveries, you know. And if we are going to do that, we have to look at phenomena that really exist. We have to look at people as they live and we've got to get out on the streets, or into the cities, or wherever the problems are. We needn't suppose that an understanding of these problems is merely an application of what has been discovered in the laboratory. On the contrary; new phenomena are created in a changing society such as ours, and they must be observed directly if we are going to get a scientific grasp on them.

Evans: To illustrate one of the ways an institute on human problems might go about looking at a crucial problem, let's discuss your studies of alcoholism (Sanford 1966b, 1968, 1970). What is distinctive about your "problem-oriented" approach to alcoholism?

Sanford: It's the interdisciplinary aspect that I would accent here. We don't separate inquiry altogether from social actions. We don't create a situation in which this group does the research and another group takes the action. If you look at the problems attendant to alcohol with a view to doing something about them, you will soon find that no one discipline has the answers. The problem itself doesn't recognize the existence of disciplines. The problem just *is*. In any instance where action is called for, you have to pay attention to all the possible consequences and implications of this action. This means that you have to take a rather comprehensive view of it. If you do that in the case of a social problem such as alcoholism, you will find that anthropologists, sociologists, political scientists, lawyers, as well as psychologists, physiologists, and so on, have had something to say about it. As a matter of fact, variables ordinarily claimed by more than one of these disciplines will be actually interacting in almost any concrete situation. This is another way of saying that if you investigate problems as they really exist, you will have to pay attention to variables that are not ordinarily considered together. In doing so you are bound to discover kinds of relationships that you would not discover if you stuck strictly to variables that ordinarily belong to a particular discipline. I have used in this connection the example of our efforts to say what might be done about teenage drinking (Sanford 1966a, 1968). For example, we recommended that the legal age for drinking be reduced from twenty-one to eighteen. We did not do that without paying a great deal of attention to the personality development in youth and to the implications of a change in this particular respect for large areas of society. If you actually recommend this change, you must consider, for instance, that all colleges would have to change their rules and their whole ways of proceeding with respect to drinking. You don't want to do this unless you know something about colleges and what the meaning would be in general if such a change were actually induced. On the other hand, you wouldn't propose it in the first place if you didn't have reason to believe that the readiness for contact with alcohol, the capacity of youth to deal with this, is greater at one time than at another time. The main point is that if you go at problems and take some responsibility for doing something about them, you can't be less than comprehensive and multidisciplinary. This is a way of advancing knowledge as well as a way of ameliorating some of our problems.

Evans: One of the most important questions concerning the logistics of such an approach is: Can multidisciplinary efforts succeed when communications among disciplines are so difficult to carry through?

Sanford: I would say that the only way you will get members of different disciplines to fully cooperate is by creating situations in which they work on genuine problems. It doesn't do any good just to house them in the same building and suggest that they discuss the interrelations of their disciplines. You have to take individuals from the departments and bring them into a situation where they meet with people from other disciplines, become interested in a problem, and begin to forget their disciplinary loyalties in the interest of really doing something. When this happens, it is just great. Everybody is stimulated. People forget to put on the mantle of their discipline every time they say something, and you get genuine involvement. The failure in communication, of course, has to do with the way universities are organized. They are organized in such a way as to pull the departments apart. You create a situation in which every department is really competing with every other, for funds, and students, and prestige, and so on. But I think we as a society desperately need a new kind of institution that is specifically devoted to the integration of inquiry and action; and that, by definition, would therefore have to be multidisciplinary. I would like to see numerous institutes organized in this fashion that would then cut across the whole university structure of departments and schools. I think that until we organize in this way, we will hardly begin to bring social science knowledge to bear upon the human problems of today.

Evans: What kinds of observations can you make for our students relative to what they might do, as they train in these fields, to be beter prepared to cope with human problems of the future?

Sanford: They should take enough psychology in college to learn something of the discipline of psychology, but three or four courses would be enough. They should then use college to get an education with the most attention to breadth. Also, they should try, even as college students, to have experiences out in the world: on jobs, or in field work that they can see in relation to their learning in college. I would like to see them try something other than schooling between college and graduate school so that they can bring to graduate school a demand for relevance, some insistence that their professors show them the meaning and significance of these courses in relation to the problems they know exist in society.

REFERENCES

Adorno, T. W., Frenkel-Brunswik, E., Levinson, D. J., and Sanford, N. 1950. *The authoritarian personality.* New York: Harper & Brothers.

Fromm, E. 1941. *Escape from freedom.* New York: Farrar & Rinehart.

Levinson, D. J., and Sanford, R. N. 1944. A scale for the measurement of anti-Semitism. *J. Psychol.* 17: 339–70.

Lewin, K. 1946. Action research and minority problems. *J. Soc. Issues.* 2: (4) 34–36.

_____. 1947. Frontiers in group dynamics: II. Channels of group life; social planning and action research. *Hum. Rel.* 1: 143–53.

Loevinger, J. 1975. *Ego development.* San Francisco: Jossey-Bass.

Sanford, N. 1966a. Psychological and developmental aspects of the adolescent years as they apply to the use of alcohol. In *Alcohol and college youth,* ed. H. B. Bruyn. Berkeley: American College Health Association.

_____. 1966b. Conceptions of alcoholism. In *Treatment methods and milieus in social work with alcoholics,* ed. S. Cahn. Berkeley: Social Welfare Extension, University of California.

————. 1967 *Where colleges fail: A study of the student as a person.* San Francisco: Jossey-Bass.

————. 1968. Personality and patterns of alcohol consumption. *J. Consul. Clin. Psychol.* 32: 13–17.

————. 1950. Community actions and the prevention of alcoholism. In *Community Psychology and Mental Health,* eds. D. Adelson and B. Kalis. Scranton, Penn.: Chandler Publishing Co.

————, and Singer, S. 1968. Drinking and personality. In *No time for youth,* ed. J. Katz. San Francisco: Jossey-Bass.

Shils, E. 1954. Authoritarianism: "Right" and "Left." In *Studies in the scope and method of "The Authoritarian Personality",* eds. R. Christie and M. Jahoda. Glencoe, Ill.: The Free Press.

SELECTED READINGS

Sanford, N. 1943. Psychological approaches to the young delinquent. *J. Consul. Psychol.* 7: 223–29.

Sanford, N. 1956. Psychotherapy and the American public. In *Psychology, psychiatry, and the public interest,* ed. M. E. Krout. Minneapolis: University of Minnesota Press.

Sanford, N. 1965. Social science and social reform. *J. Soc. Issues.* 21: 54–70.

Sanford, N. 1966. *Self and society: Social change and individual development.* New York: Atherton Press.

Sanford, N. 1967. *Where colleges fail: A study of the student as a person.* San Francisco: Jossey-Bass.

Sanford, N., and Singer, S. 1968. Drinking and personality. In *No time for youth,* ed. J. Katz. San Francisco: Jossey-Bass.

Sanford, N. 1970. *Issues in personality theory.* San Francisco: Jossey-Bass.

Sanford, N., and Comstock, C. (Eds.) 1971. *Sanctions for evil.* San Francisco: Jossey-Bass.

6

KENNETH B. CLARK

(1914–   )

Kenneth B. Clark obtained his undergraduate and master's degrees from Howard University, and received his doctorate in social psychology from Columbia University in 1940. He is currently a Distinguished Professor of Psychology Emeritus at the City College of the City University of New York, and president of Clark, Phipps, Clark, and Harris, Inc., a firm that provides professional consultation on personnel matters with emphases on human relations, race relations, and affirmative action programs. He has devoted his career as a social scientist to translating principles of human behavior into policies and programs that improve the quality of life for the poor and disadvantaged and promote improved human relations. His contributions to the literature on prejudice and the effects of segregation on blacks in America have influenced not only social psychology but also our entire culture through its impact on the Supreme Court's decision in the Brown versus Board of Education case. Dr. Clark was the recipient of the first annual Distinguished Contributions to Psychology in the Public Interest Award in 1978, and served as president of the American Psychological Association in 1971.

Why I Went to Columbia/ My Dissertation// The Problem of Selective Perception// Brown versus Board of Education/ The Doll Study/ Social Science Affecting Supreme Court Decisions// The Integrity of Social Science//Internal and External Validity// Harlem Youth Opportunities Unlimited, Inc./ The North Side Center for Child Development/ Succeeding Only in Making the Client Dependent// The IQ Controversy/Project Head Start/ Correlation Between Genetic and Psychological Characteristics// Presidential Address/ Psychotechnology/The Development of Decency and Justice Among Human Beings/ Avalanche of Criticism//The Most Important Contribution//The Responsibility of Using Social Science//

63

As we begin our discussion, Dr. Clark describes his well-known "doll studies," which he did with Mamie Clark, in which black children's preference for white dolls poignantly demonstrated the effect of racial prejudice on their emerging sense of identity. We continue by examining his movement into social activism, discussing his social science brief for the landmark Brown versus Board of Education (1954) case, as well as his active role with Harlem Youth Opportunities Unlimited (HARYOU), Inc., and the North Side Center for Child Development. Describing this stage of his career, he states, "I became an involved social psychologist rather than an isolated ivory-tower academician." At a broader level, we discuss the failure of many of the "war on poverty" programs, which naively overestimated their power to create social change and neglected the influence of political forces as well as the difficulty in implementing social service programs without promoting client dependency. He then reacts to Jensen's controversial work on racial differences in intelligence. He states, "I don't want to believe that Jensen thinks that there is a simplistic correlation between genetic determination of physical characteristics, as confused as that is, and psychological characteristics. But he suggests by his analogy that this is what he believes." We then discuss the "avalanche of criticism" he received from colleagues after his 1971 APA presidential address, in which he called for "a scientific, technological approach to decency." In closing, Dr. Clark evaluates what he considers to be his two most important contributions to psychology: teaching his students to be responsible in applying social science to help their fellow human beings, and his own efforts to integrate research activities with applied services, as at the Northside Center.

Evans: Kenneth, you received your Ph. D. in psychology and social psychology in 1940, which was in many respects an historically significant time in psychology at Columbia. What did you see social psychology focusing on when you were there?

Clark: The best way for me to answer your question is to tell you why I went to Columbia. I did my undergraduate work at Howard University, which was at that time a very exciting place. At Howard, I imbibed the spirit of intellectual excitement, stimulated by such people as Francis Sumner, Aileen Locke, Ralph Bunch, and Ernest Just, the biologist. They were all black and lived at a time when, without regard to a person's mind, the color of his skin determined that he couldn't teach any place other than a predominantly black school. That experience was a turning point for me. Otto Klineberg from Columbia came down to Howard and gave what I found out later was almost a standard talk on racial differences. I was impressed by Klineberg; I was impressed by his directness, his candor, and the fact that he was white and talking the way he was talking. I suppose I wanted to go into the field that Otto Klineberg was in.

Evans: And yet, once in graduate school, the research for your dissertation did not deal directly with prejudice and discrimination, did it?

Clark: Let me tell you what happened. I studied with Klineberg and Murphy because I knew I was going into social psychology. In that first semester they suggested that it would be desirable for me not to come on too strong in terms of my concern with racial justice. I decided that my dissertation would be indirectly related, a follow-up on the Bartlett (1932) work on remembering and the problem of selective perception, selective recall and attitudes, and how they influence human behavior. I jumped in and designed a study (Clark 1940) to test the hypothesis of the extent to which attitudes toward females who violated the stereotypical picture of the female affected groups of subjects' recall. I found that subjects, both men and women, tended to remember these females more in terms of the feminine stereotypes than in terms of the original stimulus.

Evans: Now, after you finished your doctorate, you went on to City College, where you eventually became a distinguished professor. Probably one of the most important decisions the Supreme Court has made during this century was the famous *Brown* versus *Board of Education* (1954) case. The research study that you and Mamie (Clark and Clark 1958) did probably was the first time that social science data were seriously considered in the deliberations of the Supreme Court. Could you discuss the development of this study?

Clark: The study originated with my wife, Mamie. It was her master's thesis subject at Howard University. She was interested in studying the development of self-awareness in human beings, and she had only black children available as subjects. This fact made her move toward looking at self-awareness as determined by sense of race or color. Mamie's original methods were really a modification of the Horowitz and Horowitz Show-Me Test (1939). She finished her master's and came up to New York. (She later became the first black woman to earn her doctorate in psychology at Columbia.) I was so fascinated by this study that I said maybe we ought to continue. Then I developed an extension of the method, the Show-Me Method, and used the dolls and the color test. Our primary concern was trying to understand how human beings developed a sense of their own identity, and the racial color factor was a component.

Evans: Could we pause for a moment so that you might briefly describe the methodology and results of the study? As I recall the study, even black children showed a preference for white dolls, more often selecting them when asked which doll they would rather have to play with.

Clark: At that time, there was no question about it. Two-thirds did. This was a disturbing study for both Mamie and me.

Evans: How old were these children?

Clark: From three to seven years old.

Evans: So these were not infants. These were children who were already old enough to be significantly influenced by the culture.

Clark: No question about it. We were measuring the effects of socialization when it is deleterious to self-esteem. I saw black children, in both the North and the South, being dominated by negative stereotypes about themselves. I then asked them the last question. "Now show me the doll which is like you." Some of these children would break down into tears. I remember one little girl who looked up at me when I asked her to show me which one was like her. She looked at me as if to say, "How could you do this to another human being?" and broke down in tears and ran out of the room. In the South, that wasn't as frequent; they would laugh and say, "That's a Nigger; I'm a Nigger," or something of that sort. It was so disturbing to us personally that I found the report of the study difficult to write. But Ted Newcomb and Gene Hartley, who were composing their *Readings in Social Psychology* (1958), suggested that it would be irresponsible if we didn't write it up.

Evans: So these distinguished pioneers in social psychology had begun to see that such a finding would have a tremendous impact.

Clark: I don't know if that's what they saw. I think they saw it was important. No one at that time talked about its social impact.

Evans: Now, let's move a little further. I mentioned at the beginning of this question the *Brown* versus *Board of Education* case. This was perhaps the first, and certainly an extremely important, instance of social science influencing a Supreme Court decision. How did that all come about?

Clark: Well, it came about through the lawyers of the NAACP. They decided that they were going to challenge the constitutionality of segregation without regard to alleged equality of facilities. The only way they thought they could really repeal the separate but equal doctrine was by being able to demonstrate that there was damage inherent in segregation in spite of the equality of the facilities. Robert Carter, who was Thurgood Marshall's assistant, spoke to me first. He said, "You know, it would be easy for us if we could demonstrate medical damage or broken bones or something that is concrete that everyone would agree on as damage, but the type of damage we're talking about is psychological damage, a much more subtle damage. And the only place for us to turn is to psychologists." First, they went to Otto Klineberg. Otto was a member of the advisory committee of the Mid-Century White House Conference on Children and Youth (1951). This conference was concerned with the question of personality development. They asked me about two or three months before the conference to synthesize the literature on the effects of race, prejudice, discrimination, and segregation on personality development of American children, white and black. It didn't occur to me that this was going to have any practical significance. I gave Carter a copy of the monograph and said, "You read this, and if it is at all relevant to what you and Thurgood have in mind, then maybe I can help." He read it, and within a week he said to me, "Look, it's not only relevant, but it couldn't have been better if you had prepared it for us."

Evans: So one task covered the other.

Clark: That's right. We started meeting and I advised him and the other lawyers of the group of social scientists who we would need: people like Isador Chein, Ted Newcomb, David Krech, M. Brewster Smith, and Gordon Allport. I advised the lawyers as to those whom I thought would make good witnesses. Then later, after the trial, they said, "Look, we don't know whether the Supreme Court is going to accept this or not, but we want you to pull together in a social science brief the essential points of the testimony of the expert witness at the trial level." Well, I did.

Evans: You took the core statements of these testimonies and expert witnesses.

Clark: That's right. And a summary of the White House Conference memorandum. It became the appendix to the legal brief that was the social science brief for the *Brown* versus *Board of Education* case in 1954.

Evans: This was to become a landmark involvement of the social sciences in law. Before this, the involvement of psychiatrists or clinical psychologists in sanity hearings was the typical contribution.

Clark: And you know, there were times when one of the more puristic lawyers demanded what I could not give him: proof that segregated schools in themselves created the damage. To them, that was the legal point. And I said, "Look, I don't know of any social scientist who could give you that specific kind of information." We could say that segregated schools in the context of a segregated society are damaging, but not segregated schools in isolation, because, for one thing, segregated schools do not exist in isolation.

Evans: That's right.

Clark: It was not an idyllic romance. I had to fight with the lawyers for the integrity of social science; not that they wanted me to pervert it, but some of them wanted me to make statements that I did not believe the evidence would support.

Evans: There is a fine distinction between internal and external validity of psychological data in the courtroom. Will the results of a single psychological investigation generalize to a broader societal situation? As you say, it is often impossible to demonstrate, and the scientist with integrity hesitates to make such generalizations.

Clark: You're darn right. And I insisted upon pointing out to them that my value to them was directly related to the integrity and clarity of what I provided for them.

Evans: After this decision, there was a good deal of social legislation and social action, supplementing the decision to explore what could be done on a larger scale to remedy some of the things that your study suggested were being generated by our culture. At that time, having worked with President Kennedy's Committee on Delinquency and Youth Crime, I became acutely aware of the work that you were doing with your Harlem Youth Opportunities Unlimited, Inc. (HARYOU) in New York. The issue of delinquency and opportunity has been under some fire. The point of view in the Kennedy administration was that if you can change the environment and increase the opportunities for disadvantaged youth or children, you will increase the probability that they will become constructive members of society. How did you become involved in this issue and how did you perceive this idea? I can see that by then, of course, you could no longer be just a professor of social psychology at City University. You became intricately involved in social problems.

Clark: There is no question that by that time I was an involved social psychologist rather than an isolated ivory-tower academician. Around 1950 there was an excitement in being involved in real issues. But there was also conflict. As to my work with HARYOU, it stemmed directly from my work with the lawyers and my work with Mamie as a research director at a child guidance center in Harlem, the North Side Center for Child Development. In 1940 Mamie and I founded the North Side Center for one purpose: to provide underprivileged children in Harlem with the alleged benefits of psychiatric and psychological help and counseling. We knew that if we were going to save these children it was important to do something about the environment in which they were growing up. We also knew that you couldn't really do very much if you provided help under conditions that threatened their self-esteem, increased their sense of dependency, etc. Mamie contributed the notion and practice of building the sense of self as an integral part of our psychotherapy.

Evans: Moving into social action and applied social psychology was not considered entirely "respectable" in those days, but today, of course, social psychologists are recognized more and more that they must move into applied problems and rigorously evaluate any interventions that are initiated (Evans, 1980). Speaking of evaluations, there were a number of tragedies in these projects that occurred as an outgrowth of delinquency and poverty. Innovative programs that were developed by social scientists began to get increasingly bogged down in political considerations.

Clark: I think, from my vantage point, and certainly in regard to HARYOU, that the loss of the vitality of these programs resulted from the naivete' of those of us who planned them in not taking into account the possibility, the inevitability, that programs of this magnitude and vision for social change would not be permitted to develop and function in terms of their own potential. Soon political forces would move in. It was my feeling that our experience with poverty programs was not an isolated experience. Most of them were sucked into the reality of political control.

Evans: Donald Campbell (in Chapter 7 of this volume) suggests that these types of programs should be set up in such a way that they are subject to reevaluation periodically.

Clark: Yet I don't think that factor was influential in the failures of many of the anti-poverty programs. Many of these major attempts at controlled social change never even got off the ground.

Evans: In other words, these programs were not maintained long enough to produce a measurable impact.

Clark: That's right.

Evans: Let me move a step further to the underlying philosophy involved in this issue. There is no question that today we are more skeptical of social service agencies because many of them make the client dependent on the agency welfare programs. This is something of which you became aware early, was it not?

Clark: Sure. We had kind of a sentimental view in that we believed that it would be sufficient to provide the apparatus by which they would break the prior dependence and develop a sense of their own ability to cope. It wasn't. We didn't take into account the effect of past dependence.

Evans: Even Freud implied in his famous paper written in the thirties, "Analysis Terminable and Interminable" (Freud 1950), that all he succeeded in doing was training people to be dependent on the analyst.

Clark: And all we succeeded in doing was to set up an apparatus by which there could be another kind of exploitation and hustle.

Evans: Can we really break this circularity? Isn't that still the question facing us on this issue even today?

Clark: I suppose, yes.

Evans: Let's move into another area. I know you are probably weary of the topic of the IQ controversy. Jensen's article in the *Harvard Educational Review* (Jensen 1969) looked at Project Head Start and argued that the black child might be inherently inferior in a particular type of intelligence that is more abstract than concrete and thus was unlikely to profit from such "enrichment." His position opposed the idea that the sometimes dissappointing evaluations of this program resulted from inadequate opportunities for enrichment. What disturbs me is that the issue of genetic inferiority has been brought up again in an age in which media coverage is extended, that even misconceptions can once again be brought into the culture as long as they receive strong media attention.

Clark: That's right.

Evans: How do you react when you become involved in this issue?

Clark: Well, I try to ignore it, but occasionally I react. What I'm saying is that this is the same old story; it's run and rerun all the time. Such beliefs are not so popular because they are scientific. To the contrary, this is a social, political, and racial issue directly tied to the desegregation of schools. Actually such an argument is one of the most sophisticated ways of evading the constitutional mandate to desegregate the schools, because what these people are saying in effect is that it doesn't matter whether black students have equality of education.

Evans: Kenneth, if I may, let me read a section of a published discussion that I recently had with Dr. Jensen (Evans 1976). Your reaction to it would be interesting. First, my question to Jensen: "Suppose you have in your class a black student who reads your research and in his mind it raises nagging doubts concerning his own competence?" Jensen's reply was: "In the preface to my book *Educability and Group Differences* (1973), I have something to say about this. Every person is a unique combination of genes. Your genetic background can produce so many different combinations even within one family, as I've pointed out, that you have to think of yourself in terms of what you yourself are, and not in terms of your origins. I think it's racist thinking to think of yourself in terms of your group or your ancestry. What about a Japanese fellow who's 6 foot 3 inches? Should he worry about the fact that the Japanese population as a whole is shorter than, say, the Scandinavian population as a whole? He's 6 foot 3 inches, which is tall enough to be a basketball star. Now, a person who is 5 foot 4 inches would never make it as a basketball star, not because he's Japanese, but because he's 5 foot 4 inches. It's the same thing in the intellectual realm." What is your reaction to that statement?

Clark: To me this is an incredible thing for Jensen to say because he is refuting the whole approach that he has taken in this question of race and intelligence. I don't want to believe that this man thinks that there is a simplistic correlation between genetic determination of physical characteristics, as confused as that is, and psychological characteristics. But he suggests by his analogy that this is what he believes. I would say that in itself his answer to your question could be used as a substitute for the number of articles that have been written attempting to refute him.

Evans: A few years ago, you were elected to the presidency of the American Psychological Association. Your presidential address (Clark 1971) was not what one might have expected in terms of the history of your work in black issues. Rather, you chose to talk about the human condition in general and suggested that we should consider employing psychotechnological and psychopharmacological interventions on a mass scale in order to achieve social harmony, or at least to avert social cataclysm. I'm wondering if you might talk about that presentation, and then about some of the reactions you received.

Clark: Yes, I'll be glad to. I wanted to summarize my feelings and thoughts as a psychologist, and to give the audience some notion of how I arrived at my present view of the predicament of the human being. The first two thirds was really a summing up of the different parts of psychology to which I've been exposed. The last section expressed my obsession with the development of decency and justice among human beings as it relates to the survival of the human species. I deeply believe that the events of the last three or four decades have made it clear that morality and ethics are no longer abstractions but are absolutely imperative for survival. And I wondered: How the hell do you get this? I looked at religion: that seemed to me to have failed. Education, slow. Skinnerian conditioning, difficult. My undergraduate interests in neurophysiology and psychopharmacology came back to the fore. Because the destructive potential that the nuclear physicists had imposed upon us didn't allow us the time to gradually become more decent, there was a need to accelerate the evolutionary process. We had to develop a scientific technological approach to decency that would accelerate education, that would accelerate whatever religion was trying to do. I wasn't prepared, to be quite honest with you, for the avalanche of criticism that descended around my head within the twenty-four hours following that speech. I wasn't prepared for the fact that my friends in social science and social psychology would see this as heresy and would call a press conference the very next day to have me recant. I wasn't prepared for letters accusing me of cynicism, fascism, and dehumanization, when I was really interested in humanization, you know.

Evans: Looking over your many contributions, what do you consider to be your most important one?

Clark: I think my most important contribution is my students, seeing some of them take seriously the responsibility of using social science as an instrument for helping their fellow human beings. Social science and social psychology should be and must be instruments by which people seek to help their fellow human beings.

Evans: Aside from your students, what other contributions, in research or social action, do you consider to be the most important?

Clark: Well, I guess it would be my work with Mamie, and not just the research but the development of the North Side Center. Neither she nor I was ever able to be satisfied by detached or abstract research. Our best times together were when there was evidence that what we were doing was beneficial to children and parents and human beings. I know that sounds corny.

Evans: Finally, which of the reports of your work would you especially recommend young university students to read?

Clark: I'd want them to start with *Prejudice and Your Child* (1955), which was a modification of the report I did for the Mid-Century White House Conference on Children and Youth (1951) that the Supreme Court sent for and used. I'd want them to read *Dark Ghetto* (1965). I'd like them to read a not too well known book of mine called *A Possible Reality* (1972), which deals with increasing the quality of education for low-income children in public schools. And I'd like them to read my latest book, *Pathos of Power* (1974), because it brings together a series of articles that illustrate my perspective on life.

REFERENCES

Bartlett, F. C. 1932. *Remembering.* Cambridge, England: The University Press.
Brown vs Board of Education. 1954. (347) *U.S.* 483.
Clark, K. B. 1940. Some factors influencing the remembering of prose materials. *Archives of Psychol.* 253: 1–73.

————. 1955. *Prejudice and your child.* Boston: Beacon Press.

————. 1965. *Dark ghetto: Dilemmas of social power.* New York: Harper & Row.

————. 1971. The pathos of power: A psychological perspective. *Amer. Psychol.* 26: 1047–57.

————. 1974. *Pathos of power.* New York: Harper & Row.

————, and Clark, M. P. 1958. Racial identification and preference in Negro children. In *Readings in social psychology.* 3rd ed., eds. E. Macoby, T. Newcomb, and E. Hartley. New York: Holt, Rinehart, & Winston.

————, and MARC staff. 1972. *A possible reality.* New York: Emerson Hall.

Evans, R. I. 1976. *The making of psychology.* New York: Alfred A. Knopf, Inc.

————. 1980. Behavioral medicine: A new applied challenge to social psychologists. In *Applied Social Psychology Annual,* ed. L. Bickman. Beverly Hills, California: Sage Publications.

Freud, S. 1950. Analysis terminable and interminable. In *Collected Papers* (Vol. V), ed. J. Strachey. London: The Hogarth Press and The Institute of Psychoanalysis.

Horowitz, E. L., and Horowitz, R. E. 1938. Development of social attitudes in children. *Sociometry.* 1: 301–358.

Jensen, A. R. 1969. How much can we boost IQ and scholastic achievement? *Harvard Educational Review.* 39: 1–123.

————. 1973. *Educability and group differences.* New York: Harper.

Mid-Century White House Conference on Children and Youth. 1950. Washington, D.C. *A healthy personality for every child.* 1951. Raleigh, N.C.: Health Publications Inst.

SELECTED READINGS

Clark, K. B. 1955. *Prejudice and your child.* Boston: Beacon Press.

Clark, K. B. 1965. *Dark ghetto: Dilemmas of social power.* New York: Harper & Row.

Clark, K. B. 1965. HARYOU: An experiment. In *Harlem: A community in transition,* ed. J. H. Clarke. New York: Citadel Press.

Clark, K. B. 1967. Higher education for Negroes: Challenges and prospects. *J. Neg. Educ.* 36: 196–203.

Clark, K. B. 1974. *Pathos of power.* New York: Harper & Row.

Clark, K. B., and Hopkins, J. 1969. *Relevant war against poverty: A study for community action programs and observable social change.* New York: Harper & Row.

Clark, K. B., and MARC staff. 1972. *A possible reality.* New York: Emerson Hall.

7

DONALD CAMPBELL
(1916–   )

Donald Thomas Campbell received his A.B. and Ph.D. degrees from the University of California at Berkeley in 1939 and 1947. From 1947 to 1950 he was assistant professor of psychology at Ohio State University, and from 1950 to 1953, assistant professor of psychology at the University of Chicago. From 1953 to 1979 he was at Northwestern University, where he was professor of psychology and a co-professor of bidisciplinary courses involving philosophy and sociology. His contributions reflect the diversity of his talents, and include imaginative publications in methodology, philosophy of science, the measurement of attitudes, and cross-cultural and interdisciplinary research. His landmark work on quasi-experimental design and internal and external validity has had a powrful and pervasive influence on research in social psychology that is reflected in the current trend toward research outside the laboratory, where behavior occurs in its natural setting. Dr. Campbell is the recipient of many awards, including the Distinguished Scientific Contribution Award of the American Psychological Association in 1970. He served as president of that organization in 1975. Currently, Dr. Campbell is a distinguished professor at Syracuse University.

Measurement of Prejudice/ Validating Tests/ Methodology of the Authoritarian Personality Study// Interdisciplinary Collaboration/ Cultural Anthropology// Ethnocentrism//Integrating the Behavioristic and the Cognitive// Suggestibility-Conformity/ Peer Pressure// Quasi-Experimental Design/ Multitrait-Multimethod Matrix/ Internal and External Validity// Human Nature/ Sociobiology//

Dr. Campbell and I begin by discussing his early work in developing "indirect" measures of prejudice. He comments on interdisciplinary collaboration, stating that while this can be difficult, we must be open to all kinds of evidence, including that of anthropology, sociology, and other fields. He describes the development of two competing emphases in social psychology, the behavioristic and the phenomenological, and his attempts to integrate the two. Reacting to some of the trials of psychological research, he says, "The whole process of science is tremendously wasteful, and we've got to be willing to pour ten years of work down a rat hole every now and again. Or to have it turn out successfully and be totally neglected." Speaking of his own significant and widely recognized contributions to research methodology, Dr. Campbell corrects the notion that he is an advocate of hard science approaches to the soft social sciences. Instead, his multitrait-multimethod matrix emphasizes plausibility, which "reduces the logical positivists' demand for precision, and increases the burden on intelligent human judgment." He discusses his recent efforts to integrate issues brought to prominence by the sociobiology movement: "It is a complicated point of view, and I welcome the tendency in sociology and social psychology to pay more attention to the biological."

Evans: Don, you were trained in the context of the famous work on *The Authoritarian Personality* (Adorno, Frenkel-Brunswick, Levinson, and Sanford 1950) at Berkeley. Although working with individuals not directly involved in that effort, you were already interested in some aspects of the same issue: prejudice. What did the concept of prejudice mean to you in those days?

Campbell: Well, Dick, my basic orientation toward psychology and social psychology had been formed before *The Authoritarian Personality*. I decided to be a social psychologist during my graduate work at the University of California at Berkeley in the 1930s. Social psychology in those days was an interesting mixture to which I hope we might soon return. Clearly prejudice was a dominant theme, and the prejudice literature was dominated by the work of Gardner Murphy and his students: Rensuis Likert, Eugene Horowitz, Theodore Newcomb, and others.

As to my dessertation, Harold Jones was my advisor and I focused on the measurement of prejudice (Campbell 1947). In those days we somehow felt that our measurements were more valid if the people we were studying didn't know what we were measuring. A principal gimmick was to give people detailed, factual information questions in which there was an opportunity for, shall we say, pro-Negro and anti-Negro wrong answers (Campbell 1950). I now think that was a misguided effort. On the one hand, it clearly violates our current ethics on informed consent; on the other hand, it never produced more valid measures. The measures were interesting, they often had some validity, but they were never as valid as just asking a person directly (Kidder and Campbell 1970).

Evans: Later you were to make significant contributions to the problems of internal validity and external validity. When you talk about validity, whether you're talking about direct or indirect measures, you obviously have to relate this to some behavior.

Campbell: Of course. If you want to predict whether a man belongs to the local campus reserve officers training program or the local campus pacifist organization, you can do that well with almost anybody's attitudes toward war scale; and you do it poorly if you try to make it an indirect attitude measure. That's a very good way of validating tests, considering what we have. We have no way of looking into the person's brain and measuring his true attitudes. By and large attitude scales are much more valid than personality scales, and they are impressive in predicting forms of political participation.

Evans: Edward Shils (1954) at the University of Chicago, came back with some rather rigorous attacks on *The Authoritarian Personality* (1950) studies, not only from the standpoint of measurement, but because the ideology of the investigators may have created a situation in which the high authoritarians were considered as bad guys and the low authoritarians were regarded as good guys. In fact, he speaks of authoritarianism on the left and the right. One could argue that the values of the investigators would be hard to separate here.

Campbell: I myself can make trenchant criticisms of the methodology of the authoritarian personality study, but the end product, the diagnostic F scale, is so good that a fascist rabble-rouser as well as a person who was strongly against ethnic prejudice could use it to select sympathizers. In other words, it has produced a tool that is "value-free" in the sense that people can use it to implement values exactly opposite of the original authoritarian personality research group. I think Shils, and Milt Rokeach in his later work (1956; 1960), are completely correct in pointing to the authoritarianism of the left as well as the right. Nonetheless, a highly anti-prejudiced team that hated prejudice with full-time motivational commitment can produce findings that are so paradoxically value-free that they can help implement their enemies' purposes (just as we can often trust the work of a cancer researcher who hates cancer vigorously because his mother died of cancer, if it's done scientifically enough).

Evans: That's a very interesting statement. One of the things you have emphasized in your career is the attempt to interrelate the various disciplines. Recently our social science dean was talking about implementing a cross-disciplinary doctoral program in behavioral or social science. So many such programs with the loftiest of goals seem to be instituted with optimism and discontinued with cynicism. Disciplines have greater difficulty relating to each other. They spend a lot of time talking in their own language system and they rarely understand the language system of their colleagues. Yet you obviously related quite well to cultural anthropology, and profited from your knowledge of that field. I wonder if you might comment on this and on why difficulties in such relationships seem to occur so often.

Campbell: Well, there are difficulties in all relationships, and many people forget how hard it is for psychologists to collaborate with psychologists. We have an unrealistic model of intradisciplinary collaboration (Campbell 1969a). In the 1930s every psychologist's textbook on social psychology talked about Margaret Mead's *Growing Up in New Guinea* (1930), *Coming of Age in Samoa* (1928), and *Sex and Temperament* (1938) from an anthropological point of view. In other words, it was perfectly respectable to have a lot of anthropology in a social psychology textbook. I have always had respect for what one could learn through the dramatic qualitative contrasts that anthropologists can offer. I think that we must be open to all kinds of evidence. I would like a return to such a position.

Evans: It might be interesting to consider the work on ethnocentrism. How differently would a social psychologist and a cultural anthropologist look at something like ethnocentrism, and how might these approaches be synthesized?

Campbell: Sumner developed his in-group/out-group analysis in that great book *Folkways* (Sumner 1906; LeVine and Campbell 1972). The anthropologist studying tribalism is dealing with an ethnocentrism that applies to any social group and that all group members share. If there are people living together in daily interaction with some organizational focus, a sociologist or anthropologist expects them all to be ethnocentric. All tribes try to build intragroup solidarity. The recipe of creating ingroup peace by preaching out-group hate is true of all groups from time immemorial. So here we have a version of ethnocentrism in which it's a universal sociological process dealing with group formation. Now what Dan Levinson (1950) was doing in constructing the E scale (the ethnocentrism scale) in the *Authoritarian Personality* study was measuring individual differences within one group in the degree to which people participated in this universal tendency to despise out-groups. I think that we social psychologists are probably misled by putting too much attention on individual differences and two little attention on universal human nature. I'm old-fashioned enough to believe in a universal human nature. To give a concrete illustration, I'm interested in why people's ears are 180 degrees apart. I find it of no interest why your ears are 178 degrees apart and mine are 182 degrees apart. The fact that they're on opposite sides of the head is the main thing, yet because of some interesting laws of social perception, we tend to initially notice the differences and not the common character from which these are minor deviations.

Evans: I think that another type of integration that is reflected in your work is a strong cognitive tradition that balanced the behaviorally oriented psychology at Berkeley while you were there. Today's behavioral psychologists suddenly have become more cognitive. This is a very interesting thing that you surely observed in your career, since you've been in the center of some of these developments.

Campbell: You are touching upon what I regard as a lost career. The whole process of doing science is tremendously wasteful, and if we're going to undertake it we've got to be willing to pour ten years of work down a rat hole every now and then. Or to have it perhaps turn out successfully and be totally neglected. My reputation is as a methodologist, but until recently, when I gave up, I'd always seen myself as a theorist. Integrating the behavioristic and the cognitive (or as we used to call it, Gestalt or phenomenological) was my favorite theme (Campbell 1963/1966; 1969b). Although some of that work got published, it had no effect on the field whatsoever. The social psychology in the early influential textbook by Floyd Allport (1924) is very behavioristic. Nonetheless, by 1935, and certainly by 1945, most of the social psychology books had a Gestaltish, phenomenological emphasis. Certainly the exciting textbooks when I was young had that emphasis. I think of that great first edition of Krech and Crutchfield, *Theory and Methods of Social Psychology* (1948), and that great textbook of Solomon Asch called *Social Psychology* (1952), which could be a best-seller today if reissued under the name "Phenomenological Social Psychology." The texts that were available to me when I was teaching undergraduate social psychology were Gestalt. At the same time, I was teaching in departments in which the introductory general psychology course was totally behavioristic and in which my most stimulating colleagues were hard-line behaviorists. So the discontinuity between this conscious-experience-emphasizing social psychology and the behavioristic environment gave me an interest in trying to resolve these two, and I thought I had made a major contribution toward resolving them. We don't have time to go into it deeply, but it was something like this: Take the concept of a person's "view of the world." This corresponds *not* to the behaviorist "stimulus" but rather to the behaviorist term "response tendency." So "views of the world" equals "response tendencies," and with that key you can then fit one kind of behaviorism to a conscious-experience psychology. My major empirical study motivated by that was on projection (Campbell, Miller, Lubetsky, and O'Connell 1964). It seemed to me that with this key, the concept of transference in psychoanalysis, the concept of transfer in learning theory, the concept of apperceptive projection in Harry Murray (1938), and the concept of parataxic projection in Harry Stack Sullivan (1953) all came together—making a prediction that an anxious person will tend to see others as threatening. An anxious person will tend to see new persons, whom he doesn't know anything about, as though they were the kind of persons out of his past that made him anxious (rather than an anxious person tending to see others as anxious). In any event, we had a mammoth study here in which people in twenty different dormitories rated each other on twenty traits and so on. The results of that were disappointing for any kind of projection theory. (Except for the finding that cautious people tend to see others as bold and that sort of thing. Such a contrast projection came out on a few variables.) By the empirical effort to put my theoretical integration ahead, I undermined my faith by collecting data that made it less plausible. Nonetheless, in spite of these data, I still believe my theory true, and I have a course in our catalog called "Phenomenological Behaviorism."

Evans: Now I'd like to take another concept that has been rather central to social psychology—the conformity concept. I know that you had some interesting contact with this area of research. I wonder if you'd like to comment about that.

Campbell: Conformity research started back in the 1910s with demonstrations in which dramatic lecturers would open a bottle that supposedly had a smell in it, perfume or benzene, and would then ask people to raise their hands as soon as they smelled it. Sure enough, soon the first row, then the second row hands would rise. From this kind of work, done under the term "prestige suggestion," conformity research emerged. (The prestige was from experts or from the collective vote of one's peers.) Another synonym, "susceptibility to suggestion," and conformity got lumped together as character weaknesses. Thus for a number of years, the suggestibility-conformity literature was studying what it took to be a human weakness, and individual differences in how much people had this weakness became the focus. Asch (1952) came to the field with a remarkably novel point of view: that we all depend in life on trusting the reports that other people make about a part of the world we have not observed directly ourselves. He pointed out that a great deal of what we were scoring as conformity in the laboratory was demonstrating the willingness of people to learn from the reports of other people, which should be recognized as an essential part of social process, not a weakness. From Asch's point of view, it is essential for us that we learn about most of our environment through the reports of others. It's immoral to disregard the reports of your peers, but it's also immoral to be a dishonest reporter so that your peers can't depend upon your reports. Asch didn't like it when some of his subjects fooled themselves and didn't realize they were conforming. He admired those who under this extreme pressure were independents; nonetheless, his view would be that we should be using the word "informity" rather that "conformity" in referring to this experimental paradigm. I'm ashamed to say that my own early research in this area involved measuring individual differences in conformity, so I did not provide a good example, but in my theoretical essay on conformity and even in my current "social psychology of science" writing, I stress Asch's perspective.

Evans: That's very interesting. That introduces a question that we're encountering in our research with smoking in children (Evans, Rozelle,

Mittelmark, Hansen, Bane, and Havis 1978). We find that by the time adolescents reach the seventh grade, virtually all of them believe smoking is dangerous; nevertheless, a number of social pressures seem to overcome this fear and influence them to start. One of the principal social influences, of course, is peer pressure.

Campbell: That suggests the topic of the generation gap. I think that one of the amazing things about recent U.S. civilization is the great increase of peer pressure and the great reduction of parental pressure on children. In the families that produced great violin virtuosos, great citizens, great scholars, the dominating social group for young children was the family. Children were strongly influenced by the social values of their parents. Modern American life has minimized this and has increased the degree to which peer pressure dominates. In one of my unpublished studies (with Frenkel-Brunswik and Rokeach, in continuation of the authoritarian personality research), we studied prejudice among junior high school children. We found that the students who were the most adult-oriented, those from families with many generations participating in the development of social norms, were the least prejudiced, or the most anti-prejudiced. The children who were dominated by peer pressures had the stereotypical rejection of outsiders, including people who were not in the clique. This capacity for total rejection of fellow teenagers is a little disturbing. In any event, these are important issues.

Evans: Yes. Those are very interesting statements about conformity. Of course, it is interesting to evaluate the later work on conformity by Crutchfield (1955) at Berkeley in the context of your observations.

Campbell: Well, Crutchfield, dealing with creative architects, might be absolutely right in the conclusions he reached. Nonetheless, from the point of view of civilization, we may lose things of great value if every member of the group is trying to be a novel innovator. It may be that we can only afford a certain sub-segment who has this tremendous emphasis upon novelty, so we should not make it the sole virtue.

Evans: Let's talk about your significant contributions in the area of research methodology. In the past psychology has had a conception of an ideal experiment with precisely stated hypotheses concerning relationships between independent variables and dependent variables within the context of tight experimental controls. We had many types of experimental methods, all of which suggested quite a bit of control over the environment in which the experiment was taking place. In many of the physical sciences this is possible. You began recognizing that there might be a rather serious gap between this ideal methodology and research in social psychology. To what degree can we generalize from very limited, narrow environments to the world? Looking at your elegant critiques of this type of methodology, how did you evolve your concern for moving into natural settings?

Campbell: Well, right now in the social sciences we are involved in a big debate over hard science approaches versus the more qualitative humanistic approaches. We have come through a phase in which there has been a strong emphasis upon being as quantitative as possible, being as experimental as possible. Now, through my contributions to the theory of validity in the multitrait-multimethod matrix (Campbell and Fiske 1959) and to applied experimental design (Campbell and Stanley 1963/1966) I have come to be seen by the field as advocating a hard science model for the soft social sciences. I don't see myself that way at all. Back in the early days, there was a point of view called logical positivism that carried this hard science emphasis too far, and it dominated experimental psychology. It believed in quantifying everything and picking out certain measures and regarding them as definitions. Now my multitrait-multimethod approach says that procedure won't work. If we are going to try to validate tests, all we can do is to check them against other equally imperfect measures. We should never regard any measure as perfect. E. G. Boring said in 1923 that "intelligence is defined by the Stanford-Binet intelligence test." He was a great man, but this was a stupid statement. Fortunately, E. L. Terman (1937) was in the same year revising his Stanford-Binet test to make it better, because with the help of a few theoretical assumptions he saw many biases in the 1916 edition. He saw his Stanford-Binet intelligence test, as excellent as it was, as an imperfect, fallible measure. Every measure is, as the economists say, a proxy variable, not the thing itself. That is a major theme of the multitrait-multimethod matrix: How can we still try to improve the validity of our tests without getting into the stupidity of defining anxiety by the manifest anxiety scale of 1950? We should not carry operational definitions that far, nor define drive in rats as percentage of normal body weight or number of hours since feeding. Each one of these are imperfect measures of hunger or drive or anxiety. I have given people tools that are humiliating in that if you do a multitrait-multimethod matrix on your favorite personality test, it is apt to look pretty poor. So, whereas "Campbell and Fiske" and "Campbell and Stanley" are seen as encouraging hard science, they actually undermined psychology's previous image of experimentation. The emphasis on plausibility reduces the logical positivists' demand for precision, and increases the burden on intelligent human judgment. At many levels in science we are dependent upon human judgments that cannot be made completely explicit. When we do research with people's attitudes, either the person has had to make an unroutinizable, qualitative judgment as to how to fit his beliefs into these categories or scales that we have provided him, or a coder who reads his qualitative statement has had to judge where it fits. These judgmental steps can't be made completely explicit.

Evans: Perhaps an example will help. Assume we are going to go out into the population and carry out randomized clinical trials to determine the effectiveness of a new drug on a disease. We set up placebo control groups, groups that would get the treatment, other control groups, and so on. We have a whole population of people who have given their informed consent to participate. Now in terms of your conceptions of internal and external validity, how would you generally regard this type of investigation (one that we can't often do in social psychology)?

Campbell: I think the design you described—volunteers who agree to be assigned different treatments randomly—is ideal. Nonetheless, in the medical setting there will be many occasions when we don't want to advocate randomized experiments. One of them, strangely enough, is when there is a strong medical consensus that this treatment is beneficial. If all the patients want it, and if the doctors believe it is useful, and there is plenty of it available, I don't think we can in good conscience randomize. In that case we have got to use other research designs that are not as precise in ruling out plausible alternative explanations. It is immoral to deprive the control group of something that they or the doctors believe is beneficial unless it is in short supply. We can look back at the Salk and Sabine vaccine trials for poliomyelitis. Randomized designs were possible because there wasn't yet enough vaccine to take care of everybody.

But take the infamous syphilis study of the 1930s, which experimented with no treatment at all for one long-term follow-up group. When, in 1941 or 1942, a one-week penicillin treatment for syphilis was developed, the experiment absolutely should have been stopped the next week and all of the no-treatment group been given this new therapy. In the case of penicillin the experimental evidence was compelling, but not from randomized trials. Doctor after doctor who had tried penicillin on patients they had been observing regularly saw fevers disappear, saw sores that had been running for years heal. In terms of experimental design, they were using a quasi-experimental design of the interrupted time series variety (design 7 in Campbell and Stanley 1963). Yet that syphilis study was continued with poverty-level black subjects up until 1960 or 1965. This was absolutely immoral curiosity! Doctors may have learned something from it, but they should have done without it.

Evans: In your presidential address a few years ago at the APA (Campbell 1975), you presented what the psychological community felt was a rather startling position for a social psychologist. If we are going to relate to some of the other social sciences, and even to society and policymakers, we certainly must relate to biology. How can we take a field like social psychology, which has been so dominated by learning and the influence of culture on behavior, and suddenly introduce the idea that there may be some genetically programmed processes that may even override or be as significant as these social and cultural processes?

Campbell: The notion of a universal human nature is implicit in much of our work. We assume that human beings are going to act in their own best interest. I believe this is a valid assumption on the grounds of my interpretation of biological and evolutionary theory. I take sides with a group that emphasizes individual selection and denies the possibility of group selection. But whichever group of biologists is right, their theory of evolution is relevant to the issue of whether individuals act to optimize their own well-being or whether they act to optimize collective purposes. My own view is that biological evolution produces among us vertebrates an opportunistic, selfish animal. We find in a lot of our social customs, like the Ten Commandments, the Seven Deadly Sins, the List of Temptations, and the exhortations of people to love and live for others, a cultural emphasis designed to curb a stubborn, selfish part of human nature. That's the theme of that presidential address, and it cuts into the current sociobiology area in a complicated way. It joins the sociobiologists in saying that evolution produces an average, typical human nature. Some of the extreme cultural relativists or the extreme learning theorists say that everybody is born a completely blank slate, a tabula rasa, and that all character is a product of past environments. I say there is an average human nature, a prototypically human nature that includes certain types of aggression, opportunistic selfishness, and the like. So I disagree with the complete anti-biological group, but I also disagree with major themes in the sociobiological literature that say our biological tendencies have produced a human nature that is just right for collective social living. I am more sympathetic to that pessimistic tradition in many of the great religions that says animal human nature has to be distrusted. It is a complicated point of view and I welcome the tendency in sociology and social psychology to pay more attention to the biological. But I distrust that major theme in sociobiology that says biological evolution has produced just the kind of altruistic animal we need for modern social conditions. I think that in itself is disloyal to biological evolutionary theory. There are many reasons, including new features of our environment, why we want to call "sinful" tendencies that are built into biological human nature (Campbell 1979).

Evans: Of your many contributions, which do you consider to be the most significant?

Campbell: I feel that I have indulged myself in the freedom to meander in my interests. I have made a contribution here and a contribution there as I saw the opportunity to do something useful. Many of my major thrusts have turned out to be blind alleys. For instance, the indirect attitude measurement effort: ten years down the drain. The effort to unify behaviorism and phenomenology seems to have been another blind alley. In any event, in this meandering career I feel lucky to have made contributions that other people have appreciated, and at the same time to have kept doing things that were new and stimulated my curiosity. So I don't want to pick from this career: I don't have the perspective. I will say this: as Asch would tell me, I can't help but be affected by other people's reactions, and in terms of the feedback I get, my contributions to methodology are the most important. I am currently investing more in that area by going into philosophy, epistemology, philosophy of science, and the like, but I'm not doing it in the traditional philosophical way. I'm doing what I call descriptive epistemology, or theory of science, rather than philosophy of science (Campbell 1959; 1974). So I'm becoming a methodologist who is trying to rethink methodology. Surprisingly enough, my preoccupation with both biological evolution and social evolution is fitting into that. The experience of having tried to be scientific in an area in which it's particularly difficult to be scientific makes people like you and me much more interested in philosophy of science than, shall we say, a successful physicist.

REFERENCES

Adorno, T. W., Frenkel-Brunswik, E., Levinson, D. J., and Sanford, R. N. 1950. *The authoritarian personality*. New York: Harper & Bros.

Allport, F. H. 1924. *Social psychology*. Boston: Houghton Mifflin.

Asch, S. E. 1952. *Social psychology*. Englewood Cliffs, New Jersey: Prentice-Hall.

Boring, E. G. 1923. Intelligence as the tests test it. *The New Republic*. 34: 33–36.

Campbell, D. T. 1947. The generality of a social attitude. Unpublished doctoral dissertation, University of California, Berkeley.

———. 1950. The indirect assessment of social attitudes. *Psychol. Bull.* 47:(1): 15–38.

———. 1959. Methodological suggestions from a comparative psychology of knowledge processes. *Inquiry* 2: 152–82.

———. 1963. Social attitues and other acquired behavioral dispositions. In *Psychology: A study of a science* (Vol. 6), *Investigations of man as socius*, ed. S. Koch. New York: McGraw-Hill.

———. 1967. Stereotypes and the perception of group differences. *Amer. Psychol.* 22: (10) 817–29.

———. 1969a. Ethnocentrism of disciplines and the fish-scale model of omniscience. In *Interdisciplinary relationships in the social sciences*, eds. M. Sherif and C. W. Sherif. Chicago: Aldine.

———. 1969b. A phenomenology of the other one: Corrigible, hyothetical and critical. In *Human action: Conceptual and empirical issues*, ed. T. Mischel. New York: Academic Press.

———. 1974. Evolutionary epistemology. In *The library of living philosophers* (Vol. 14-I), *The Philosophy of Karl R. Popper*, ed. P. A. Schilpp. Lasalle, Illinois: Open Court Publishing.

———. 1975. On the conflicts between biological and social evolution and between psychology and moral tradition. *Amer. Psychol.* 30: 103–1126.

———. 1979. Comments on the sociobiology of ethics and moralizing. *Behav. Science* 24: 37–45.

———, and Fiske, D. W. 1959. Convergent and discriminant validation by the multitrait-multimethod matrix. *Psychol. Bull.* 56: (2) 81–105.

———, Miller, M., Lubetsky, J., and O'Connell, E. J. 1964. Varieties of projection in trait attribution. *Psychol. Monogr.* 78 (Whole No. 592).

———, and Stanley, J. C. 1963 and 1966. Experimental and quasi-experimental designs for research on teaching. In *Handbook of research on teaching*, ed. N. L. Gage. Chicago: Rand McNally. Reprinted as *Experimental and quasi-experimental designs for research*. Chicago: Rand McNally.

Crutchfield, R. S. 1955. Conformity and character. *Amer. Psychol.* 10: 191–98.

Evans, R. I., Rozelle, R. M., Mittelmark, M. B., Hansen, W. B., Bane, A. L., and Havis, J. 1978. Deterring the onset of smoking in children: Knowledge of immediate physiological effects and coping with peer pressure, media pressure, and parent modeling. *J. Appl. Soc. Psychol.* 8: 126–35.

Kidder, L. and Campbell, D. T. 1970. The indirect testing of social attitudes. In *Attitude measurement*, ed. G. F. Summers. Chicago: Rand McNally.

Krech, D., and Crutchfield, R. S. 1948. *Theory and problems of social psychology*. New York: McGraw-Hill.

LeVine, R. A., and Campbell, D. T. 1972. *Ethnocentrism: Theories of conflict, ethnic attitudes and group behavior*. New York: Wiley.

Levinson, D. J. 1950. The study of ethnocentric ideology. In *The authoritarian personality*, T. W. Adorno, E. Frenkel-Brunswik, D. J. Levinson, and R. N. Sanford. New York: Harper & Bros.

Mead, M. 1928. *Coming of age in Samoa*. New York: William Morrow & Co.
———. 1930. *Growing up in New Guinea*. New York: William Morrow & Co.
———. 1935. *Sex and temperament*. New York: William Morrow & Co.

Murray, H. A. 1938. *Explorations in personality*. New York: Oxford University Press.

Rokeach, M. 1956. Political and religious dogmatism: An alternative to the authoritarian personality. *Psychol. Monogr.* 70 (Whole No. 425).
———. 1960. *The open and closed mind*. New York: Basic Books.

Sullivan, H. S. 1953. *The interpersonal theory of psychiatry*. New York: Norton.

Sumner, W. G. 1906. *Folkways*. New York: Ginn.

Shils, E. 1954. Authoritarianism: "Right" and "Left." In *Studies in the scope and method of "The Authoritarian Personality,"* eds. R. Christie and M. Johoda. New York: Free Press.

Terman, L. M., and Merrill, M. A. 1937. *Measuring intelligence*. Boston: Houghton Mifflin.

SELECTED READINGS

Campbell, D. T. 1959. Methodological suggestions from a comparative psychology of knowledge processes. *Inquiry* 2: 152–82.

Campbell, D. T. 1969a. Ethnocentrism of disciplines and the fish-scale model of omniscience. In *Interdisciplinary relationships in the social sciences*, eds. M. Sherif and C. W. Sherif. Chicago: Aldine.

Campbell, D. T. 1974. Evolutionary epistemology. In *The library of living philosophers* (Vol. 14-I), *The Philosophy of Karl R. Popper*, ed. P. A. Schilpp. Lasalle, Illinois: Open Court Publishing.

Campbell, D. T. 1979. Comments on the sociobiology of ethics and moralizing. *Behav. Science* 24: 37–45.

Campbell, D. T., and Fiske, D. W. 1959. Convergent and discriminant validation by the multitrait-multimethod matrix. *Psychol. Bull.* 56 (2): 81–105.

Campbell, D. T., and Stanley, J. C. 1963 and 1966. Experimental and quasi-experimental designs for research on teaching. In *Handbook of research on teaching*, ed. N. L. Gage. Chicago: Rand McNally. Reprinted as *Experimental and quasi-experimental designs for research*. Chicago: Rand McNally.

8

DAVID MCCLELLAND

(1917–   )

David McClelland took his undergraduate degree from Wesleyan University and his master's from the University of Missouri. In 1941 he received his doctorate from Yale. After posts at Weslayan and Bryn Mawr, he moved to Harvard University where he is now professor in the department of psychology and social relations. his research in the area of motivation, in particular the need for achievement and the power motive, has been highly innovative. It has led to significant theoretical contributions and highly creative measurement tests. In addition his research findings have been applied to a wide variety of social problems in such areas as management and organization, alcoholism, and increased productivity in the world's underdeveloped nations.

Biological and Social Determinism/The Discrepancy Hypothesis/A Theory of Expectancies/Learning Affects Adaptation Levels/Some Universal Incentives/Achievement/Challenge/Power/The Desire for Impact//The Achievement Motivation/The Need for Achievement/Defining the Field/Measurements/N-Ach/V-Ach/Achievement and Values/The Origins of Achievement/It's Never Too Late to Learn Achievement/Some Very Important Applications//Power Motivation/Historical Perspective/Authoritarianism/Looking at the Motive/TAT/Folk Tales/Cross-Cultural Studies//The Achievement Motivation and Underdeveloped Countries/You Do It Because They Want You To//Research Ethics/Academic Freedom/The LSD Controversy/Reactions to Criticism/It Troubles Me Very Much/Introducing Measurement to a Soft Area/ The Cause and Cure of Heart Disease!/A Look at the Future//

Dr. McClelland and I discuss his early work on social motivation, and he recalls the development of the theory of expectancies, the discrepancy hypothesis, and his work on adaptation by the organism. He describes the techniques used to measure achievement, and his systematic study of the need for achievement in humans—achievement motivation. He explains what he means by both need for achievement and value achievement, and what he believes to be the origin of these needs. He reacts to questions concerning the heritability of IQ, and offers an interesting alternative: ". . . one of the worst things that is inherited is the opportunity structure. It's got nothing to do with your genes; it's got to do with society." He then tells how achievement-motivation training has been effective in working with problems of school children from deprived environments, underdeveloped nations of the world, and in business opportunities for minority groups. We discuss his current research on power motivation, and he connects it up with the serious problem of alcoholism. Dr. McClelland tells how the TAT is used to measure fantasy in delineating both the achievement and the power motivation, and the interesting and novel way he applied this concept to cross-cultural studies. We discuss research ethics and academic freedom, and he then reacts to criticisms of his work. In conclusion, he outlines some of his current research, including the relationship of power motivation to stress and alcoholism.

Evans: Dr. McClelland, looking back at the evolution of your thinking, one notes that even in your earlier work, such as your 1951 textbook on personality (McClelland 1951) you were trying to demonstrate how social motivation develops, anticipating a social-learning mode that is becoming extremely important in psychology today. The traditional homeostatic model, of course, defines motivation as all the conditions that arouse, direct, or sustain the organism, and argues that certain unlearned, primary drives are part of the inherited nature of the organism, while drives of a higher order, social drives, are learned. This thinking has been challenged by ethologists such as Lorenz (Evans 1975*b*) who believe that what we call social motivation, the need for social approval, may really be programmed in the genome and that we are overestimating the importance of learning. In fact, they say such motives as social approval may be as innate as the need for food, the hunger drive. How would you react to this?

McClelland: You will remember from that book, that I had developed a somewhat different theory that combined biological with social determinism, what I called the discrepancy hypothesis. The basic idea involved a certain relationship between a stimulus and the adaptation level of the organism for that stimulus, which either gives pleasure or pain. That provides for both learning and biology, because learning affects adaptation level. I used the example of adapting your mouth to a saline solution. If you adapt at a certain level, you can then take a new level that would seem pleasant to you in relation to the adaptation level, but would be very unpleasant without that adaptation. I applied this idea, generally, to expectancies. My basic theory of motivation was, and I guess still is, a theory of expectancies. If you expect something will happen—100 percent—and it does happen, you don't get any particular reaction on the affective side. It just confirms, and if anything, you get boredom. It may even be a bit negative if you have the same expectancy confirmed over and over again. So far as motivation like the achievement motivation is concerned, it still looks clear to me that it's a discrepancy between what you expect and what happens. If the discrepancy is small, it interests you, it catches your attention and challenges you, and you're more attracted to that particular situation. If it's too different from what you expect, you avoid it. So approach and avoidance motivation are basically tied to this biological thing.

Evans: Actually, that's not too far removed from what the ethologists would agree with.

McClelland: I developed this theory right out of ethology at the time. I haven't done much with it for the past twenty years because I found it very hard to measure, very hard to get at. It makes good theoretical sense, but in practice it's very hard to determine on what level people are adapting. I don't think it's untrue; I think it's one of those theories that gets left behind because it hasn't been tested. The person who has worked with it the most is Jerry Kagan (1970) at Harvard. He has worked a lot with infants, on what causes an infant to smile—the pleasure response— if it sees a face that is a little different from the face it is used to seeing; if the face is very different, the infant may not smile and may even avoid it. Now in the social motives, it's clear to me that there are certain incentives that are quite universal, however they are derived. In the case of achievement motivation for example, the incentive of challenge—something just a little beyond what you can probably do—is universal for members of the human species. In the case of power, it's more apt to be the desire for impact.

Evans: One of your many innovative contributions to psychology that students will identify immediately is your work on achievement motivation. Going back to the area of measuring achievement, we think of Murray's (1938) classification of needs, such as need for avoidance, need for affiliation, and of course, need for achievement. Did your work begin from the kind of thing Murray was talking about, or had you become interested quite independently?

McClelland: What I borrowed from Murray was, essentially, fantasy as a technique for measuring motivation, but I brought to it an experimental approach. I did it systematically. What is the effect of hunger on motivation? What is the effect of achievement arousal—what I used to call ego involvement?

Evans: I know it's impossible to be absolutely precise in constructs like this, but what did you mean by "need for achievement"? What were you describing?

McClelland: There are three different ways to answer that question. First, we had an arousal technique: we aroused what we felt was the achievement motive in people and detected its effect on fantasies. That's a little like injecting somebody with something and taking a blood sample to see what happens. Then second, we had a coding definition; that means we coded fantasies to find instances of achievement—imagery, we called it. That is probably the closest to a good definition; the concern for doing something well, or better than it has been done before. The third way was the actions shown by people high in this need, whose fantasies were high in need for achievement. We know these people act in ways that maximize their feedback on how well they're doing. They like situations that are moderately risky because they have a chance of succeeding, and they like to be personally responsible for what's going on, so if they do succeed, they can take the credit. They want feedback on how well they're doing, so they do something concrete. All of this suggests that the motive is the desire to do something better, *measurably* better.

Evans: Another interesting thing I recall is from a series of lectures you gave quite a few years ago. This was your description of two directions in which achievement motivation could move. In one direction is the individual who attempts to achieve in terms of social reinforcement, for the immediate reward, so that people will applaud him. But you also talked about another direction, not "n-ach," the need for achievement, but "v-ach," value achievement, a type of achiever who exercises his need for achievement in such a way that he doesn't care about external reinforcement, about people saying he's great. It's more a personal sense of satisfaction, the kind of thing that Maslow and Rogers (Evans 1975a) imply when they talk about a higher level of individuation. Is this kind of artisan's self-satisfaction the kind of achievement you were thinking about?

McClelland: I think it's analogous. This is the person with a high need for achievement as we measure it in fantasy, who could be happy on a desert island constructing a swing in a palm tree. If it worked, he'd get satisfaction out of building some little gadget, even though nobody else knew he'd done it. The person with high v-ach, and we measure this essentially from self-ratings, rates himself high in achievement motivation. We find such people to be influenced by what experts consider to be good, and other people think is right. They are more apt to be influenced by that.

Evans: There seem to be two problems that confront the scientist in this area. One is the question of measurement which we've discussed and the second is the source. Where does it come from? One line of thought relates it to early childhood rearing practices. If the child receives a great deal of independence training, right from the start, there seems to be a great achievement-need developing, while too much of a dependency relationship results in somewhat less need for achievement. Is that what you were speculating?

McClelland: I was very much influenced by the culture and personality field that argued that basic things like motives were laid down early in life, that they were laid down preverbally so they weren't terribly conscious, and that they continued to influence you disproportionately for the rest of your life. We found evidence that mothers who encouraged their sons and set high standards for them, who gave them lots of encouragement in achievement areas, tended to have sons with a higher need for achievement. At the time, it seemed that the encouragement had to come at just the right time, so that the child's reach would just exceed his grasp. I found that fathers who were authoritarian tended to discourage their sons from developing achievement motivation. I'm less sure now that it's some particular thing that happened at a particlar time of life. We've been giving achievement-motivation courses for adults, and we can teach them achievement motivation when they're twenty-five, forty-five, or sixty-five. It's never too late to learn achievement.

Evans: You're saying, then, that first you were thinking in the tradition of Freud's early five years of life, or what Adler described as a kind of life style that's embedded and almost irreversible. Then you began to find that it's not irreversible, that persons can be retrained to become more achievement-oriented.

McClelland: I was also influenced in all this by the civil rights movement in the sixties, because all this early childhood training looked like it was fatal to the blacks, seemed to condemn them forever. It was believed that their character couldn't be changed. We found, in fact, that they could be changed. I began to think of it like learning to play tennis. If may be easier to learn certain things about tennis when you're young, but you can certainly learn them when you're older. In fact, you may learn it better because you can hold the racquet better.

Evans: The point you made about black children brings to mind the stir and furor that has evolved around the work of such people as Herrnstein, Jensen, and Shockley. Take Jensen (1969) for example, who began to look at Head Start and such programs designed to take children from so-called deprived environments—the kind of environments that may deprive them of the enrichment that may lead to higher need for achievement. These programs try to provide this enrichment and intercept these deficits so that the child can function better. Jensen is a very thoroughly statistically minded psychologist, out of the tradition of Thorndike and Spearman, and he began to think this deficit couldn't be accounted for entirely in terms of environment; that perhaps as much as 80 percent of intellectual functioning might really be genetically based. If there is some limit fixed by heredity, and one that is racially linked, what effect would this have on training children in achievement motivation?

McClelland: Jensen is just wrong about saying that compensatory education doesn't work. Lots of compensatory education doesn't work, but achievement-motivation training *does* work. There's a very careful study by Richard DeCharms (1975) in St. Louis, done with a variant of achievement-motivation training that he called "origin training." He trained the principals and teachers in black districts of St. Louis, and there were very marked changes over a two-year period in the test scores of the kids, after motivation training. Psychologists don't believe in motivation training; they believe in skill training. I would argue that the motivation problem is central, that we do know how to work on it and that we have worked on it successfully. DeCharms showed that it really worked there.

Evans: Then you believe this training can overcome the deficits some of these children face, even if the problem is inherited?

McClelland: Undoubtedly, there are some things that are inherited— skin color, eye color, things like that—and one of the worst things that is inherited is the opportunity structure. If you're black, you inherit less opportunity, all along the line. It's got nothing to do with your genes; it's got to do with society. If you develop some goals, some reasonable goals for a young person to make, and then you are systematically prevented from achieving those goals, not from your own lack of ability, but simply because you're black, that discourages your achievement motivation. That's another kind of inheritance. I went back and looked at the famous studies of Terman (Terman and Oden 1947) that everyone quotes about IQ, and which are usually cited as an example of the heritability of intelligence. If you'll look at his data, you'll discover that the kids with high IQs came from better families; their families were richer and could help them more—to go to college, for example, and pay their way through college. These kids were happier; money helps people be happier, and they inherit money along with whatever genes they inherit. You can't conclude from Terman's studies whether it was better opportunities that led them to be more successful, or better achievement motives, or higher IQs.

Evans: You are saying that achievement motivation is an overriding factor; that even the person with a high IQ is still going to function in a context of achievement motivation?

McClelland: I would say some motivation. There are all kinds of other motives, but you're absolutely right. He's not going to use his intelligence at all unless he's motivated to do something.

Evans: Moving away from achievement motivation, I'd like to talk about another motive that I know you're presently interested in. In fact, I believe you have a book soon to be published on power motivation (McClelland 1975). Historically, the older philosophers semed to see the world operating in terms of power. Nietzsche talked about man in terms of a power-oriented organism, and Jung (Evans 1976) disagreed strongly with Freud in the juxtaposition of power versus sex. Jung clearly felt that power was a very important motive and they must have had some interesting discussions because their own relationship was really a power relationship. What seems to be strange is that here we have a very important motive, central to the behavior of man, and yet it has not been studied in a systematic way. Why do you feel there is such a resistance to studying power as a motive?

McCelland: We have been studying it very intensely for the past five years, although a lot of the work hasn't been published yet. As to why it wasn't studied earlier, I think the answer is very clear. American social scientists, and I would say Americans in general, are afraid of power. They don't like it, they're against it, they don't think it should be exercised, they dislike people who have it, and of course, there are some very good historical reasons for this. Almost everyone knows stories about fleeing from tyranny, about Nazi tyranny, about the exercise of power. Power was a terrible thing. It was associated with authoritarianism, race prejudice, everything bad. *The Authoritarian Personality* (Adorno, et al. 1950) kind of killed the field.

Evans: You think *The Authoritarian Personality* killed the field?

McClelland: It made power a swear word. Authoritarianism is definitely a bad thing. You shouldn't have power motivation. Obviously power motivation can take that form, but I'm saying that power motivation is much broader than that. A mother is exercising power when she protects and nurtures her young, and we consider that good. it's still the power instinct, the power drive.

We started systematically measuring it about ten years ago and a very good book has come out by David Winter (1973) called *The Power Motive.* Then my own work on alcohol, described in *The Drinking Man* (McCelland, et al. 1972), turned out to be related to power motivation. We discovered that drinking increased power fantasies, and we tied that into power motivation.

Evans: How did you study these motives? The historical pattern is to name a motive, then define it . . .

McClelland: Wait, let's be clear. We do not define in advance. We define only well enough to arouse it, and in the case of power motivation, we used three different ways. We used student candidates who were awaiting election returns, and had them write TATs while they waited. We figured their power motives would be aroused. We compared their scores with the scores of other students under neutral conditions—a very careful comparison, almost phrase by phrase—and out of that, we got a base line. Next, we put somebody in the role of experimenter—that's a powerful role—and then we had subjects watch a hypnotist, a power-related experience and we had them write fantasies under these conditions. We found the result were similar in all the conditions.

Evans: You mentioned the TAT—the Thematic Apperception Test—and it might be interesting to have you describe a typical power response, or a typical achievement fantasy, to show the distinction.

McClelland: Well, let's say we show a picture of a guy in shirt sleeves working at what appears to be a drawing board. A typical story might go: "This is George. He's working late on some project. He's new on the job and eager to do well. He's working on a new system that's going to save the company money, and he works late and succeeds and goes home happy, and gets promoted." It's a simple story, but full of achievement imagery because he clearly wants to do better, wants to find a new way, and he's happy because he succeeds. Even if he had failed, it would have scored for achievement because the concern is still with doing well. Another story might go, 'This is George. He's working late and he wants to come up with something that will win him the prize in some kind of architecture competition because he knows the person who wins that prize will be proclaimed the greatest architect in the world. His wife will respect him more if he wins because she had some doubts about his being an architect. If he wins that prize, he will get worldwide recognition and fame, and his wife will love him. And he does." That's clearly not concerned with doing a better job or with performance; he's wholly concerned with recognition.

Evans: You have done some very interesting cross-cultural studies with achievement motivation. How do you approach the measurement of something like the motivation achievement or the achievement of power from one culture to another?

McClelland: We code the fantasies the same way, and there are certain actions that are similar the world round, like moderate risk taking. The thing that varies from culture to culture is the area in which people take risks. That varies enormously from culture to culture and even in our own culture, between the sexes. There are great differences because of culture patterning, of what men do, typically, and what women do. Women may take moderate risks and act like achievers in, say, the social area, and men may take more risks in the mechanical area.

Evans: You say *moderate* risks. The amount of risk is a form of innovation, isn't it?

McClelland: It leads to shortcuts.

Evans: What type of material did you use in the cross-cultural studies? Obviously the TAT cards would not work in every case.

McClelland: Whole cultures produce something very much like fantasies, namely folk tales, so we started coding these folk tales. We coded them for achievement motivation and found it enabled us to predict certain things, such as the number of entrepreneurs, and so on. Although social psychologists had completely discarded the study of "group mind," we found we could get measures of motives on countries through coding children's stories—stories in children's textbooks—and from them tell if the country had developed rapidly, whether it would go to war, and so on.

Evans: One thing that has characterized your career is your idea of starting out with a theory, developing a measure and then putting this together in a "training package." You have even gone into underdeveloped countries to attempt to train them in such things as achievement motivation, haven't you? How did you happen to get involved in this?

McCelland: When I finished my book, *The Achieving Society* (McCelland 1967), I had traced the role of achievement motivation in the dvelopment of entrepreneurs and the relationship of that to economic growth, and I had done historical studies showing that countries that were high in achievement motivation developed more rapidly. I conceived the idea that maybe we could develop achievement motivation, and I had a little ambition—a very power-oriented ambition—to create an achieving society, to influence history, so to speak. It was a long, hard struggle because people found it difficult to take me seriously. There is a strong prejudice that psychologists have that it's hard to change something like motivation in adults. Well, we've done it at least a dozen times, all over the world, and we've done a number of careful follow-up studies, and the results are very predictable. We always get about two-thirds results. That is, about two-thirds of the people are turned on by this training. Our trained people do about twice as well as untrained people who are otherwise comparable. We're doing it on a large scale for minority business enterprises in this country—blacks, the Chicano communities—and we're having real success. There's no question about these people doing better—their profits are up 90 percent, on the average, in six months. We did our first work in India, and that is written up in a book called *Motivating Economic Achievement* (McClelland and Winter 1969). It's the first of the evaluation studies. We started there twelve years ago, training small businessmen in one city, matched with a control city where there was no training. We don't know whether it was because of what we did—we like to think it was—but the city where the businessmen were trained is doing much better today than the control city.

Evans: There's a criticism that I'm sure you've heard, about your moving into these underdeveloped countries and trying to make them become more achievement-oriented. There are those who say, "Why can't we leave quiet, cooperative, nonproductive countries alone?"

McClelland: The answer is simple. You do it because they want you to. Our first talks take approximately the following form: "You've got dysentery. You've got all kinds of aches and pains. Do you like that? Do you want to be rid of it?" And the answer is usually, "Yes." You say, "You've got to quit drinking the water from the pond. It has organisms in it that cause the trouble." Now, is that wishing your western way of life on him? I think not. I think that's giving him information he didn't otherwise have. It's still up to him whether he wants to do anything about it.

Evans: Now here's a question I'm sure you've heard before. The power of the experimenter has been involved in several recent examples of research—Stanley Milgram's (1974) obedience to authority work, and Philip Zimbardo's (1973) simulated prison experiment are two that have caused a great deal of stir—and the question of experimenter ethics is being given a lot of attention. Your own experience at Harvard, when Leary and Alpert were involved in their research with LSD, represented one of the early ethical challenges to psychology's use of subjects. Do you feel that your actions at the time were justified in light of more recent concerns about ethics?

McClelland: That's a complicated issue. The concern for ethics is extremely important. Some experimenters find it easier, and I honestly suspect some of them find it more fun, to shock people than to do something nice for them. Margaret Mead once said to me, "You can't lie to subjects." And I said, "What do you mean, you can't lie to subjects?" She said, "They know something is wrong." There's a lot in that, and I've never forgotten it. The LSD controversy didn't involve deceit; the subjects in that study were all too willing to take LSD. It involved the question of how far you can stretch the mantle of academic freedom over innovative research. And it was a case of somebody doing something that was very unpopular and somewhat dangerous, more than misuse of subjects. The kickback on personality research in the long run was more serious. Other psychologists are always suspicious of personality people because personality people, by definition, work with the more difficult, delicate areas of human behavior—sexuality, homosexuality, criminality—all of the things that make people nervous. They make psychologists nervous too. Unfortunately, that's our job as psychologists, to understand those phenomena and just keep working on them. It might interest you to know that I've kept records from that time, and of all the graduate students involved at that time in LSD research, none takes LSD today, to my knowledge. Leary is the only one who, as far as I know, continued to recommend its use and to take it himself.

Evans: What are some of the criticisms of your work that have troubled you? Perhaps "troubled" is too strong.

McClelland: No, it's not. It troubles me very much. I've never understood why it's so difficult for psychologists to take work based on fantasy seriously. After all, the instructions for writing a story are not very different from the instructions for a memory task, running nonsense syllables on a memory drum. I've followed all the rules, statistical tests, experimental controls, everything that a good psychologist ought to do, but I feel that my data have never had the same acceptance as they would if I had stuck to something more traditional. That seems unfair to me.

Evans: It would be interesting to hear you assess your own work. What do you consider to be your own most important contribution?

McClelland: I'd like to think it's measurement in the area of motivation. Everybody has talked about motivation, but until I got around to measuring it, we weren't really able to make the kinds of breakthroughs I think we have now. I think, overall, that's the major contribution I've made. I introduced measurement into a very soft area that otherwise is dealt with by "common sense," "good clinical judgment," "conventional wisdom," and so on.

Evans: In assessing your contributions, it seems to me that you have moved into a very devastating problem with alcoholism and have come up with a whole new direction of research. Could you describe some of that work?

McCleland: We discovered that people who drink too much are people who want a "power rush." Drinking produces an adrenaline response, and this gets into fantasy in the form of power imagery, particularly for people who don't have power, or who have had power and have had it taken away from them. Let's say an army officer is passed over for promotion, and his former subordinates are now kicking him around. He turns to the bottle, not to "drown his sorrow," but just to feel stronger for a little while. We've done a very carefully controlled study with severe alcoholics in which they learned why they were drinking and how to discover alternative outlets for their power drives. A control group received the standard AA group therapy, outpatient treatment at the veterans' hospital where we conducted the study. At the one-year follow-up, about 25 percent of those who got the standard treatment were still on the wagon. Of those who got the additional power-motivation training, 50 percent were doing better. It works because we had more specific knowledge of what was wrong in the first place, so we could treat it better.

Evans: You focused on the power dimension very precisely. We've found in our own research in persuasive communication that specificity is a far more important variable in communication than the character of the message. You're applying this specificity to a very complex problem.

McClelland: One thing that psychologists really know is that feedback works. The human organism is so constructed that it can adjust very quickly, but if your feedback is fuzzy, it's very hard to have learning. In the area of alcoholism, people were telling alcoholics that all sorts of things were wrong with them, but these things weren't pinpointed.

Evans: What are you working on at the present time?

McClelland: I have just finished writing a paper on the stress syndrome and power motivation. People high in power motivation have a higher resting level of adrenaline production; they act as if they're under stress even when they're not. You keep pouring adrenaline into your circulatory system and eventually you damage the cardiovascular system. You get this circulating adrenaline that's not burned up by large muscles, and some people become addicted to what I call the "power rush." What we need to do is a longitudinal study on high power motivation in adolescence and how it correlates with essential hypertension in the thirties and heart attacks in the forties. A very fascinating study by Herbert Benson (Wallace and Benson 1972) at the Harvard Medical School has shown that meditation techniques specifically decrease the secretion of adrenaline and the whole stress syndrome associated with it. So I have now given you the cause and cure of heart disease! It will need to be checked out, of course.

Evans: But it's a very interesting set of hypotheses. It is most interesting the way you take a particular motive, like power, make a subtle conversion into a specific damaging disorder, and then use your training methods and evaluation procedures to yield long-term longitudinal data. If you get the long-term changes, you're going to have a lot of people knocking at your door. They probably already are.

REFERENCES

Adorno, T., et al. 1950. *The authoritarian personality.* New York: Harper.
DeCharms, R. 1975. *Enhancing motivation: a change project in the classroom.* New York: Irvington.
Evans, R. 1975a. *Carl Rogers: The man and his ideas.* New York: Dutton.
———. 1975b. *Konrad Lorenz: The man and his ideas.* New York: Harcourt.
———. 1976b. *Jung on elementary psychology.* New York: Dutton.
Jensen, A. 1969. How much can we boost I.Q. and scholastic achievement? *Harvard Educational Review,* 39: (1) 1–123.
Kagan, J. 1970. Attention and psychological changes in the young child. *Science* 170: 826–32.
McCelland, D. 1951. *Personality.* New York: Free Press.
———, et al. 1953. *The achievement motive.* New York: Appleton.
———. 1967. *The achieving society.* New York: Free Press.
———, and Winter, D. 1969. *Motivating economic achievement.* New York: Free Press.
———, et al. 1972. *The drinking man.* New York: Free Press.
———. 1975. *Power: The inner experience.* New York: Irvington.
Milgram, S. 1974. *Obedience to authority.* New York: Harper.
Murray, H., et al. 1938. *Explorations in personality.* New York: Oxford.
Terman, L., and Oden, M. 1947. *The gifted child grows up.* Stanford, Calif.: Stanford University Press.
Wallace, R., and Benson, H. 1972. The physiology of meditation. *Sci. Amer.* 226: 84–90.
Winter, D. 1973. *The power motive.* New York: Free Press.
Zimbardo, P., Haney, G., and Banks, C. 1973. Interpersonal dynamics in a simulated prison. *Int. J. Criminology and Penology* 2: (1) 69–97.

SELECTED READINGS

McClelland, D. C. 1951. *Personality.* New York: Free Press.
McCelland, D. C., Atkinson, J. W., Clark, R. A., and Lowell, E. L. 1953. *The achievement motive.* New York: Appleton-Century-Crofts.
McCelland, D. C. (Ed.) 1955. *Studies in motivation.* New York: Appleton-Century-Crofts.
McCelland, D. C., Baldwin, A. L., Bronfenbrenner, V., and Strodtbeck, F. L. 1961. *Talent and society.* Princeton, N. J.: Van Nostrand.
McCelland, D. C. 1975. *Power: The inner experience.* New York: Irvington.

9

IRVING JANIS
(1918–   )

Dr. Janis has been a central figure in social psychology for more than three decades. He received his B.S. from the University of Chicago in 1939 and, following work as a research psychologist in the War Department from 1943–1946, earned his Ph.D. at Columbia University in 1948. During his career he has made seminal contributions to social psychology in the areas of persuasive communications, attitude change, psychological stress, and decision making. His integrative contributions to theory and research have earned him numerous awards, including a Guggenheim Fellowship (1973–1974) and the Socio-Psychological Prize of the American Association for the Advancement of Science in 1967. Dr. Janis is now professor of psychology at Yale University, where he has been since 1947.

Mass Communications// Otto Klineberg// Attitude Change/ Cognitive Dissonance//Psychological Stress// Role Reversal// Alcoholics Anonymous/ Cohesive Group Experience// Personality Correlations/ Interactions Rather Than Main Effects// Decision Making// Pre-Decision Stress Pattern// External Validity// Experimental Method// Incentive Theory// Groupthink// Crisis in Social Psychology//

As we begin our discussion, Dr. Janis describes his early training under Carl Hovland, during which he studied the effects of mass communications. "I learned from Hovland the necessity for very rigorous testing of hypotheses, [even] under field conditions." Dr. Janis describes his series of studies of the effects of role-playing on attitude change, and his experiments on the effects of fear-arousing communications. He then discusses his imaginative experiment on "emotional role playing," in which the combination

97

of fear-arousal and psychodramatic role playing as terminal can-
cer patients proves potent enough to alter the attitude and beha-
vior of heavy smokers: "Some of the young women in the first
study went so far as to throw away their cigarette packs as they
left the laboratory." Dr. Janis also describes his more recent
work exploring what makes groups like Alcoholics Anonymous
so effective. Highlighting his concern with real life problems, he
discusses his integration of his work on psychological stress and
his interdisciplinary study of decision making. He questions why
people's decisions are not better than they are, and states,
"People make errors because of the kind of stress coping pattern
they are using." Reacting to the controversy that surrounded his
"incentive" theory of attitude change, he throws light upon
some aspects of what his colleague William McGuire labeled
the "twenty dollar misunderstanding." Finally, Dr. Janis re-
sponds to the prevalent concern that social psychology is facing
a scientific crisis: "It seems to me that the crisis is being sur-
mounted and there is every reason to be hopeful of making so-
cial psychology into an additive science."

Evans: Dr. Janis, as you look over your career in social psychology,
what were some of the things that you saw as you moved from the more
traditional social psychology at Columbia to the less traditional orientation at Yale?

Janis: The transition actually took place for me during World War II,
before I got my Ph.D. degree at Columbia. I was drafted into the Army,
into the research branch of the Information and Education Division,
where I worked directly under Carl Hovland, who was developing his
program for studying the effects of mass communications. Specifically,
his group researched the effects of communications like the "Why We
Fight" film series that were designed to influence morale of the American
soldiers in a positive way. I learned from Hovland the necessity for very
rigorous testing of hypotheses, including the application of experimental
methods to situations like the showing of a film under field conditions
and assessing the attitude changes that were produced. So it was that
wartime experience that generated a switch in my interests in the direction of doing as rigorous research as possible on attitude change.
However, I never did lose, at any time, my broader interests in tackling
any problem that one can get a handle on. And I have done something
that is beyond the pale as far as many experimentalists are concerned. I
have written a book consisting entirely of historical case studies, the
book on *Victims of Groupthink* (1972). I believe in retaining a broad

range of interests and tackling any problem for which a reasonable source of evidence is available.

Evans: You're saying we're not locked into a point of view that was either too narrow or too broad. You could see the virtues of a more rigorous experimental approach as well as of the hypothesis-gathering looser "field work." You knew Otto Klineberg; how did he influence your perspective?

Janis: Well, the thing that stands out most was the integrated character of his approach, the use of data from all sources of social science. He was one of the broadest based social scientists I have ever encountered, relying heavily on social anthropology and sociology as well as psychology (e.g., Klineberg 1954). In the book that Leon Mann and I have just published, *Decision Making* (1977), you will find that maybe six or seven different disciplines are represented there in terms of the literature that we take very seriously. For example, research by political scientists and economists is included along with work by anyone else who has done studies bearing on the behavioral aspects of decision making, irrespective of academic discipline.

Evans: Harold Kelly and you worked with Carl Hovland on *Communication and Persuasion* (1953). As you look back at that work, what do you think some of its most important features are?

Janis: Communication and Persuasion was a progress report on the first five years of the project that Carl Hovland had set up at Yale to investigate systematically the variables that influence the effectiveness of communications designed to persuade people. It is the general approach that has had the greatest carry-over value. The general approach is to formulate sharply the hypotheses that deal with important variables, and then to design studies and find suitable settings in which to investigate those variables. Finally, we rigorously assess the effects, not just the main effects but also "interactions" between two or more variables.

On the substantive side, the things that have emerged from that volume that interest me most have to do with the effects of role playing. I did some work in collaboration with Bert King (Janis and King 1954) that indicated under certain conditions saying is believing. When you are assigned a role to argue in favor of a given position, as debaters often do, that participation tends to change your attitude in the direction you are arguing. Herbert Kelman did some important work at about the same time on essay writing, showing that children tended to change their attitudes after producing essays they wrote in order to try to get a prize. That early work led to a major development in social psychology. It took flight when Leon Festinger came along and reinterpreted those results in line with the theory of cognitive dissonance, which he was developing in the fifties. His 1957 book *A Theory of Cognitive Dissonance* discussed our experiments in great detail and then added some more experiments to it. Subsequently, he and Merrill Carlsmith did the classic study (Festinger and Carlsmith 1959) that led to the "twenty dollar misunderstanding," as William McGuire labeled it, referring to the misunderstandings surrounding the differences between my self-persuasion theory and Festinger's cognitive dissonance theory of role-playing effects. That area has led to an understanding of the importance of factors such as the improvization of new arguments and a person's sense of personal responsibility, which determine whether or not playing the role will change one's attitudes.

Evans: You became involved in some carefully controlled experimental work that led to the classic study in the area of fear arousal and how this affects dental hygiene behavior (Janis and Feshbach 1953). How did you happen to get involved in this research? (Certainly, dental hygiene was not an area that had generally involved social psychological research.)

Janis: I was interested in the dynamics of fear from my work on fear in combat. I had the responsibility for writing the chapters on that subject in the volumes on combat and its aftermath of *The American Soldier* (Stouffer, Lumsdaine, A. A., Lumsdaine, M. H., Williams, Smith, Janis, Star, and Cottrell 1949). It seemed to me that studying fear appeals in persuasive messages in public health communication would provide an opportunity to investigate some of the important aspects of what fear does to people and how it can be both constructive and destructive in its effects. At the same time, I was investigating fear among surgical patients, which led to a book, *Psychological Stress* (Janis 1958), that reported a series of studies I had carried out. One reason I chose dental hygiene was that it seemed to be a specific area where the fear would be realistic. Also, most people, including high school students, were not following the recommendations of the American Dental Association to brush their teeth immediately after meals, despite their dental hygiene courses. I have felt from the very beginning that research on persuasion should never be oriented toward problems that are going to be of help to the propagandists or the people who are trying to manipulate the public to buy things they don't want, but rather should be oriented toward the problems of people in public health and others who are trying to do some public service.

Evans: So you and Hovland were already considering this long before most psychologists had become interested in preventive medicine. Could you briefly review the methodology of the studies on fear appeals and rebate some of the conclusions? You might make a comment on how the problems of internal and external validity present themselves in a study of this sort.

Janis: Well, we did the first study in conjunction with the hygiene course in a high school, during the early 1950s (Janis and Feshbach 1953). Seymour Feshbach and I had the opportunity to work with a large number of students in classrooms where they were given this kind of course. We prepared a film-strip lecture with a speaker on a tape recording. Taking into account the problem of internal validity, we prepared three different versions to represent three different levels of fear, holding everything else constant. One version was minimal fear arousal, the second moderate fear arousal, and the third was all-out as far as we could go: showing pictures of people with cancer of the mouth and horribly deformed teeth and all that sort of thing, as well as saying very dire things about what could happen from tooth neglect. It was a selective presentation of certain materials that would have emotional impact. As in all controlled experiments, students were assigned at random to the three versions. Our results showed that the minimal fear appeal was the most effective. In presenting the results, we were very careful to say that we thought there were special circumstances in which this result would occur, and that in other conditions one might find a moderate or high fear appeal to be the most effective. One of the important circumstances affecting the generalizability of the findings was that the students who were exposed to the very strong fear appeal were given only the single recommendation to brush their teeth in the proper way, using the proper kind of toothbrush. This recommendation may have seemed incommensurate with the magnitude of the diseases they were seeing. It was hard to accept that just by brushing your teeth you can get rid of all those threats. With regard to the problem of external validity, we expected that in other situations where fear appeals are used, if people are reassured by the recommendations, and are no longer in a state of high fear at the end of the presentation, a strong intensity of fear arousal would be more effective. We mentioned that in our publication. However, the story that got picked up in textbooks and in other reports usually emphasized that the high fear appeal had a boomerang kind of effect, that it produced the opposite effect from what was intended. This was not what we found. We showed that it was effective, but significantly less so than the minimal fear appeal. That notion caused lots of unnecessary controversy in the literature, but I think by this time it has been clarified.

Evans: In fact, it sounds to me as though you anticipated what Higbee (1969) concluded in his review of the fear arousal literature—that situational factors were very important in determining the impact of varying degrees of fear arousal.

Janis: Right. I think that one of the most important things about our study was that it opened up research on effects of emotional arousal on attitude change. It showed that one can get meaningful results on a problem that had previously not been worked on systematically, and it did lead to very productive work by you (Evans, Rozelle, Lasater, Dembroski, and Allen 1973), Leventhal (1965), Berkowitz (1960), and a number of other investigators.

Evans: You mentioned earlier some of the work that you and King did on the idea that if you get someone to play a role involving an attitude or behavior that is at odds with his or her own, this could be a technique for changing those attitudes or behaviors. Jacob L. Moreno (e.g., 1972), in his historic work in psychotherapy, had been using an intense form of role playing called psychodrama. How similar is this to the work you were doing?

Janis: Well, my work is close to an outgrowth of Moreno's psychodrama research, role reversal. For example, in role reversal you take the role of a person you are having a controversy with in order to understand the other side of the dispute. I first became interested in this phenomenon when I heard a lecture by a Norwegian philosopher of science, Arne Ness. Ness (1938) had practicing lawyers present arguments in favor of various social attitudes and then studied the nature of their logic. As an incidental finding, he mentioned that a number of these lawyers told him that they found their attitudes had actually changed in the direction of the position they had been arbitrarily assigned to defend.

That intrigued me, and I wondered if the same sort of thing happens in debates. So I began investigating debating teams at Yale. The phenomenon seemed to be absolutely rampant; almost everybody who participated indicated that at the very least they had to struggle against adopting the position that they had been assigned to defend. But then it occurred to me that the "saying-is-believing" phenomenon could be because of selective exposure, that they saturated themselves in the evidence that was in favor of the assigned position. The question was: If you held the amount of information constant, was playing the role going to be sufficient to change attitudes? It is precisely at this point that you need an experiment to be able to control all the other factors, like exposure to information, in order to pin something down. You can't just rely on interviewing debaters. That's what led me to do the first experiment on self-persuasion in collaboration with Bert King (Janis and King 1954).

Later Leon Mann and I did some studies on a different kind of role-playing, in which you play the role of yourself in a future situation that could give rise to attitude change. This was the sort of thing we did with smokers (Janis and Mann 1965). We asked them to imagine themselves in a situation where a physician tells them that they have cancer of the lungs and that as a result they have to have surgery. We planned it in real psychodramatic fashion, encouraging our subjects to be good method actors or actresses, responding exactly as if they were personally experiencing this kind of disaster. So the experimenter put on a white coat and had some props around, like an X-ray plate showing a mass that was obviously cancerous, and enacted the role of the physician. The subject played the role of the patient at the moment when he or she was given the diagnosis. This psychodrama had a very powerful emotional effect, so much so that some of the young women with whom we did our first study went so far as to throw away their packs of cigarettes as they left the laboratory. We used this psychodramatic device in later studies with people who voluntarily came to a smoking clinic for help. This type of "emotional role playing," as we call it, seems very effective in getting people not only to change their attitudes but to change their behavior as well.

Evans: One of the things that is interesting when you are dealing with addictive behaviors, such as smoking, is that as long as you have cooperation and involvement from the participants, things go pretty well. But time and time again, as the reviews of this literature by Bernstein and

McAllister (1976) and in our recent review (Evans, et al. 1970; Evans, Henderson, Hill, and Raines 1979) have pointed out, there is a tendency toward a regression in these difficult behaviors. What must we begin thinking about in terms of this regression?

Janis: Well, we have experienced the same sort of thing that all clinics throughout the country experience when they try to help people to lose weight or to give up smoking or to change any other kind of difficult habit that affects their health adversely. As you say, after a few weeks or months they regress to their original behaivor. We have had some follow-up studies that go on for anywhere from six to eighteen months, which is well beyond the critical period, because most of the regressing back to the original habit takes place after a month or two following the termination of the clinical contact. One of the studies that shows persistent effects is a study of the effects of emotional role playing that Leon Mann and I did with smokers (Mann and Janis 1965). A year and a half later people who played the role of a lung cancer victim were still showing a significant reduction in reported smoking as compared with controls who were exposed to the same information but did not play the role (Janis and Mann 1968). To some extent we have also had this kind of success in an experiment on the buddy system that David Hoffman and I did (Janis and Hoffman 1971).

Evans: This buddy system research sounds like you have systematized observations of spontaneous groupings such as Alcoholics Anonymous or Weight Watchers.

Janis: Yes, I had always been intersted in Alcoholic Anonymous. In my lectures to undergraduates, I often refer to the clinical scandal of our times. This grass roots movement, Alcoholics Annonymous, has obtained far better results than professional psychiatrists and clinical psychologists have in their work with alcoholics. What is scandalous is that the scientific community has not been studying the "how" of this thing, to try to find out what makes groups like Alcoholics Anonymous so effective. Using the approach that Hovland used, which was to consider our knowledge of social influence and to discern the key variables, you can arrive at dozens of possibly effective variables. I singled out the buddy system as one of the variables to investigate systematically. Alcoholism was much too complicated and difficult a problem to study in a field of experiment, so I chose smoking as more appropriate. We set up pairs of smokers who were instructed to be in daily contact, to phone each other every day. When we compared them with a group that had contact only once a week in the clinic, we found a big difference (Janis and Hoffman 1971). In the short run it doesn't show up because everybody improves as a result of coming into the clinic and working with the psychologist. Over the long haul, after the clinic sessions were over, the difference emerged. Our original notion was that it was the social support that was doing it, the fact that they had somebody they could always rely on whenever they felt tempted to go back to heavy smoking. That turned out to be much too simpleminded, because we discoverd that the contact with the buddy stopped within a month after the last session at the clinic. And yet, there was a sustained effect a year later, despite the lack of social support. So we feel it has something to do with the group dynamics that were created by the buddy system, with the internalization of norms that came about by virtue of their being members of a cohesive group that was created by their daily contact during that short period of time. And I would see this result in relation to what happens with encounter groups, T-groups, and other groups in which people have a very intensive reaction over a short period of time. It seems that they internalize certain of the norms they picked up as a result of that cohesive group experience.

Evans: Turning now to a slightly different area—psychosomatic medicine—there is a concern about the effects of stress on behavior and bodily well being. This was precipitated by results of the Western Collaborative Group Studies of Friedman and Rosenman (1974), which linked Type A behavior to cardiovascular disease in an eight-and-one-half-year longitudinal study. Such behavior seemed to be a reaction to the stress of time urgency and competition. The term "stress" seems to be too broadly used in the literature. Also, stress is difficult to measure. Some years ago you did a very widely discussed book on psychological stress (Janis 1958). Would you like to comment about the way you looked at psychological stress then and how you feel about this construct today?

Janis: My work does not really tie in with that of Friedman and Rosenman or the others who have been concerned with individual differences in susceptibility to illness. Individual differences do exist, and personality factors can make a difference with respect to stress. When you try to measure the individual differences, however, they appear to be very slight. It is much more likely that you are going to find bigger effects if you look at personality in relation to situational factors. I was especially interested in the role of warning information and reassuring communications in people's reactions to stress. One of the things that I noticed in the work with soldiers during the Second World War was that there were signs that the battle inoculation course they went through made a big difference in their level of fear and their effectiveness in performance. There were also many indications that for the Air Force personnel who flew the flying fortresses the situational factor of having a fixed number of missions made a tremendous difference in their fear symptoms, their going on sick call, and so on. Starting in the late forties and early fifties I did a series of studies with surgical patients that were reported in the book *Psychological Stress* (1958). Again, one of the things that impressed me was that the amount of information the patients had about what was going to happen to them seemed to make a very big difference. It was that stress inoculation aspect that I subsequently pursued.

Evans: You were developing ways of training people to cope with stressful situations. In a way this anticipated some very significant lines of research in the attitude and belief areas, for example McGuire's (e.g., McGuire and Papageorgis 1962) work and Lazarus' (1966) work on coping with stress.

Janis: In a way quite unexpected to me, the work that I was doing on stress also prefigured my own subsequent work on decision making (e.g., Janis and Mann 1977). In the 1950s I was very concerned with the problems of warnings, such as warnings for community disasters, like floods, hurricanes, and tornadoes, as well as for personal disasters, like having cancer. I did a good deal of work on the various coping patterns people show in response to the warnings. Some patterns seemed helpful and adaptive, but others were ineffective, maladaptive, and even life-threatening. Many years later I began studying personal decision making, including career decisions, marital decisions, and decisions involving people's health. I was struck by the fact that making these consequential decisions can be very stressful, and yet there has been relatively little psychological research into the effects of this stress upon the soundness of the decision-making process. It occurred to me that maybe some of the things we learned from disaster studies might have some application to the broader problems of decision making.

Evans: Speaking now of that work in decision making, I suspect that no area of research is more significant for an entire culture, as well as individuals. There has been much work in this field in industrial-organizational psychology, political science, bargaining and negotiation, sociology, administrative sciences, and in the field of education. Charles Osgood (1961) and Herbert Simon (1976) are two names that come to mind as having made particularly interesting contributions in this vast field. What has particularly interested you in this area?

Janis: We have been interested in looking at all of the behavioral phenomena associated with decision making, especially focusing on the problem of why decisions aren't better than they are. Why is it that people make so many foolish errors that they later recognize and regret? Some of the answers are provided by an analysis of stress coping patterns. Other answers come from work of people like George Miller (1956) who have studied the limitations of cognitive abilities. People are just not able to keep in mind all the complexities of a problem. There is a limitation to their immediate memory and the number of categories they can work with. But over and beyond those cognitive limitations, and beyond the effects of misinformation, people make errors because of the kind of stress coping pattern that they are using.

Evans: So you are suggesting that methods for coping with stress in decision making can be developed to prevent errors that people later regret.

Janis: Yes. First we start descriptively, trying to understand which factors contribute to errors. Then insofar as our hypotheses are worth their salt they should tell us what can be done to avoid those errors. Then we move from the descriptive hypotheses to prescriptive hypotheses that tell us something about what could be done by a decision counselor to help people to make more effective decisions. It is the latter problem that I'm working on at present.

Evans: In a way, you have gone beyond Festinger (1957), who was describing post-decision dissonance, by asking how one makes dissonance-producing decisions in the first place.

Janis: Incidentally, we make extensive use of Festinger's work in our decision-making book. Festinger has elucidated beautifully the defense we call the bolstering form of avoidance; that is, when instead of considering the alternatives carefully a person just grasps on to one of them. He then commits himself to it, builds it up for all it's worth, plays up all the positives, plays down all the negatives, and thus is impervious to new information that might make him realize that he is not doing the right thing. Finally, the feedback gets to be so negative that he realizes he has made a bad mistake, but by that time it may be too late for him to recoup his losses. We are concerned with early prevention of that kind of error so that the individual can correct the situation before the full impact of the negative consequences has hit.

Evans: So you are saying that this pre-decision stress pattern may be one of the most important types of stress with which we can deal. The literature on decision making is quite extensive. How did you develop your own particular focus?

Janis: We decided to focus on observations of real life decisions. The vast majority in the literature were laboratory studies that have been done under simulated circumstances. Those lab experiments may be of value for understanding certain aspects of cognitive processes, but they are misleading when it comes to how people behave in real life decision-making contexts.

Evans: So again you are raising the question of external validity.

Janis: Right. We have given priority to research from different disciplines that have some degree of inherent external validity because they are dealing with real life decisions rather than artificial ones, like the prisoner's dilemma game. There isn't much mention of prisoner's dilemma type of research in our book, because although it may have some value, it is not relevant, in my opinion, for elucidating how people cope with real life decisions.

Evans: So you're continually trying to address yourself to these real life situations. Apparently you feel that if you are going to make a contribution to this field, you can't be limited by a narrow experimental base.

Janis: Except that I do not want to be misunderstood as meaning that investigators should not use the experimental method. I think the experimental method is still the method par excellence, absolutely essential for working out causal sequences. The trick is to be able to use the experimental method with real life kinds of decisions and attitudes. You need to work out causal sequences that have external validity rather than ones that deal with artificial laboratory materials.

Evans: Considering some of the criticisms of your work, which have troubled you the most?

Janis: I guess it was the running battle that I had for many years with the cognitive dissonance theorists, especially over the role-playing or as they call it "forced compliance" type of experiments (Festinger and Carlsmith 1959). There was a constant battle of interpreting and reinterpreting the results of the various experiments. I now regard that as a controversy that was not very productive. What bothered me most were the misunderstandings about the position I was maintaining. For example, I proposed an incentive theory, referring to the incentives that a person arrives at through the use of his own imagination in producing arguments (Janis and Gilmore 1965). Considerable controversy arose in connection with the "twenty dollar misunderstanding," which pertained to the effects of paying people varying amounts of money. The cognitive dissonance theory position was that if you pay a person a large amount of money, it creates little dissonance and therefore produces little attitude change. My position was that as an incentive, payment has mixed value in self-persuasion. On the one hand, a person may want to work hard to earn his pay, but on the other hand, he is disturbed about being paid to argue against his own beliefs. He may be suspicious or may castigate himself for selling out, for not sticking by his guns just because he is being paid a lot of money.

Evans: Again, you are suggesting that such processes are always more complex at a cognitive level than some of the earlier dissonance researchers may have recognized.

Janis: And also at the motivational level.

Evans: Right.

Janis: Part of the controversy involves semantics. I theorized that when people engage in role playing and improvise arguments that provide new incentives for adopting a position, they may persuade themselves. Because I called it "incentive theory," many psychologists thought that the incentives I was talking about were money payments, and that the more the external incentive, the more the attitude change. That was not my position; rather, it was to analyze the effect of any external incentive on the internal incentives that come from improvising new arguments. Monetary payments could have some positive effects and some negative effects, and we should not be at all surprised to find that under some conditions they make no difference. It's partly as a result of that controversy that I came to realize there is no single experiment that can ever stand up against criticism of people who want to tear it down. There are always several different ways that you can interpret results. The ultimate conclusions must rely on the convergence of evidence from many different investigators that replicate the same basic phenomena over and over again in different settings. As you will see in *Decision Making*, we try to pick up the aspects of cognitive dissonance research that we think have lasting value, and the aspects of our own research that we think are valuable, and try to make use of the best of both worlds.

Evans: Irv, looking back at your many and varied contributions, which of these do you consider to be the most significant?

Janis: Well, you know how it is. It's always the last baby that gets spoiled, on whom most affection gets showered. So the work on decision making, especially the use of a model based on the patterns of coping with stress, is what I would hope would prove to be a lasting contribution. I also think the work that is opening up the field of decision counseling—trying to find out the conditions under which counseling can be effective in helping people improve the quality of their decisions that they make, the degree to which they are satisfied with their decisions, and the degree to which they are able to adhere to them in the long run—is important. We are giving special attention to health-related decisions, like losing weight, but are also considering career decisions along the same lines. We have been investigating the type of self-disclosures that are made, the type of verbal feedback given by the counselor, the type of commitment that is made to the counselor, and other factors that can affect the nature of the relationship. It seems to me that these factors are vital aspects of the social influence process. It is really the degree of cohesiveness with the counselor that is influencing the clients' behavior. We are studying the conditions that promote the kind of cohesiveness characteristic of a group in which everybody follows the norms. It is the internalization of the norms conveyed by the counselor that is the heart of the problem.

But I don't want to imply that I think this kind of social bonding always has positive effects. My book *Victims of Groupthink* (1972) looks at some of the negative effects of cohesive groups. Unfavorable effects on the quality of decisions may occur if the maintenance of a pleasant social atmosphere becomes more important than engaging in hard-headed, critical thinking. In that book I examine case studies of a number of major fiascos, including the Bay of Pigs, the escalation of the war in Vietnam by Lyndon Johnson's group of advisors, and the failure of the naval group at Pearl Harbor to be prepared for the Japanese surprise attack. The problem is to determine what circumstances allow a group to have a constructive function in helping each individual to arrive at a better decision and what the conditions are under which you have groupthink, or other kinds of adverse effects that make for poor quality of decision-making.

Evans: Many of us in social psychology are aware of a so-called crisis in our field. What do you see this crisis as being, and how do you believe it will be resolved?

Janis: I think that the crisis has come about mainly because some of the major findings in social psychology that have captured people's imaginations have not stood up well in replication studies or have been found to be weak and attributable to artifacts. I think the main trouble is that most of the evidence comes from artificial laboratory situations. The variables that influence how people behave in real life often play a very minor role in the laboratory. A great deal has been learned about demand characteristics, apprehension about being evaluated, and other aspects of the social psychology of the social psychological experiment. I think that the solution to the crisis has been correctly recognized by a large number of social psychologists who have been moving away from artificial laboratory situations into real life settings where systematic field experiments can be done on consequential attitudes and decisions, such as those involving a person's health. It seems to me that the crisis is being surmounted and there is every reason to be hopeful of making social psychology into an additive science.

REFERENCES

Berkowitz, L., and Cottingham, D. R. 1960. The interest value and relevance of fear arousing communications. *J. Abnorm. Psychol.* 60: 37–43.

Bernstein, D. A. 1969. Modification of smoking behavior: An evaluative review. *Psychol. Bull.* 71: 418–40.

_____, and McAllister, A. 1976. The modification of smoking behavior: Progress and problems. *Addic. Behav.* 1: 89–102.

Evans, R. I., Rozelle, R. M., Lasater, T. M., Dembroski, T. M., and Allen, B. P. 1970. Fear arousal, persuasion, and actual vs. implied behavior change: New perspective utilizing a real-life dental hygiene program. *J. Pers. Soc. Psychol.* 16: 220–27.

_____, Henderson, A. H., Hill, P. C., and Raines, B. E. 1979. Current psychological, social, and educational programs in control and prevention of smoking: A critical methodological review. In *Atherosclerosis Rev.*, eds. A. M. Gotto and R. Paoletti. 6: 203–43.

Festinger, L. 1957. *A theory of cognitive dissonance*. Evanston, Illinois: Row, Peterson.

_____, and Carlsmith, J. M. 1959. Cognitive consequences of forced compliance. *J. Abnorm. Soc. Psychol.* 58: 203–10.

Friedman, M., and Rosenman, R. H. 1974. *Type A behavior and your heart*. Greenwich, Connecticut: Fawcett.

Higbee, K. L. 1969. Fifteen years of fear arousal: Research on threat appeals: 1953–1968. *Psychol. Bull.* 72: 426–44.

Hovland, C. I., and Janis, I. L. (Eds.) 1969. *Personality and persuasibility*. New Haven: Yale University Press.

_____, Lumsdaine, A. A., and Sheffield, F. D. 1949. *Experiments in mass communication*. Princeton: Princeton University Press.

Janis, I. L. 1958. *Psychological stress*. New York: Wiley and Sons.

_____, and Gilmore, L. B. 1965. The influence of incentive conditions on the success of role-playing in modifying attitudes. *J. Pers. Soc. Psychol.* 1: 17–27.

_____, and Hoffman, D. 1971. Facilitating effects of daily contact between partners who make a decision to cut down on smoking. *J. Pers. Soc. Psychol.* 17: 25–35.

————. 1972. *Victims of groupthink: A psychological study of foreign-policy decisions and fiascos.* Boston: Houghton Mifflin.

————. (Ed.) 1978. *Counseling on personal decisions: Theory and research on helping relationships.* New Haven: Yale University Press.

————, and Feshbach, S. 1953. Effects of fear arousing communications. *J. Abnorm. Soc. Psychol.* 48: 78–92.

————, Hovland, C. I., and Kelley, H. H. 1953. *Communication and persuasion: Psychological studies of opinion change.* New Haven: Yale University Press.

————, and King, B. T. 1954. The influence of role playing on opinion change. *J. Abnorm. Soc. Psychol.* 49: 211–18.

————, Lumsdaine, A. A., and Gladstone, A. I. 1951. Effects of preparatory communications on reactions to a subsequent news event. *Pub. Opin. Quart.* 15: 487–518.

————, and Mann, L. 1965. Effectiveness of emotional role-playing in modifying smoking habits and attitudes. *J. Exper. Research Personal.* 1: 84–90.

————, and Mann, L. 1968. A follow-up study on the long term effects of emotional role playing. *J. Personal. Soc. Psychol.* 8: 339–42.

————, and Mann, L. 1977. *Decision-making: A psychological analysis of conflict, choice, and commitment.* New York: Free Press.

————, and Wolfer, J. A. 1975. Effects of a cognitive coping device and preparatory information on psychological stress in surgical patients. *J Exper. Soc. Psychol.* 11: 115–65.

Klineberg, O. *Social psychology.* (Rev. Ed.) 1954. New York: Henry Holt & Co.

Lazarus, R. S. 1966. *Psychological Stress and the Coping Process.* New York: McGraw-Hill.

Leventhal, H., Singer, R. P., and Jones, S. 1965. Effects of fear and specificity of recommendation upon attitudes and behavior. *J. Personal. Soc. Psychol.* 2: 20–29.

McGuire, W. J., and Papageorgis, D. 1962. Effectiveness of forewarning in developing resistance to persuasion. *Pub. Opin. Quart.* 26: 24–34.

Miller, G. A. 1956. The magical number seven, plus or minus two: Some limits on our capacity for processing information. *Psychol. Rev.* 63: 81–97.

Moreno, J. L. 1972. *Psychodrama.* (4th ed.) New York: Beacon House.

Ness, A. 1938. *"Truth" as conceived by those who are not professional philosophers.* Oslo: Hos Jacob Dybwad.

Osgood, C. E. 1961. An analysis of the cold war mentality. *J. Soc. Issues* 17: 12–19.

Rozelle, R. M., Evans, R. I., Lasater, T. M., Dembroski, T. M., Allen, B. P. 1973. Social approval as related to the effects of persuasive communications on actual, reported and intended behavior change—a viable predictor? *Psychol. Reports* 33: 719–25.

Simon, H. A. 1976. *Administrative behavior: A study of decision-making processes in administrative organization.* (3rd ed.) 1976. New York: Free Press.

Stouffer, S. A., Lumsdaine, A. A., Lumsdaine, M. H., Williams, R. M., Jr., Smith, M. B., Janis, I. L., Star, S. A., and Cottrell, L. S., Jr. 1949. *The

American soldier: II Combat and its aftermath. Princeton: Princeton University Press.

SELECTED READINGS

Hovland, C. I., and Janis, I. L. (Eds.) 1959. *Personality and persuasibility.* New Haven: Yale University Press.

Janis, I. L. 1958. *Psychological stress.* New York: Wiley and Sons.

Janis, I. L. 1972. *Victims of groupthink: A psychological study of foreign-policy decisions and fiascos.* Boston: Houghton Mifflin.

Janis, I. L. (Ed.) 1978. *Counseling on personal decisions: Theory and research on helping relationships.* New Haven: Yale University Press.

Janis, I. L., Hovland, C. I., and Kelley, H. H. 1953. *Communication and persuasion: Psychological studies of opinion change.* New Haven: Yale University Press.

Janis, I. L., and Mann, L. 1977. *Decision-making: A psychological analysis of conflict, choice, and commitment.* New York: Free Press.

10

MILTON ROKEACH

(1918–   )

Milton Rokeach took his B.A. at Brooklyn College and his M.A. in 1941 from the University of California. He recived a Ph.D. in psychology in 1947 from the University of California at Berkeley where he was a member of the authoritarian personality research group. He has held positions as professor of psychology at Michigan State University and the University of Western Ontario, and he is presently professor of psychology and sociology at Washington State University. Professor Rokeach has extended authoritarian study into the broader field of ideology and personality in his work on dogmatism, and his current research involves an intensive examination of human values as they affect behavior.

Trapped into a Concrete Mode of Thought/Rigidity and Ethnocentrism/ A Phenomenon That Pervades All Areas of Human Life/The Authoritarian Personality/Not Left or Right/ A Structural Analysis/ The "And Besides" Syndrome/Isolation/Only a Simple-Minded Fool/The Opinionation Test/Race versus Belief/Two Kinds of Prejudice or One?/Opinionation/Dogmatism/Ethnocentrism/ Authoritarianism//The Three Christs of Ypsilanti/Self-Confrontation/Values/Beliefs/Attitudes/Opinions/No Correct Way/ Only Fruitful Ways/Value Has a Transcendental Quality/Terminal Values/End States/Instrumental Values/Behavior/Changing Values Changes Attitudes/The Possibility of Genuine Long-Term Change//

Dr. Rokeach was involved with the group that did the seminal work on the authoritarian personality. His doctoral dissertation was a study of the relationship between rigidity in thinking and ethnocentrism. The authoritarian-personality work evoked criticisms of a nature that persuaded Dr. Rokeach to try and build a structural foundation for such concepts, which would be broader, more basic and nonideological. In testing qualities such as prejudice with questions designed to elicit the quality no matter what its manifestations, he collected some surprising results that are still difficult for some of his critics to accept. Pursuing his interest in belief systems as they relate to human dissonance, he brought together three mental patients, all of whom thought they were Jesus Christ. A great deal of Dr. Rokeach's later work has been in the area of human values, with an extensive effort to define terms and with experiments conducted in efforts to change values and thus to modify behavior. He outlines these findings, and I ask him some of the questions his critics have asked about his work. We end our discussion on the subject of ethics, which, when it comes to the manipulation of human values, is crucial. Reacting to the possibility that value change could be negative as well as positive, Dr. Rokeach is willing to allow itself to be changed in one direction, but not the opposite. "I can influence you to grow, but I cannot influence your values in the direction of retrogression; I think there is a built-in protection."

Evans: Dr. Rokeach, looking at your impressive career, one recalls that your significant contributions really began while you were completing your doctorate at the University of California at Berkeley. It is well known that that was a very exciting period in the social psychology group there. Out of that group of innovative behavioral scientists came the classic work on the authoritarian personality (Adorno, et al. 1950). Your doctoral dissertation became one of the significant investigations during this period. Could you tell us a little bit about that early research? It had to do with the matter of rigidity and ethnocentrism, is that not correct?

Rokeach: Yes, it did. It was an attempt to relate an ideological or attitudinal variable, ethnocentrism—or in plainer English, prejudice toward outgroups—on the one hand, and a variable that could be called a purely cognitive variable, a variable that had to do with the ability to solve problems. I thought that I saw a connection that had something to do with rigidity or structural rigidity of thinking. And to study it, I picked a problem that was well known to me as a result of my studies with Solomon Asch, the Gestalt psychologist, and that was the problem of *Einstellung,* worked over extensively by Luchins (1942), Wertheimer (1945), and others. It attempted to find out whether people who are rigid in solving problems involving the development of sets, or *Einstellung,* are also more likely to be prejudiced. I remember vividly as an undergraduate student at Brooklyn College first learning about *Einstellung* and its influence from Solomon Asch, who argued that the conditions that led to a person being rigid had to do only with the field conditions and that personality had nothing to do with it. I myself couldn't believe that personality counted for nothing.

Evans: As I recall, in one of your particularly intriguing experiments you had a group of individuals given an opportunity to solve arithmetic problems that were really simple enough so that they could do them in their heads. They were given scratch paper and pencil, and one of the measures you used was the amount of scratch paper they actually used, which related to what might be called "concreteness," or what the authoritarian-personality group called "extraceptiveness." You found that those who are prejudiced are likely to use more scratch paper than those who are not. How did you conceptualize that?

Rokeach: They seem to be related to two very different things, but in my reading of the literature on the determinants of rigidity, I discovered that one of the major determinants of rigidity in problem solving is the inability to think abstractly, or being trapped into a concrete mode of thought.

Evans: You were in a rather unusual position to react to this entire authoritarian-personality study. In fact, you did your doctorate under Nevitt Sanford (Adorno, et al. 1950), one of the original coauthors of the volume, and you had the privilege of working with people like Else Frenkel-Brunswik (1945). They started out studying anti-Semitism, then proceeded to study ethnocentrism. Interrelationships among such concepts suggested to them a "prefascist" or "authoritarian" personality. They drew a picture of the high authoritarian as being very rigid, black-white, overly conventional, an individual who is likely to stereotype, and to think in concrete dichotomies.

Rokeach: Who is intolerant of ambiguity.

Evans: Yes. The picture one gets is of a rather distasteful individual. Now, Dr. Shils (1954) at the University of Chicago, reacting to this work on the authoritarian personality, felt that the background of the investigators might have led them to a kind of self-fulfilling prophecy. They hated nazism; some of them had escaped from Nazi Germany. They hated authoritarianism, and so they were almost bound to find the authoritarian personality a bad guy rather than a good guy. A lot of people, therefore, questioned this study on the grounds that it might have reflected more the values of the investigators than genuine scientific findings. Do you think those criticisms were justified?

Rokeach: Well, yes, I think they were justified, but I also felt that the Shils criticism that the workers on the authoritarian personality had neglected the authoritarianism of the left was just as self-serving and just as ideologically motivated as the original workers contending that it was the Fascist who was the bad guy. I felt that there was something tremendously self-righteous about the proposition that it's those guys, the "theys," who are the authoritarians and bigots. I felt that the phenomena of authoritarianism, of bigotry if you like, were phenomena that pervade all areas of human life. I saw these phenomena to be manifest at all points along the political spectrum and in the academic world as well. I noticed that psychoanalysts were intolerant of behaviorists, Gestalt psychologists were intolerant of psychoanalysts; they were all anti-anti-Semitic. Those people who read my work from secondary sources, not from my own work, are under the impression that all I've done was to insist that authoritarianism exists on the left as well as on the right. I would vigorously deny it. What I was saying was that this is a phenomena that has to be studied independently of the left-right continuum. And for this reason, I launched into what I called a structural analysis, a study of the structural properties of authoritarianism that would allow us to make statements about it regardless of ideological content. I came up with such Lewian properties as the "degree of isolation" of belief-disbelief systems, "degree of differentiation," "time perspective," and the like.

Evans: I wonder if you could elaborate on those concepts. They were very central to your thinking at that time.

Rokeach: Well, take the concept of isolation. That refers to two ideas coexisting in two adjacent regions but with no communication between them. They are in a state of isolation, or what is more commonly known, of compartmentalization. One might believe two logically opposite things but not realize that they are opposite because of isolated boundaries. Whenever a person uses too many arguments that have a certain form, like, "No, that's not so, and besides, . . ." which I call the "And Besides Syndrome," that tips me off to a condition of isolation. A good illustration of that is my coming home one day and seeing my son, Marty, who was then five, hitting a kid smaller than he was. I bawled him out, and he answered me, "Dad, I didn't hit him, and besides, he hit me first, and besides, I didn't hit him very hard." Well, that suggests a condition of isolation between three cognitions, each of which contradicted each of the others. So in my own work on the authoritarian, on dogmatism, I tried to reformulate the concept so that it structured the properties of authoritarianism as it might exist in any area of human endeavor. Whether I succeeded is another matter, but that's what I tried to do.

Evans: There was a test developed called the F-Scale, which was supposed to measure the authoritarian personality in a broad sense; as a matter of fact, it's still being widely used. Take a test like the F-Scale, even there authoritarianism principally seems to be related to something like the right and left on the political spectrum. You feel there is the need for something a little less value-loaded; perhaps the term, dogmatism. Would that be a fair statement?

Rokeach: Yes. Let me illustrate. One of the items in the F-Scale and the scale for the measure of predisposition toward facism, states, "There are two kinds of people in this world, the weak and the strong." Now, to agree with it is to agree with a fascist idea, but it only captures an authoritarianism of the extreme right. Hoping to measure the same trait, but at all points along the continuum, I reworded it to read: "There are two kinds of people in this world, those who are for the truth and those who are against the truth." Now notice that agreeing with that idea doesn't instruct us on what the person thinks is the truth, but whether he is a Freudian, a Leninist, a Hitlerian, a Nietzscheian, or a whatever, he would still agree with it if he were authoritarian. So I think that that insight allowed me to proceed from the very specific concept of fascist authoritarianism to the more general, but in so doing, I had to get rid of the content.

Evans: At this point, however, you found it more valuable to begin calling this dogmatism, or open- and closed-mindedness rather than using a word that was somewhat more value-laden like authoritarianism. Is that correct?

Rokeach: Sure, but this is not to say that open-mindedness is not value laden. I'd be the last one to deny that it is. But even so, it is not ideologically value-laden. I found that the fundamental way of defining prejudice was equally objectionable. The traditional way that social scientists have developed for measuring prejudice is to find out how people feel about this or that ethnic or racial group, how they like Jews, blacks, Chicanos, Japanese. The more you say you dislike them, the more prejudiced you are. And yet, I found phenomena of prejudice among people who wouldn't be caught dead with an anti-Semitic statement, or with an antiblack statement; it was another form of bigotry that simply escaped attention. I therefore conceptualized this phenomenon of bigotry, not in terms of how much you like or dislike ethnic or racial groups, but in terms of how much you like people who agree with you or disagree with you, whatever they may be. And liking somebody because they agree with you is no less a manifestation of prejudice because it has a qualificational string attached to it than disliking people because they disagree with you. So I invented this test I called the "Opinionation Test" that had phrases like, "Only a simple-minded fool would say that there is a God," and "Only a simple-minded fool would say there is no God." And what I expected from the tolerant person was to disagree vehemently with both of these things in order to qualify as tolerant; if he agreed with either one of them, I considered this a manifestation of prejudice. This was the same structural strategy of getting at prejudice regardless of the content of prejudice. From there, of course, I moved to the whole question of whether there are two kinds of prejudice or one. You are the coauthor with me on that research (Rokeach, Smith, and Evans 1960), and there the question was, What happens if you pit a racial variable against a belief variable? How do you feel about a white person who is an atheist and a black person who is an atheist or a white person who believes in God and a black person who believes in God? By systematic design of studies of that kind, we were able to begin to ask, How much do people like other people on grounds of belief similarity rather than on grounds of racial similarity? That has led to some interesting research controversies.

Evans: Right. That study, among several others, was the culmination of approximately ten years of work: *The Open and Closed Mind* (Rokeach 1960) was published in 1960. What were some of the reactions to that book, which is now certainly regarded as very significant?

Rokeach: Well, there were some fairly interesting reactions. When I first mentioned the work on race versus belief to a very prominent social psychologist, I explained to him that this work was done at Michigan State University, and I asked him if he would take a look at the results. He believed that the results would show that people would like a person of their own race who disagreed with them more than a person of the opposite race who agreed with them about something important, because everybody knows how important race is. When I told him that the vast majority of the subjects do exactly the opposite, he said, "Oh, the reason why you got these results is because the subjects are at a liberal midwestern university, and you brainwashed them. They know what answers you wanted. If you were to repeat this study in a southern university, you wouldn't get this sort of thing." Whereupon I told him the study had also been done at a southern university; then I mentioned your work, Dick (Rokeach, Smith, and Evans 1960), and pointed out that the results were no different at the University of Houston than they were at Michigan State University.

Evans: I would have completely agreed with him and was probably just as surprised as he with what we found down here.

Rokeach: His next reaction was, "Oh, I know what's happening. This is all at the verbal level, but at the behavioral level, you wouldn't get this sort of thing." Well, I had no answer for him, there. But it did lead to further work, the work that I did with Mezei (Rokeach and Mezei 1966) that was eventually published in *Science*. That work required us to do field experiments. In one case it involved unemployed workers who didn't even know they were in an experiment. They were asked to make choices between persons they wanted to work with, whether they wanted to work with two people of the same race as they, or two people who agreed with them on a particular issue. So we replicated the work on race versus belief in a natural behavioral field condition, and we found the same thing. Whereupon the criticism shifts once more and this time it's, "But work isn't all that important. They're not marrying each other." And so, as each point was responded to with the next experiment, the criticism shifted to a new level. Rather than concerning themselves with the theoretical, political, social, and economic implications of these findings, the critics are rather preoccupied with thinking up alternative interpretations designed to deny and to trivialize the results. I guess the only response that I have left is to say that as far as I can tell, the belief principle works up to and including marriage, as evidenced, for example, by the fact that belief congruence is found to be more important than race as a determinant of marriage, say, in Hawaii where the social constraints against interracial marriage are considerably weaker than they are in the United States.

Evans: You mentioned the use of the Opinionation Scale. Of course, a widely used scale in psychology is also the Dogmatism Scale, the D-Scale. Do you see any difference between what you were measuring in the Opinionation Scale and the Dogmatism Scale?

Rokeach: Yes, I think the relationship between opinionation and dogmatism is the same as the relationship in the authoritarian personality research between ethnocentrism and F. Ethnocentrism is the attitudinal correlate of bigotry that is supposed to be somehow casually related to that which underlies it—authoritarianism. Opinionation, similarly, is the tolerance variable that is supposedly causally related to the dogmatism that supposedly underlies it.

Evans: One of the most unique research efforts by a social psychologist is reflected in your book, *The Three Christs of Ypsilanti* (Rokeach 1964). Could you tell us a little bit about what this is all about and some of the things you found?

Rokeach: Well, basically, it's a clinical study. I had lots of quantitative data, but I deliberately left them out. It's a story of three paranoid schizophrenics, each of whom believes that he is Jesus Christ. I brought these three people together.

Evans: They were all in the hospital?

Rokeach: Two of them were in different parts of the same mental hospital, and one was in a different hospital. I brought them together and put them to work in the same laundry room; they ate at the same dining table; they slept on three adjacent cots. Every day, day in and day out, for a period of two years, they were living in each other's environment. The purpose of this confrontation was to create the maximum human dissonance that I could imagine; each one had to live with two other people who constantly thought they were he. I was motivated by my interest in balance and dissonance and by my lifelong interest in the structure of belief systems. I wanted to find out, in this clinical context, what happens when the most fundamental of all beliefs that I can imagine was constantly being challenged in a way that it could not possibly be challenged in our daily lives. It's much too complicated to discuss here, but in my book, *The Three Christs of Ypsilanti,* I tried to describe the sequence of changes of beliefs that took place in these three people over a period of two years. I think I learned what it is to confront other people with contradictions, and I also think I learned something about what it means to confront one's self. Basically, this work laid the groundwork for the work that I'm now doing on changing values, and with it, changing behavior by what I call the method of self-confrontation.

Evans: By and large, the term "conflict of values" has been anathema to experimenters in psychology, because values are something that are considered almost in the spiritual realm, not subject to scientific investigation. As Skinner (Evans 1968) says, we can arrange the contingencies in the environment, reinforce the right response; so why worry about values, attitudes, beliefs? Even non-Skinnerians argue, What is a value? What is an attitude? What is a mood? How do all these things tend to differ? So maybe we ought to start right there. What is the difference between a value, a belief, and an attitude?

Rokeach: Well, it was about 1964 that Gardner Lindzey invited me to write the article on attitudes for the *International Encyclopedia of Social Sciences* and after much thought, I decided I would. Then I spent approximately six months reading the literature on what the social sciences—sociology, psychology, and other areas, but mainly those two—have to say about attitudes. And I became acutely aware that these social sciences seemed to be using that word interchangeably with other words—opinion, value, value system, ideology. What began to grate on me was that the specialists in the field had only the dimmest perception of what the difference was, if any. The field was in chaos. Now intuitively I knew there had to be some very profound distinction between attitudes and values. I was forced to face up to the question. How shall I tell myself and others what it is that makes a thing a value, and that question led to my current interest in values.

Evans: You see the words *belief* and *belief systems;* you use the term *value* and the term *attitude;* and in fact, you use the word *opinion* (Rokeach 1968).

Rokeach: First of all, I must say that there is no correct way of defining concepts. There are only fruitful ways. The question is, Is it a difference that makes a difference or is it a difference that makes no difference? So having said this, I can only say that I've attempted to make certain distinctions on the assumption that such distinctions make an important difference. What's the difference between an attitude and an opinion? To me, an opinion is nothing more than a verbal expression. An attitude is that which underlies the opinion; it may be exactly the opposite of the opinion expressed. For me, an attitude is a hypothetical construct that I can only infer from all the things a person says or does, and I've got to take my chances on being wrong. Perhaps more important, in my thinking, is the difference between an attitude and a belief. For me, an attitude is a set of beliefs that are focused on a particular object or a particular situation. For instance, a Likert Scale is a set of statements, each of which was the same subject, Jew, or black, or church, or God. A Likert Scale measures attitudes toward God through a set of statements, each of which asks the person to agree or disagree with a belief that he has about the properties or attributes of God.

Evans: And how do you define values?

Rokeach: Value has a transcendental quality. It is not focused; it's across objects, across situations. I distinguished two kinds of values. One kind of value concerns a desired end-state of existence, a state of equality, a state of happiness, a state of inner harmony. I prefer to call these terminal values. The other kind of a value is what I call an instrumental value, an idealized way of behaving, cutting across objects and situations —honesty, for example. You're never taught to behave honestly only with respect to whites and not with respect to blacks. Honesty, responsibility, courage, helpfulness, cleanliness, politeness, obedience—these would be instrumental values. So one set of values, terminal values, relates to prescribed end-states, and the other set of values, instrumental values, relates to idealized behavior.

Defining values and attitudes this way, one can immediately infer that there must be thousands of attitudes, but only a small number of values. You can't have thousands of end-states, or thousands of ideal modes of behavior, but there are thousands of objects toward which we have attitudes. To me this was a very important distinction.

Evans: What are the implications of this, as you see it?

Rokeach: Distinctions aren't worth making just to be made, at least not in science. Science in an activity that leads to theoretical constructions, which lead to predictions of behavioral effects that will take us beyond what we know. So what I was really after in distinguishing the concepts of value from attitude was to try to conceptualize why people have the attitudes they do, and beyond that, with what are the behavioral consequences of these attitudes? Beyond this, there is the question, Is it possible to change values, and if so, can we thus change attitudes, and with it, behavior? So, I began to move away from where my colleagues in the field were focused—I might almost use the word fixated—the concepts of attitude change and the theories of persuasive communication designed to change attitudes. I moved to theories of value organization and value change, to a consideration of the consequences of value change for attitude and behavioral change.

We are now looking through the literature on attitude change in the *Journal of Personality and Social Psychology* to determine how long after the experimental treatment the posttest is administered. I am reasonably sure, intuitively, from my reading of the literature of the past quarter of a century, that this literature is a literature of short-term attitude change. By short-term I mean changes taking place a few minutes after an experimental treatment, sometimes a day or so afterward, rarely a week or more. This literature doesn't tell us anything about the changes we look for in therapy or in education and reeducation. It's a literature of the things that would be more useful to Madison Avenue and propagandists rather than to educators, therapists, and counselors. Moreover, the closer the posttest is to the experimental treatment, the more it is suspect because the more it is vulnerable to alternative interpretations.

Evans: Dr. Leon Festinger (1964) reviewed the literature on attitude change to see if there was a relationship between attitude changes and behavior changes. He found that the relationship was rarely, if ever, demonstrated. Do I understand you correctly, that your research on values introduces the possibility that modifying values can affect behavior? In your book *The Nature of Human Values* (Rokeach 1973) you do incorporate studies that report actual behavior and demonstrate that a change in values will affect behavior, not only for a short period of time but for a long period of time. As I recall, there was a study that had to do with joining the NAACP that illustrated this? Is that correct?

Rokeach: Yes. It involved attempting to change the values that underlie civil rights behavior. What we did, by feedback to the subjects about their own and others' values, was to increase experimentally their own values for equality and freedom. One hundred days later and again four hundred and sixty-five days later, the NAACP solicited them to join. The experimental findings are very clear on the point. They showed that approximately two and a half times as many experimental subjects joined the NAACP as control subjects. And in my book, *The Nature of Human Values* (1973), I report other independently obtained behavioral effects of the experimental treatment that had changed values, for example, actual enrollments in courses on race relations obtained from official registration figures of the university, or changes of majors from physical science or natural science to social science. When we look at all the results from all these studies, it is unlikely that you can explain away the behavioral differences between experimental and control groups on the purely methodological grounds.

Evans: There is probably no doubt that there are certain types of behavior that have a strong compulsive component, like smoking, overeating, or alcoholism. That's a case of behavior that we sometimes call addictive, and that we find extremely difficult to change. The relative complexity and really compulsive nature of this type of behavior is a factor that obviously has to be dealt with. Isn't it a lot more difficult, even with your approach, to change a compulsive behavior than one that is not compulsive?

Rokeach: Well, I can respond very briefly by saying I'm sure that compulsive behavior is going to be more difficult to change than noncompulsive behavior, but in principle, I see no theoretical reason why it would be impossible to change. In any case, presently known empirical findings show that both compulsive types of behavior, namely smoking, and noncompulsive types of behavior, namely joining a political organization, and others that I haven't mentioned, can be changed on a relatively long-term basis by first changing the values that underlie such behavior.

Evans: Of course, this is very exciting and could be a significant breakthrough for those interested in behavior modification. However, Skinnerian theory of behavior modification (Evans 1968) is obviously extremely attractive because of its simplicity. It doesn't require complicated value constructs; it suggests that by simply controlling the contingencies of the environment the probability that certain behavior will occur is increased. So the Skinnerian would say that consideration of values is irrelevant and needlessly complicated.

Rokeach: All you're really saying is that the Skinnerians offer an alternative interpretation of the known facts. We need to examine this alternative interpretation in order to ascertain whether it will indeed account for the known facts. Well now, Skinnerian behavior modification requires that a change of the contingencies of reinforcement would involve at least several treatments, so that behavior can be shaped gradually. No Skinnerian study that I've ever heard of claims to change the contingencies of reinforcement over a long-term period by a single-shot experimental treatment. I would then ask. How would one account for a change observed twenty-one months after a single experimental treatment? And if the observed behavioral consequences are remote, and if there are demonstrable cognitive mediators of those consequences, you have to account for all the cognitive changes that are observed to occur three weeks later, three months later, fifteen months later, all as a result of a single experimental intervention. That's why I don't believe that a Skinnerian interpretation is a viable alternative interpretation of the known empirical facts.

Evans: Dr. Rokeach, I've already mentioned a few criticisms of your work; are there others that bother you?

Rokeach: I naturally anticipated that if a psychologist claims behavioral change as remote in time as I have claimed, as the result of a single experimental treatment, it will be regarded with the gravest skepticism. I know that I myself would regard it with great skepticism because all of our training tells us that this is beyond what is presently known. In my book, one of my chapters is entitled, "Some Alternative Interpretations." I felt especially obligated to consider all the conceivable alternative interpretations of the data. I raise statistical arguments, methodological arguments, alternative substantive arguments; in all, perhaps ten different types of alternative interpretations that might represent threats to validity. I've done the best job I possibly could in considering fairly all these alternatives. After doing so, I'm forced to the conclusion that any one of them can reasonably account for some of my experimental findings, but that none of them could account for all of them. Therefore, I am left with the interpretation that a single experimental self-confrontation, one that demonstrates a contradiction between a person's values and his self-conceptions, can create an effective state of self-dissatisfaction that has long-term cognitive and behavioral consequences that cannot be accounted for in any other way except to assume they are results of genuine, long-term value changes.

Evans: I would like to ask you about an issue that plagues social psychology, perhaps all of psychology, now more than ever before in history. This was generated partly by applications of Skinnerian notions, which appears to control behavior, but also in experiments such as Milgram's (1974) and Zimbardo's (Zimbardo, et al. 1973) that expose subjects to certain kinds of conditions that may be aversive or uncomfortable, even though they are operating with informed consent. There are charges that we are not operating ethically. What right do we have, as social scientists, to control behavior or to engage in experiments that disturb human subjects?

Rokeach: Well, you're really raising the question of ethics. What right have I got to decide which values to change in which direction? For a long time I worried about it because I genuinely felt that if we could change behavior in one direction, we could change it in the other. I no longer think so. I believe that the self is so constructed that it is willing to allow itself to be changed in one direction, but not the opposite. Thus, I think I would have a good chance of persuading you, or anyone else, to increase your value for a world at peace, but under no circumstances do I

think I could persuade you to decrease it. Similarly, I believe I could persuade you to increase your value for wisdom, but not to decrease it, to
increase your value for a world of beauty, but not to decrease it. Self-
conceptions are learned by human beings in the context of a society that
socializes each person; it teaches the individual how to obtain mileage for
himself, how to increase or maintain his self-conception as moral and
competent, and that mileage can be obtained by changing one direction
but not the other. So, for this reason I no longer worry about whether I
could manipulate a person arbitrarily, to change him in a direction opposite to his own need to self-actualize. My theory is really a theory of self-
acutalization. I can influence you to grow, but I doubt that I can influence your values in a retrogressive direction; so I think there is built-in
ethical protection against arbitrary value manipulation.

Evans: Can you demonstrate the validity of what you're saying?

Rokeach: Yes, we're about to embark on some actual research designed to demonstrate the "unidirectionality hypothesis," namely, that
values can be changed in one direction for any one person, but not in
both directions.

REFERENCES

Adorno, T., et al. 1950. *The authoritarian personality.* New York: Harper.

Conroy, W., Katkin, E., and Barnett, W. 1973. Modification of smoking behavior by Rokeach's self-confrontation technique. Paper presented at the annual meeting of the Southeastern Psychological Association in New Or-
leans, April 7, 1973.

Festinger, L. 1964. Behavioral support for opinion change. *Pub. Opin. Quart.*
28: 404–17.

Frenkel-Brunswik, E., and Sanford, N. 1945. Some personality factors in anti-
Semitism. *J. Psychol.* 20: 271–91.

Luchins, A. 1942. Mechanization in problem solving. *Psychol. Monogr.* 54: 6.

Milgram, S. 1974. *Obedience to authority.* New York: Harper.

Rokeach, M. 1960. *The open and closed mind.* New York: Basic Books.

_____. 1964. The three Christs of Ypsilanti. New York: Knopf.

_____. 1968. The nature of attitudes. In *International Encyclopedia of the
Social Sciences,* ed. E. Sills, New York: Macmillan.

_____. 1968. *Beliefs, attitudes and values.* San Francisco: Jossey-Bass.

_____. 1973. *The nature of human values.* New York: Free Press.

_____, and Mezei, L. 1966. Race and shared belief as factors in social choice.
Science 151: 167–72.

_____, Smith, P., and Evans, R. 1960. Two kinds of prejudice or one? In *The
open and closed mind,* ed. M. Rokeach, pp. 132–68. New York: Basic
Books.

Shils, E. 1954. Authoritarianism: "Right" and "Left." In *Studies in the scope and method of "The Authoritarian Personality,"* eds. R. Christie and M. Jahoda. New York: Free Press.

Wertheimer, M. 1945. *Productive thinking.* New York: Harper.

Zimbardo, P., et al. 1973. The mind is a formidable jailer: A Pirandellian prison. *New York Times,* p. 38, April 8, 1973.

SELECTED READINGS

Rokeach, M. 1960. *The open and closed mind.* New York: Basic Books.

Rokeach, M. 1964. *The three Christs of Ypsilanti.* New York: Knopf.

Rokeach, M. 1968. The nature of attitudes. In *International Encyclopedia of Social Sciences,* ed. E. Sills. New York: Macmillan.

Rokeach, M. 1968. *Beliefs, attitudes and values.* San Francisco: Jossey-Bass.

Rokeach, M. 1973. *The nature of human values.* New York: Free press.

Rokeach, M., and Mezei, L. 1966. Race and shared belief as factors in social choice. *Science.* 151: 167-72.

11

LEON FESTINGER

(1919–   )

Leon Festinger received his B.S. in psychology at the College of the City of New York in 1939, and his M.A. and PhD. from the State University of Iowa in 1942. He has held positions at the University of Rochester, Massachusetts Institute of Technology, and was program director of the Research Center for Group Dynamics of the University of Michigan. He was professor of psychology at Stanford University before moving to his present position as Distinguished Professor of Psychology at the New School for Social Research. The American Psychological Association awarded him its Distinguished Scientific Contribution Award in 1959, citing in particular his group dynamics work. Professor Festinger's cognitive dissonance theory has generated a vast amount of creative research. Moving away from the social psychological field, he is now exploring perception from a physiological stance.

I Was with It When It Opened Up/The Evolvement of the Small Group Studies//Simply a Nonfitting Relationship/A Definition of Cognitive Dissonance/With Some Contemporary Examples//Behavior Commits You to Something/The Cognitive Components of Feelings and Attitudes//Looking at the Question Behind It/The Shift from Social to Physiological Psychology//Criticism/Validity /A Look at the Future//

Dr. Festinger and I discuss his early work in the area of small groups, and he describes some of the studies that opened up this field, recalling his work as a graduate student with Kurt Lewin. He traces the thinking that led up to the publication in 1957 of A Theory of Cognitive Dissonance, and then applies the theory to some real-life situations, including smoking and health and contemporary politics in the United States. We discuss the relationship between attitudes and behavior and the effects of rewards in reducing dissonance. He reiterates his strong feelings that changing behavior can change attitudes and values. He describes his shift from research in social psychology to the perceptual-sensory work in which he is currently engaged. Reacting to questions about criticisms of his work, he comments, "I have never been bothered by any of the criticisms of my work. There should be criticism in science. One hopes that the criticism will be constructive, leading to improvement."

Evans: Dr. Festinger, an intriguing thing about your career is that you became well known, and deservedly so, for your contributions to social psychology and to psychological theory in general. Then you began to look at the effects of certain physiological factors on behavior. Had you become disenchanted with social psychology?

Festinger: It's probably more accurate to say that I became somewhat disenchanted with the rut I was in. I felt I wasn't making any significant contributions to social psychology any longer.

Evans: You did your graduate work with Kurt Lewin, who in my opinion is one of the truly creative and profound thinkers in the history of psychology. It would be very interesting to hear how working with him might have affected your own career as you went into social psychology.

Festinger: Of course, I was very much influenced by him. There was a very good group of people working with him at the University of Iowa at that time—Ronald Lippitt, Dorwin Cartwright, and quite a number of others. I mention those two because they were also with me later at MIT at the Research Center for Group Dynamics. One of the things about Kurt Lewin was that he really understood the role of theory in science, and even more than that, had a superb understanding of the relationship between theory and data in the empirical world. Those, in particular, are the things I learned from him.

Evans: There's a very profound paper that Lewin wrote on the distinctions between Aristotelian and Galilean modes of thought (Lewin 1935) that seems, at a highly sophisticated level, to look at the core of one of psychology's problems: the historical versus the contemporaneous examination of phenomena. Did working with a man of this philosophical sophistication present any problems for his students? Did his exposure to the European tradition of philosophical training give him a different slant than most psychologists?

Festinger: I'm not sure of the different slant. There was a trend in

American psychology at one point toward a highly empirical orientation. They used to call it "dust-bowl empiricism." But that trend was on the wane then. People like Hull, Tolman, and Spence were all theoretical people. Some of Lewin's theoretical contributions were, indeed, on a much more philosophical level—what you might call describing a framework within which theory could be built. But a lot of his contributions at a theoretical level were very precise hypotheses about the empirical world. Lewin's (1951) work on tension systems, satiation, and resumption of interrupted tasks all involved very specific theory. I don't think there is a great gap.

Evans: With your knowledge of Lewin, what do you consider to be his most important contribution, aside from his tremendously interesting general perspective?

Festinger: I don't think the general framework of topological psychology ends up as a very important contribution because it has waned without really influencing psychological theory, although for him, it was a fruitful, heuristic framework within which to think and in which to work. His major contributions are specific theories about tension systems and their effects, the new areas he opened up for investigation, such as level of aspiration, and the psychological effects of interrupted tasks; the whole experimental approach to social psychology.

Evans: As you began to develop your interests as a social psychologist, you first worked with small groups—group dynamics—and some of this work was included in a book that you did with Schachter and Back, *Social Pressures in Informal Groups* (Festinger, Schachter, and Back 1950). What were some of the key findings you reported that you still consider to be of some importance?

Festinger: I would say, mainly the conclusions about how groups generate pressures toward uniformity, how groups react to deviance, and the whole notion of the variable of cohesiveness of a group as affecting the strength of those pressures. The theories that we developed explaining those results led to a whole series of laboratory experiments attempting to test and develop them further. Most of that work is embodied in my article on informal social communication (Festinger 1950).

Evans: That article appeared in the *Psychological Review* in 1950. What were some of those findings that you still consider to be significant? That's a big test.

Festinger: That article is entirely theoretical, and it attempted to explain and account for the data concerning pressures toward uniformity in groups, the variable of cohesiveness as its affected those pressures, reactions to deviance, and the implications of this whole process for interpersonal communication within a group.

Evans: The whole area of group dynamics continues to be important, yet there is no doubt that as a field, group dynamics has been somewhat replaced by exotic applications of small group theory, such as sensitivity training and encounter groups. This seems to be a tremendous jump from the set of theoretical principles that you formulated to attempt to solve an array of complicated human problems. How do you feel about this?

Festinger: Forgive me a little bit of skepticism. I think sensitivity groups and training groups represent a big jump, but I don't think they jumped off from any theory that I developed, or that anybody else developed that was based on empirical evidence. They took off on a big jump out of ideology, and they may or may not be worthwhile, but I don't see any scientific evidence for these procedures. It doesn't mean that they are not valuable. Science may learn something from them, but so far I don't see the connection.

Evans: Even though some of the people in these groups talk about some of the same constructs that you talk about—group pressures, dealing with deviance, etc.—you don't feel that it is really theory-based? You think it has evolved at a more pragmatic level.

Festinger: I think so, but then my particular talents don't seem to include the application of scientific knowledge to practical problems. Other people may see firmer connections than I do.

Evans: Perhaps one of the few constructs in contemporary psychology that has really become a part of the concurrency of thinking at almost all levels is your notion of cognitive dissonance. Your book, *A Theory of Cognitive Dissonance* (Festinger 1957), in which you brought together a group of papers expanding this notion, is obviously considered a classic in the field, still much referred to and widely circulated. It would be interesting for our students to have you trace the development of dissonance theory. One widely held belief is that it might have begun out of a homeostatic model—the physiological notion that many psychologists have adopted in their motivational theories—that the organism seeks balance and that much of the function of the organism can be understood as a process of balance and imbalance. Would that be a fair assumption, that dissonance theory might have been rooted in a homeostatic model?

Festinger: No, I don't think so. In the introduction to that book, I really state very specifically and accurately how it arose, but I guess nobody believes it. Or else nobody reads introductions to books! I had been going through the literature on rumor transmission, and was interested in the problem of how rumors spread. It's a question of whether somebody feels strongly enough about the rumor so that he has to communicate it to others. I came across an article on rumors (Prasad 1950) that I really had difficulty understanding. This study was done in India after a big earthquake, and the rumors were collected among people outside the area of destruction. Most of the rumors predicted even more catastrophic things to come in the future, and it was just difficult for me to understand at the time why people would be spreading and believing frightening things like that. Generally, we don't go around frightening ourselves. One possible explanation that occurred to me was that these people had felt this enormous quake and were frightened and couldn't turn the fear off. Since they were outside the area of destruction, looking around, they didn't see anything different. There was nothing to justify that fear, so they invented things to justify it. It is the idea of cognitive invention, cognitive distortion, cognitive change to make your view of the world fit with how you feel or what you are doing; that was the basic idea out of which the formulation of dissonance theory developed.

Evans: How would this idea that you're describing differ from the Freudian defense mechanisms, such as rationalization?

Festinger: That's an impossible question for me to answer directly, but let me answer it tangentially. There are all kinds of mechanisms and techniques available to the human being, and any of these that are in his repertoire can be used in the service of many different things. Assuming that Freud is correct, and in some areas I am sure he is, people use these mechanisms to protect themselves from such things as guilt. They also use these mechanisms to get rid of dissonance. The mechanisms may be identical, but the basic theories involved are about different processes.

Evans: That's an interesting point. To put it another way, you're giving more specificity to a general concept, and not necessarily relating it to more generic defense mechanisms, such as rationalization.

Festinger: Dissonance is highly specific; it is something that one can define with reasonable specificity. Mechanisms can be used for the purpose of reducing dissonance as well as for many other purposes.

Evans: There's a paper in your 1957 book that has been receiving attention again because of the current concern for smoking and public health. You were reporting a state-wide study that had to do with the effects of the surgeon-general's report on smoking, and how heavy smokers, moderate smokers, and nonsmokers perceived that information. There were two aspects of it: whether or not people were aware of the message on the relationship between smoking and health; and secondly, if they were aware of it, how likely were they to believe it. It clearly showed that heavy smokers were less aware of the message; but if they were aware of it, they were less likely to believe it. As I recall, you used this study to illustrate dissonance theory.

Festinger: That's right. The main thing was the relationship between how much people smoked and the extent to which they believed this information. Heavy smokers tended not to believe it.

Evans: A number of studies have shown that almost everybody now believes that smoking is bad for health, heavy smokers and nonsmokers alike. There are a very few people who don't believe these data. Now the data, as I see it, are probability data—they don't say that if you smoke, you will definitely get these diseases and die young—we're talking about probabilities, risk-taking. You're taking more of a risk if you're a heavy smoker, but there is no certainty. It's very clear that handling dissonance by simply not believing the data is almost impossible now. How would dissonance theory deal with continued smoking, even heavy smoking, on the part of the individual, given this type of information?

Festinger: It's no trouble to specify all the ways you can deal with this dissonance, even though you can't deny the harmful effects of smoking any longer without being unrealistic. But you can persuade yourself that your life expectancy reduction is really relatively small, that it's real-

ly a choice of how you want to die, that after all, lung cancer is a
relatively painless death. You can persuade yourself that you can equal-
ize your life expectancy by avoiding other situations, like driving a car. If
you don't drive a car and you do smoke, your life expectancy is longer
than if you don't smoke and do drive a car. And you can persuade yourself that if you avoid all the things that are just as dangerous as smoking,
you can end up just lying in bed, and that's dangerous too. And who
wants to live to the age of ninety-eight anyhow?

Evans: Another interesting aspect of dissonance theory deals with doing something that is at odds with one's convictions. For example, let's
take the people around Nixon. We could argue that some of these individuals started out as bright young lawyers, with the idealism that
bright young lawyers often have, and surely any in that group, by their
own testimony, were idealistic. As they begin to carry out orders that are
discrepant with these idealistic beliefs, the question becomes how the dis-
sonance-resolution process is involved in terms of the rewards that may
or may not be present. I believe that it's historically rather important that
we analyze things like this, because we see so much of this in our society
today.

Festinger: The question you're asking is not why they did these acts,
but what would dissonance theory say about the subsequent effects on
their behavior, on their attitudinal structure, from having committed
these acts.

Evans: Exactly.

Festinger: The consequent effects of these actions would depend, according to dissonance theory, on how much pressure there was on these
people to do those things. If there were huge pressures, so that the actions could be justified in their own minds in terms of this pressure, I
don't think there would be any subsequent changes in ideology or in attitudinal structure. But what probably happens is that there is relatively
little pressure applied to do these things, and the first things that are done
are not so horribly dissonant with prior ideology. Dissonance is created
because the actions are dissonant with existing ideology and the pressure
to engage in those actions was relatively weak. Then they persuade
themselves (or try to persuade themselves) that what they did wasn't
really very bad, and that the purposes for which they were doing it were
very, very important. Once that process starts, it can go on and on, to
end up with their believing that they didn't do anything wrong, that
what they did was for national security. Very gradually and subtly their
attitudes change. On the surface, their ideology may have remained the
same, but there are all kinds of exceptions in their minds for national
security, and there are all kinds of redefinitions of what represents
national security.

Evans: It seems to me that dissonance theory can be useful in describing the corruption process. Moving in to another area now, *When
Prophecy Fails* (Festinger, Riecken, and Schachter 1956) is still a very interesting study. Could you tell us how you happened to get involved in
this particular study?

Festinger: That occurred very early in the period where we were developing dissonance theory. If you start with the notion that if a person has two beliefs or two cognitive items that don't fit together, there will be a process going on that tries to change one or the other of them so that they fit together better. It's easy to ask the question: What happens if both pieces of information that are in a dissonant relationship with each other are very, very resistant to change? It occurred to us at the time that some lovely instances of this kind of thing were available in historical movements where groups of people were predicting the end of the world and the second coming of Christ. If you really believe the second coming is going to occur and the world as it exists today is going to vanish, you don't go about your life in a normal manner. Material possessions don't mean anything, jobs don't mean anything. You just prepare for the second coming. We started looking into these historical movements. Many of these movements predict a specific day for the end, and when the event doesn't occur, these people are left with a very large dissonance between their belief system and their behavior on the one hand, and the fact that the predicitons didn't come true on the other. They have incontrovertible evidence that their belief system was wrong. Yet it is very difficult for them to change their belief system because they are committed to it by all their behavioral acts, which can't be undone. One way to lessen the dissonance would be to go out and persuade more people that your belief system is correct—perhaps this one little prediction was somewhat erroneous—but the general belief system is correct. So these discomfirmations of the belief system could lead to greater proselytizing efforts. And in all the historical movements that we could find, that seems to have occurred. Then we ran across this small newspaper article about a group that was predicting a specific date and time for the end of the world—not a millennial group in the traditional sense—but they were predicting that the world would be destroyed by flood on a specific date. In the hope that this would not occur, we thought we could have a live study and see whether there was an increase in proselytizing after this discomfirmation. That's why we did the study, and indeed, that is what happened.

Evans: You were actually able to study this right in the field, you were able to follow it up right after the predicted event failed to occur.

Festinger: Oh, yes, we were right there.

Evans: From the standpoint of a naturalistic study it was really beautiful. Now let me recall a paper that you presented at the American Psychological Association several years ago in which you challenged the field of psychology to think carefully about the relationship between attitudes and behavior. You were saying that there isn't much evidence that changing attitudes will change behavior. This led to a lot of thinking about whether we should be involved in attitude-change research at all if changing attitudes doesn't change behavior. On the other hand, dissonance theory seems to suggest that if we change behavior, a change in attitude will follow. This was the model that was demonstrated in the historic 1954 Supreme Court decision, *Brown* versus *Board of Education,* that implied if we developed laws to change our segregation practices, the attitude changes would follow. How do you feel about this theory?

Festinger: There are two different things that are embodied in your question. One is the relationship between behavior and attitudes, and the other is the relationship between attitude change and behavior change. By and large, I'm sure you will find a relationship between the attitude that is held and the relevant behavior that is overtly exhibited. The question is, if you change the attitude, will you then change the behavior or will that attitude simply slip back? At the time I could find no evidence in the literature to support the idea that if you could change the attitude, the behavior would change and stay changed. Whatever evidence existed, and it was very little, seemed to say that the attitude would just slip back. I would still maintain that if you change attitudes with the idea of wanting to change behavior, you'd better get some commitment about the attitudinal change so that the dissonance-reduction processes will drag the behavior into line with it. Usually, if you want to create a change to which a person is committed, it's much easier to get that person committed to a behavioral change, and if you do that, without too much pressure, I think you will find that attitudes will slide into line with the behavior.

Evans: Now the people involved with the behavior-modification movement have increasingly focused on behavior, on modifying or arranging the contingencies in the evironment to increase the probability that the desired behavior will occur. For their purposes, cognitive proceses involved in attitude are more-or-less irrelevant. That is, of course, an extreme view, but do you feel that it is sufficiently sophisticated to be adopted generally by psychology? Would we be losing a lot to ignore cognitive constructs, such as attitudes, altogether?

Festinger: As a practical mechanism for creating certain kinds of changes, perhaps we could look at behavior and nothing else. But from the point of view of understanding humans, if you look at nothing but behavior, you're ignoring a vast world that exists for human beings.

Evans: You mention something very interesting here—the point of view of understanding. Characteristically, we talk about three different areas psychologists are concerned with—understanding, prediction and control. With behavior modification, we're talking about controlling behavior, possibly predicting it, but we're not really concerned with understanding behavior. In other words, behavior modification says that we should go where the action is. But you're saying that we shouldn't ignore understanding. Do you think that progress would be seriously thwarted in psychology if we focused primarily on controlling and/or predicting behavior, forgetting about the understanding?

Festinger: It's very easy to control behavior. I can point a gun at you, and if you believe I'm ready to use it, you will do what I tell you to do. That's not what you really mean by controlling behavior. You're concerned with creating a change in behavior that lasts and endures in the absence of supervision. That means that something has to have gone on inside the person. You may find a technique for doing that in some limited area, but unless you understand the processes that are involved, unless you have a good theory about it, you don't know where it is going to work and where it isn't going to work. You aren't going to make progress. It's a little like the economic indicators. Every time they don't work, they post hoc create another economic index.

Evans: That's very well put. And if we look at what's happening in the behavior-modification movement, we can take the very interesting work of Albert Bandura (1973), who has introduced the concept of modeling and who is talking about such things as vicarious cognitive dimensions in modifying behavior. Some of the behavior-modification people are talking about "intraceptive conditioning," which introduces some form of cognitive component (imagination) into behavior change. I think what is happening in this movement bears out what you're saying, that you have to enrich what you're doing beyond the simpler delineation of behaviors in its own right.

Festinger: The history of science is filled with demonstrations that the more you understand about the dynamics of a process, the better your prediction is, and the better your control of relevant events is.

Evans: One facet of your work in dissonance theory involves the concept of public commitment—a tool used quite often by propagandists—that if you make a public commitment to a point of view that is essentially at odds with your "real" point of view, this commitment can have an effect on altering your "real" point of view.

Festinger: That's from the point of view that once a dissonance is created, how can you reduce it? If you have a public commitment or any other kind of commitment to something, changing that cognitively will be very difficult. The person will attempt to reduce the dissonance by trying to work on these cognitions, those aspects of the situation that are less resistant to change. By creating a commitment, making the cognition about that behavior very resistant to change, the dissonance-reduction processes will be oriented toward the other, less-resistant items.

Evans: In your more recent work, you have shifted rather radically to research at the physiological level in the area of vision. What got you interested in studying the properties of vision?

Festinger: It's a rather long story. It emerged primarily out of the fact that I didn't feel I was making much progress, theoretically, with dissonance. And without making progress and having new ideas, I became dissatisfied with myself. So I returned to the old question of what happens if there's a dissonance between two pieces of information, both of which are highly resistant to change. It occurred to me that one of the things that makes a piece of information resistant to change is to have that information come to you through your own sense experience. If I see something is white, it's very hard for me to persuade myself that it's red. If you put wedge-prism spectacles on a person and he looks at a straight, vertical line or edge, that line appears curved. If he rubs his hand up and down that edge, the information from his arm tells him that it's straight.

There would be two pieces of information, both from direct sense experience, that would be dissonant with each other. We tried that, and it turned out to be a very bad way to study dissonance reduction because no dissonance was created. What happens is that the arm feels it is moving in a curved pattern. I later discovered that Gibson (1933) had pointed this out in an article in 1933! But the attempt to understand that led me into the study of vision, and I was willingly trapped by all of the fascinating problems about vision and the visual system.

Evans: Briefly, could you describe the gist of your present work in vision? I know this work is very intriguing to a number of people who are familiar with it.

Festinger: I can tell you briefly what I'm working on currently, although how I got there, and why I'm working on it, and why I find it fascinating, I cannot tell you briefly. That would take time. But the visual system is a relatively peculiar system in that the perceptual system does not get any information about eye movement or eye position based on feedback information from the muscles that move the eye. If you move your arm, for example, there is feedback, primarily from the joint receptors, that tells the central nervous system something about the position of the arm. There is no such information fed back to the perceptual system from the extraocular muscles, the muscles that move the eye. Any information that the perceptual system has about eye position or eye movement is based on monitoring of the efferent output to the eye muscles. The perceptual system knows the position of the eye only insofar as it knows where the eye was told to go. Because of that situation, anything the perceptual system knows about the eye position and eye movement has to be information that was contained in the efferent command at the point at which it was monitored by the perceptual system. Because of that, the visual system becomes a window onto the workings of the efferent output system, which you can't get as cleanly with any other system. What I'm working on primarily is trying to understand and pin down the information contained in those efferent output commands to the eyes at various stages in the transmission chain.

Evans: In looking over your great number of contributions, both in social psychology and in vision, what criticisms of your work have bothered you?

Festinger: I have never been bothered by any of the criticisms of my work. I have felt that some of them were rather useless, but that is the prerogative of other people. There should be criticism in science. When something is published, one imagines that it is not perfect; one imagines that others will criticize it; one hopes that the criticism will be constructive, leading to improvement.

REFERENCES

Bandura, A. 1973. *Aggression: A social learning analysis.* Englewood Cliffs, N.J.: Prentice-Hall.
Brehm, J., and Cohen, A. 1962. *Explorations in cognitive dissonance.* New York: Wiley.
Festinger, 1950. Informal social communication. *Psychol. Rev.* 57: 271–82.
_____. 1957. *A theory of cognitive dissonance.* Stanford, Calif.: Stanford University Press.
_____. 1964. Behavioral support for opinion change. *Pub. Opin. Quart.* 28: 404–17.
_____, Schachter, S., and Back, K. 1950. *Social pressures in informal groups: A study of human factors in housing.* New York: Harper.
_____, Riecken, H., and Schachter, S. 1956. *When prophecy fails.* Minneapolis: University of Minnesota Press.
Gibson, J. 1933. Adaption aftereffect and contrast in the perception of curved lines. *J. Exper. Psychol.* 16: 1–31.
Lewin, K. 1935. *Dynamic theory of personality.* New York: McGraw-Hill.
_____. 1951. Selected papers by K. Lewin in *Field theory in social sciences: Selected theoretical papers,* ed. D. Cartwright. New York: Harper.
Prasad, J. 1950. A comparative study of rumours and reports in earthquakes. *Brit. J. Psychol.* 41: 129–44.

SELECTED READINGS

Festinger, L. 1950. Informal social communication. *Psychol. Rev.* 57: 271–82.
Festinger, L., and Katz, D. (Eds.) 1953. *Research methods in the behavioral sciences.* New York: The Dryden Press.
Festinger, L. 1957. *A theory of cognitive dissonance.* Stanford, Calif.: Stanford University Press.
Festinger, L. 1964. Behavioral support for opinion change. *Pub. Opin. Quart.* 28: 404–17.
Festinger, L., Schachter, S., and Back, K. 1950. *Social pressures in informal groups.* New York: Harper & Brothers.
Festinger, L., Riecken, H., and Schachter, S. 1956. *When prophecy fails.* Minneapolis: University of Minnesota Press.

12

HAROLD PROSHANSKY
(1920–   )

Harold Proshansky is one of the founders of environmental psychology and has promulgated much theory and research in this area, especially with respect to urban envirnoments. Dr. Proshansky's approach to psychology is problem-oriented and interdisciplinary, and attests to his concern with solving important social problems. He has been a leader in the development of the Society for the Psychological Study of Social Issues Division of the American Psychological Association. He took his B.S. from the City College of New York, earned his M.A. at Columbia University, and received his Ph.D. at New York University in 1952. He has held positions at New York University, Brooklyn College, the University of Michigan, and is currently the president of the graduate school and University Center of the City University of New York, as well as professor of psychology.

Social Perception/ Prejudice/ Ways the Research Failed// Open Methodology/ Exploratory Research/ Measurement Does Not Always Mean Quantify// Interdisciplinary Efforts//Environmental Psychology/ Place Identity// Ecological Psychology/ Physical Settings//Theoretical Analysis// Middle Range Theory// Complex Human Problems/A Science That Solves Problems//

As we begin our discussion, Dr. Proshansky talks about his early training in experimental studies of perception and the development of his interest in social psychology: "I envisioned complex issues being solved by evolving new sets of principles, and nothing could stop us, period!" He reacts to the relative failure of psychology's involvement with the phenomena of prejudice, suggesting that the laboratory experimental work was not sufficiently complex to enable psychologists to intervene in the real world. He discusses the desirability of using methods that

136

allow you to "preserve the integrity of the phenomenon you study" and of becoming thoroughly familiar with the phenomena as they occur before trying to do research. Dr. Proshansky relates his endeavors to cooperate with other disciplines in solving complex social problems, and cautions that interdisciplinary efforts are plagued with difficulties, which are multiplied by the lack of mutual understanding and communication. He draws from his experience to describe an approach to interdisciplinary cooperation that optimizes the potential for productive research and problem solving. Then, turning to his specialty, environmental psychology, Dr. Proshansky discusses the rising importance of the urban environment as one of the determinants of behavior that deserves our attention. He talks about his research on the impact of different household settings on style of life, an innovative study in which he utilized photography, group interviews, and the "hot-line" technique to gather and cross-validate data. He responds to what he views as unrealistic expectations for social changes from redesigning physical settings, emphasizing that the environment is just one of the several factors involved. Finally, Dr. Proshansky expresses his conviction that complex human problems require appropriate methodologies: "I am absolutely convinced that if we start and end in the laboratory experimentalist model, we are going to be playing with lint in our belly buttons."

Evans: Dr. Proshansky, in looking over your career I notice your early work in social perception, before you began to invest your efforts in the field we broadly call environmental psychology. What did the field of social psychology look like to you as you finished your training at New York University?

Proshansky: Going back to the 1950s (I got my Ph.D. in 1952, but had completed my master's in 1941), for me social psychology was the end-all of end-alls. I viewed it as not only the field I wanted to be in but as a field with incredibly great promise. I had been a strong proponent of laboratory rat psychology and the behavioristic approach, and then the learning theory based upon memory drums. Since my interests and training were in experimental method in perception, I thought I would continue to study perception at a social level, to find out about human perception in terms of social interaction processes. So, for example, I became very interested in first impression formation. At the same time, ethnic prejudice was a great interest to me, as well as attitudes toward work, on which I subsequently did work in 1959 and 1960, and 1961. I was oriented toward the laboratory, toward the field when necessary, and rooted in general experimental psychology; I envisioned complex issues being solved by evolving new sets of principles, and nothing could stop us, *period*. That was my view of social psychology at that time. You could find evidence for it in my great admiration for the work of Sherif, Festinger, Pepitone, Morton Deutsch, and Bill McGuire (who came a few years later). So up until the time when I got to Michigan, I was absolutely convinced that social psychology, as defined and established by those key figures, was the proper direction.

Evans: Now, it would be interesting to hear you discuss the Society for the Psychological Study of Social Issues. You were in a particularly good position to see its development from basic research to action research in the area of prejudice. Social psychologists have been accused of spending a great deal of time studying prejudice, but, in spite of some very important landmarks, such as Gordon Allport's book *The Nature of Prejudice* (1954) and the work of the California group on authoritarianism (Adorno, Frenkel-Brunswick, Levinson, and Sanford 1950), social psychology has not been very successful in actually increasing tolerance in the United States. How do you feel about that?

Proshansky: If I had to give an answer, my feeling is that I agree with that accusation. There was nothing wrong with the intention; social psychologists ought to study prejudice if they claim they are interested in establishing principles of social behavior and applying them in a way that will resolve major social problems. Prejudice is a major social problem. In my mind, it turned out to be a bust; while the research was useful in revealing the length and breadth of prejudice, and establishing how resistant it was, in other ways the research failed. First, before we understood prejudice we were already involved in the process of change. That involvement was predicated on the assumption that we knew enough about the phenomena to produce change. That is one reason we failed: we did *not* know enough. Second, whatever we knew and understood about prejudice within the realm of social psychology was based on systematic research that had nothing to do with the real phenomena of race or ethnic prejudice. It was based on ridiculous attitude scales that measured nothing but a set of verbal responses. Not only were the techniques bad, but we defined prejudice in very limited terms so that the extent to which it could operate was never actually grasped by any social scientist. We made a rather simplistic assumption. If a person makes a particular statement, he is prejudiced more or less. Third, there was a great need to constantly quantify these phenomena long before we knew what we were talking about. Fourth, and most important, everything that we did in analysis and study of prejudice was based upon a laboratory experimental model, as if prejudice was a series of responses that were made by a person because he was prejudiced, if you provide the stimulus you get the response. For all the lip service that social psychologists gave to the total person, the nature of the situation, and so on, the fact is that we never conceptualized settings, we never conceptualized social environments. We constantly treated the person as if he made responses to situations. We acted as if that small, highly extreme group that we call entrenched bigots represented what prejudice was. What is the answer? The answer is that ethnic prejudice is not one phenomenon, it is probably many different phenomena. Each one of those phenomena is relevant to a set of conditions and may express itself in a different way. The best illustration of this was the fact that Hovland and his group at Yale did not find any confirmation in the real world with the measures that we were using.

Evans: Now, the historic decision *Brown* versus *Board of Education* (1954) cited the work of Kenneth and Mamie Clark, who did a simulated study involving dolls which showed that by a certain age even black children prefer white dolls to black dolls (Clark and Clark 1947). This demonstrated how prejudiced attitudes became inculcated, even in relatively young children. The Supreme Court apparently utilized data from that study in rendering its anti-segregation decision. The cynic might ask if that was the best we could produce in 1954. Does that reinforce what you were saying?

Proshansky: Yes. The decision, as far as I am concerned, was a great one. But I reviewed the studies that utilized these picture tests and although some showed that black children wanted to be white, others did not show this. There were many methodological problems.

But none of that dampened my interest in developing some kind of model and methodology that would address itself to major social problems. My attraction to the field of social psychology was not interest in conceptual analysis or knowledge for its own sake. I was constantly attracted by the desire to understand major social problems and to solve them. I learned by 1962 that not only was the methodology wrong, but that we never really taught our students to think conceptually, to discover and understand the dimensions of the problem. American graduate students in psychology are essentially atheoretical people. They do not know how to think conceptually. All they know how to do (and I was one of them) is to see how quickly you can put the problem into a mold and gather data.

Evans: As you know, there is a very important methodological emphasis that is beginning to permeate psychological training. The emerging quasi-experimental methodology that Don Campbell and others developed (e.g., Campbell and Stanley 1963) says that the traditional methodology does not make much sense when you go out into the field. How do you feel about this new type of open methodology and the new emphasis on evaluation research?

Proshansky: Some people think if you work in the field rather than in the laboratory you are less experimental: untrue. Open methodology allows us to deal with problems face-on and use a methodology that will keep the phenomena intact. Unfortunately, I find that people tend to bring laboratory techniques out into the field, structuring the situation in ways that provide data but destroy the phenomenon. It is the same old techniques simply used outside. What I have emphasized is preserving the integrity of the phenomenon that you study. Don't destroy it in the process of studying it. I have a prior question to ask when I get to evaluation research; just because you move into a complex area does not necessarily mean that you are ready to do research in it. Suppose it is unresearchable for the moment; suppose that it will take time before one has enough understanding. Maybe the methodology should be just spending time with the problem and finding out what is happening and asking yourself the question: Is this the time for research and systematic data collection? Or should you wait upon that and merely be anecdotal, recording the phenomena, keeping an account, and simply looking? That is what I call exploratory research; it is nothing more than looking around.

A final problem worries me in open methodology. If you decide to go into quasi-experimental designs and look at birth records or number of times people come into the hospital or what have you, make sure that what you are doing is relevant to a meaningful problem. Not, as sometimes happens, that it really doesn't matter what the problem is, as long as we are good on our methodology. A set of principles that I would like to see applied in methodology would go this way. One, before you do anything, spend a long enough time understanding the dimensions of the problem even if all you can do is write little things down on a piece of paper. Each day you learn a little more. Two, if it is time to measure, make sure you understand what you mean by the word "measure"; make sure that you understand that measurement does not always mean quantify. It may mean record, it may mean qualitative information systematically collected. Three, if you go ahead, don't use one method or technique, use two or three. Four, don't interview unless you are sure that the phenomenon, whether it is an attitude or value or feeling or knowledge, really exists in the person. We have learned that 75% of the time people make responses to their physical environment and are completely unaware of it. Incidentally, stop studying phenomenon between Monday at two o'clock and Wednesday at three o'clock. Most of the problems we are interested in, Dick, are problems that have a time dimension. They have a duration, and if we take two and three years, that is the nature of the work we do. What is important is the problem, and you cannot fit it into a schedule. I wouldn't even use the word "longitudinal" in research. If the phenomenon has a time dimension to it, that is the only way to study it. The difficulty with all of this is not only that it is time-consuming, but it is money-consuming; it is costly research. I am not against using the experimental method when it is appropriate, but I am happy about the Campbell emphasis and I am happy about the desire to move out in an exploratory fashion.

Evans: Another thing that characterizes your perspective is that you have been an advocate of cross-disciplinary, interdisciplinary efforts to deal with problems. You have been involved in projects where you worked with sociologists, cultural anthropologists, economists, political scientists, and so on. Many programs could benefit from interdisciplinary or multidisciplinary input, but to carry it off is very difficult. These programs sound good, they make sense, but a lack of communication among disciplines still appears to persist. How do you feel about this?

Proshansky: Beginning as early as the time of my degree in 1952, one of the great dreams I had was that not only would social psychology do it, but it would do it holding hands with a number of other disciplines. I have functioned my entire professional life touching other disciplines. Most of those efforts have failed; such efforts will continue to fail unless we know where and how we are going. Let me be very precise. First, interdisciplinary has many meanings. One of the earliest meanings was that if you took a large problem area, brought people from different disciplines together to work on it, and let them all do their own thing, somehow or other the work would fit together and solve the problem. Nothing could be farther from the truth. That is not the interdisciplinary that I have in mind. Second, as you mentioned, language and communication are problems.

Third, there is an assumption made when we are interdisciplinary that we have enough knowledge in each area so that all we have to do is think about the relationships of each of our disciplines to the problem and we will arrive at a solution. This involves a more dubious assumption than one must make as a social psychologist or an environmental psychologist, for example. If we don't have our own concepts developed, how the hell are we going to relate them to the other guy who also doesn't have his own concepts developed? The only way an interdisciplinary approach can ever work is when a problem is first clearly understood by one or two people who then sit down with all the other relevant people and make a decision about which part of the problem to attack first.

Fourth, what "experts" are you bringing together? The police commissioner of the city of New York and I once talked about research by behavioral scientists on police-community relations, the quality of police work, relationships to criminals, and what have you. The commissioner said to me, "You know that I am identified with research, but I don't want your kind of research." I asked why not. He said, "Look, if you want to help us, then it is essential that behavioral scientists come in and become part of the scene that we call police-community relationships. It is impossible to come in, muddy up the water, think you understand it, and then tell us how to solve it. It just can't be. This is a complex problem." The interdisciplinary efforts that I know of have brought in behavioral scientists from laboratories; they did not know the phenomena, they were unable to communicate with the practitioners, and they did not understand the larger context in which problems occur. They were immersed in an Alice in Wonderland world, their definitions and understanding of the problems out there were relatively nil because none of them had ever been out there. They were doomed to failure.

Evans: How can we make these interdisciplinary projects more productive?

Proshansky: What I have done in environmental psychology is to first look at a problem from the point of view of a psychologist, then allow each step of the analysis to tell us at what point we need input from another level or another discipline; we are problem oriented. Also, we understand our limitations, we make no promises. The only way an interdisciplinary approach can ever work is when a problem is first clearly understood by one or two people who then sit down with all the other relevant people and make a decision about which part of the problem to attack first. Let me give you an example. I have a project going on right now in the area of the quality of the delivery of urban services. We are using continuously working groups of teams, including a union official, a consumer who will operate over a long period of time, practitioners responsible for the program (policemen and firemen), and only one behavioral scientist. The program has only one objective: to see if we can come up with interdisciplinary, meaningful, possibly researchable questions on the issue of responsiveness in urban services. Just the questions. If we can come up with these questions, then will come the task of formulating the problem in research terms.

Evans: Now let's move into the area that many people describe as your specialty, the field of environmental psychology, to which you just referred. It might be best to start by simply asking the question: What is environmental psychology?

Proshansky: It always seemed to me so unusual to find that no matter what problem was discussed—proverty, prejudice, occupation, sex conflict—the physical environment was always taken for granted by the social psychologist. This intrigues me because while I don't think the physical environment contributes a great deal to the variance of behavior, it contributes some. For me, environmental psychology has a specialized meaning: It is really a field that focuses on attempting to establish the relationships between the nature and organization of physical settings and human behavior and experience. It is interdisciplinary; our work often takes place with the architects, designers, and what have you. We design space, we develop it for roles. The key word now is "urban." I would argue that if you want to understand human behavior apart from applied problems, you can't talk only about the determinants of genes, the determinants of social interaction, and the determinants such as love and hate; you also have to ask about the space we make. Man makes the built environment, and the built environment in turns acts on man. I am not leaving out natural environment, but for the largest number of people now it is the technological world of the city. That is what I mean by environmental psychology. "Place identity," a term that I helped introduce, reflects the idea that we internalize places and that they help to establish who we are, much as do ethnic groups, families, mothers, attitudes, and what have you.

Evans: The field of ecological psychology appears to exist along with the field of environmental psychology. Is there some intended distinction when we hear about ecological psychology?

Proshansky: Yes. Ecological psychology identified with Barker's (1963, 1965) very specific approach and in many ways I identify with it, but Barker was not interested in environmental psychology as I define it. He is not really interested in the physical environment as a set of determinants. It merely is a context within which to establish social norms and social behavior for large numbers of people defined in physical terms. It looks at those normative aspects of behavior rather than at the physical environment. Environmental psychology takes a slightly different view. Obviously, there is no physical environment that is not social and cultural, but for the moment, let's reverse figure and ground. Let's make the physical the most important, look at its relationship to behavior, and worry about social and cultural as we get into a much more complex analysis of the problem.

Evans: I'm sure that from the start you have been confronted with the idea that somehow we can take a slum, tear it down, replace it with ecologically attractive structures, and somehow a lot of good things will happen: the crime rate will decline, the delinquency rate will decline, the school dropout rates will decline. The belief is that changing that part of the environment we call housing would somehow have these vast sociological, economic, and political implications. What is your reaction to the failures of such efforts?

Proshansky: Many people have grandiose notions about what space can and cannot do, like, "If he had not grown up in that dirty rotten apartment he would not be a crook," or "If we build a college dorm this way and that way, then all the couples who come to live there are going to be happily married." That's nonsense. Anyone who thinks that redesigning a physical setting will produce changes in the behavior of people is absolutely out of his mind. These ideas will be advanced out of commercial and self-interest: buiders, real estate people, and what have you. Space may facilitate, it may inhibit, it may influence to some degree, but things don't happen only because of space. If someone comes to us and says, "Could you help us design this space so that all the ethnic groups that mill around here are going to like each other?" that would be an impossible demand. If tomorrow I could with a snap of my fingers redesign cities so that everybody would be living in beautiful places, you would still have all kinds of problems. A: Since these people are of a particular background and experience, would they know how to deal with it? Would they know how to keep it up? It is not just living in it, it's maintaining it. B: Are you guaranteeing them jobs to provide the income to keep it up? C: Is that environment now so different and so new that in terms of their own training and experience it threatens them more than helps them? If you want to change the existence of minority groups and large numbers of other people, if you want to eliminate crime, you are going to have to start with the redistribution of money and power. There is no substitute.

Evans: Could you briefly describe the sequence from starting with a problem, doing some exploration concerning possible solutions, and finally implementing a solution?

Proshansky: A good example would be the research I am doing concerning the relationship between style of life and housing experiences. We wanted to look at the kinds of behaviors people have in their physical settings, what we call the household, in an urban setting. We got permission to work with people who have residences in New York City: one-family homes, high-rise project housing, and old-time tenements that were not high rises. We made sure that we had both black and white. What was crucial was our desire to explore and find out how people use the space: where they do things, who controls the space, and what it means when you introduce a number of concepts about privacy and comfort. We were not interested in interviewing and sampling hundreds of people in New York City because we had very little confidence in the interview. We recognized from the beginning that all of those questions could be completely irrelevant, that people had not thought about them. So first we introduced the hot-line technique, which was what that we could telephone the people at any hour up to midnight and as early as six in the morning to ask them a series of questions such as "Where are you now? Where are the other people in the family? Who is doing what?" Second, we photographed spaces. Third, we used what we call the group interview. If you ask each member of the family about the space, the stories are always from somebody's vantage point. One kid will say, "It's my room," and then the other kid will say, "Well, I use it more than she does." Or the mother says that this is his room and the kids tells you later, "Yeah, she gave me the room, but every time I want to go in there and play she kicks me out." So we used the group interview. Amazingly, there was a self-correction. Our hope in the first two years was to come out with some feeling about what really happens in space so that at least we could say this interview approach was backed up by all the other information. This is the kind of research we are doing.

An example at the other end of the spectrum would be the very simple research we are doing on the movement of people in crowded subway stations. Based purely on empirical observation, we were able to make a series of recommendations for decreasing congestion in the given stations. By moving a number of exits, changing the number of staircases, we could decrease the congestion because it resulted mainly from the space having not been well designed for people who move in what we call hoards rather than as individuals.

Evans: It seems to me that you are describing fairly inductive rather than deductive research. You are really not starting with *a priori* hypotheses; you were looking for possibilities, rather than testing hypotheses.

Proshansky: The purpose of this sometimes quick and dirty research is not only to satisfy a client but also to immediately run back to the office and sit down and begin with what I call theoretical analysis. Environmental psychology has to be as theoretical as it possibly can be. I don't mean a grand scheme and I don't mean a Skinnerian system. Morton

Deutsch called it middle range theory and I call it even less than middle range. Place identiy came to me, not out of any piece of research, but from thinking to myself how the physical environment has an influence on self-identity. We must have space that has meaning to us. I can predict certain things about Evans' desk and office. Places are very important to us; they also define our identiy. So I coined the term "place identity." Most of us are unaware of it, but people have all kinds of conceptions about spaces and places. All you have to do is disturb them in some way—an earthquake, a disaster—and suddenly it is clear.

Evans: Looking over the many contributions you have made as a social psychologist, what would you consider to be your most important?

Proshansky: Of everything that I did, I would say it was being part of that small group that pushed for environmental psychology as I have defined it (Proshansky and O'Hanlon 1977). Not so much because of its contribution to solving problems—that may or may not occur—but in raising the whole question of what represents an appropriate methodology when we are interested in complex human problems. I am absolutely convinced that if we start and end in the laboratory experimentalist model, we are going to be playing with lint in our belly buttons.

Evans: A concluding question: What are some of the criticisms of your work that have troubled you the most?

Proshansky: One criticism that has been leveled at me in particular is that my greatest contribution is framing out the grand statement, but not the specifics that ought to proceed to any given end. I am now convinced that in the behavioral sciences the only thing that really will matter is the extent to which we develop a science that can solve problems as well as provide understanding.

REFERENCES

Adorno, J. W., Frenkel-Brunswik, E., Levinson, D. J., and Stanford, R. N. 1950. *The authoritarian personality.* New York: Harper.

Allport, G. W. 1954. *The nature of prejudice.* Reading, Mass.: Addison-Wesley.

Barker, R. G. 1963. *The stream of behavior.* New York: Appleton-Century-Crofts.

———. 1965. Explorations in ecological psychology. *Amer. Psychol.* 20: 1–14.

Brown versus *Board of Education.* 1954. 347 *U.S.* 483.

Campbell, D. T., and Stanley, J. C. 1963. *Experimental and quasi-experimental designs for research.* Chicago: Rand McNally.

Clark, K. B., and Clark, M. 1947. Racial identification and racial preference in Negro children. In *Readings in social psychology,* eds. T. M. Newcomb and E. L. Hartley. New York: Holt.

Proshansky, H. M., and O'Hanlon, T. 1977. Environmental psychology: Origins and development. In *Perspectives on environment and behavior: Theory, research, and application,* ed. D. Stokels. New York: Plenum Press.

SELECTED READINGS

Landau, M., Proshansky, H. M., and Ittelson, W. H. 1962. The interdisciplinary approach and the concept of behavioral science. In *Decisions, values and groups* (Vol. 2), ed. N. F. Washburne. Proceedings of the Conference of the Air Force Office of Scientific Research at the University of New Mexico. New York: MacMillan.

Proshansky, H. M., Ittelson, W. H., and Riulin, L. G. (Eds.) 1970. *Environmental psychology: Man and his physical setting.* New York: Holt, Rinehart and Winston.

Proshansky, H. M. 1972. For what are we training our graduate students. *Amer. Psychol.* 27: 205–12.

Proshansky, H. M. 1972. Methodology in environmental psychology: Problems and issues. *Human Factors* 14: 451–60.

Proshansky, H. M. 1973. Theoretical issues in "environmental psychology." *Rep. Research in Soc. Psychol.* 4: 93–108.

Proshansky, H. M. 1976. Environmental psychology and the real world. *Amer. Psychol.* 31: 303–10.

13
STANLEY SCHACHTER
(1922–   )

Stanley Schachter studied at Yale University, Massachusetts Institute of Technology, and in 1950 completed work for a Ph.D. at the University of Michigan. He was a Fulbright professor at the University of Amsterdam and spent several years at the University of Minnesota before accepting a position at Columbia University in 1961. There he has served as professor and chairman of the social psychology department and as Robert Johnston Nivens Professor of Social Psychology. Professor Schachter has done landmark research in the fields of group dynamics and communications, and, in 1969 received the American Psychological Association's Distinguished Scientific Contribution Award. His current research involves the more physiological aspects of motivation related to such areas as hunger, stress, and smoking.

Why People Want to Be Together/The Need for Affiliation//How Can I Describe What I'm Feeling?/Social/Cognitive/Physiological Interrelationships//How Do You Extinguish a World of Food Cues?/ External Cue Determination of Behavior of Obese Humans//The pH Factor/Smoking and Stress//Crime and Chlorpromazine/Some Intriguing Extrapolations of the Adrenaline-Emotion Studies//Go Where the Problems Lead You//

Dr. Schachter and I discuss the influences that led him to his well-known work on affiliation. He outlines the experiments that clearly defined the area of need affiliation and generated several broad new lines of research. We draw some comparisons between his research on obesity and parallel studies on smoking behavior. Dr. Schachter describes his current research on the physiological components of nicotine addiction in such a way that even the beginning student can follow the design of the experiments, the development of the hypothesis, and the intriguing

147

results. He then comments on the theoretical implications of the adrenaline-produced anxiety studies with some possible generalizations to the criminal psychopath. Reacting to the question about his work in several areas, Dr. Schachter comments, "There's no such thing as a tough area. An area's tough only if you don't have an idea." In conclusion, Dr. Schachter discusses the work he has found most personally satisfying in an outstanding career.

Evans: Dr. Schachter, although your more recent work has moved in other directions, your early work in the field of social psychology is still widely discussed in introductory and social psychology textbooks. One area of particular interest is your work on affiliation. What led you into this line of research? How did you first become interested in the need for affiliation?

Schachter: I had been working with Leon Festinger and Kurt Lewin on the whole business of social influence, social comparison, how people evaluate their opinions, the social determinants of opinions, and so on. It simply struck me that though we had paid a great deal of attention to the consequences of being with other people, we had paid almost no attention to why people bothered associating at all. Social psychology started from the premise that people do affiliate; they do associate, they do want to be with each other, and it goes on from there to examine what happens when they are together. I became very curious as to why, in a nonobvious way, people want to be together at all.

Evans: You say in a nonobvious way. Could you expand on what seems to be a key to your whole program of research, as I see it?

Schachter: There are certain needs that obviously you can satisfy only with other people—sex is a clear one, and bridge and tennis, and so on. You have to do these things with other people. However, people spend immense amounts of time together beyond such simple need-satisfactions, and it's really not obvious why. Historically, the thing that got me into affiliation was a talk by Don Hebb (1949) about his sensory deprivation work. If you remember these studies, they involved putting people into social isolation and sensory isolation, sometimes for days on end. Hebb reported tremendously dramatic effects. Many of his subjects had hallucinations, most of them seemed to suffer a great deal. I wondered how much of this was due to sensory deprivation, as Hebb claimed, and how much to the fact that they were simply alone. So I read a number of autobiographical reports of people who had spent a great deal of time alone—people who had sailed around the world alone, monks, prisoners, hermits—and it did appear that the state of being alone, in and of itself, was immensely painful.

Evans: Can you recall some of the early studies that you did in that area?

Schachter: I tried a couple of case studies in which paid volunteers lived in a room alone, seeing no one for days at a time. There was some evidence of suffering; but from these cases alone, it was difficult to figure out just why this should be the case. And so I started a series of experiments on the relationship of anxiety to the affiliative need—a pure guess, at first, that if you're upset and frightened, you want to be with other people. It turned out that if the subjects were badly frightened, they wanted very much to be with other people, and if they were calm, not nearly so much so. Comparatively, the intensity of their need to be with others was far less when the subjects were calm than when they were anxious.

Evans: Is it possible to take a need, like the need for affiliation, and separate it from social needs that seem to overlap in so many ways? For example, the need for social approval might overlap with this, or be a problem of the sort David McClelland (1953) had with the need for achievement. We're not always sure that we're getting that specific thing. Did you have any problems in looking at this, in measuring it?

Schachter: I never assumed there was anything such as a generalized need for affiliation. I simply didn't think in terms such as McClelland's notions of needs, or those of his forefather, Henry Murray (1938).

Evans: This is a very important point because in Murray's original list of needs, he set up a pattern that stated, if you did a factor analysis, that you'd find all these specific needs, which, without measurements, is pretty hard to do. You weren't thinking, then, in terms of this framework.

Schachter: No. It seemed to me that if you talk about something like a need for affiliation, you assume there must be some people who are high in this need and some who are low. You would expect people who are high to want more to be with older people than those who are low. From casual observation, however, there seem to be times when people want very much to be with other people and times when they want very much to be alone. So my view was: What are the situations that lead people to want to be with others? What are the situations that lead them to want to be alone? I never thought of it in trait terms which I think essentially is what McClelland and Murray have done.

Evans: This is the distinction I was trying to evoke, the idea that a trait concept of a need is really quite different from yours. Do you feel that your need for affiliation has sometimes been presented incorrectly in introductory textbooks?

Schachter: No, not particularly. To pursue the contrast between my approach to affiliation and the trait view, it did seem to me that implicit in the notion of a traitlike need affiliation is the expectation that no matter what the circumstances, people who are high in that need will want to be with others more than people who are low in that need. In some of our experiments we deliberately manipulated conditions to show that there are situations where such people want to be with others, and there are situations where they want *not* to be with others. With such a pattern of results, it is simply more useful to think in terms of what people get out of being with one another rather than in terms of a traitlike need affiliation.

Evans: I'm glad you underlined that. Looking at some of the specific studies, what are the one or two experiments that you find particularly intriguing, as you look back on that work?

Schachter: The very first experiment, of course, the one in which we simply manipulated fear, making some subjects anxious and some calm, and then gave them a choice of being together or being alone. That they wanted to be with others when they were frightened opened up the whole problem. It was a real phenomenon, a real fact, we had a *finding*. What the hell did it mean? That question led to the whole series of experiments described in my book.

Evans: *The Psychology of Affiliation* (Schachter 1959). Those experiments must have led you to look at this whole area much more closely.

Schachter: The only other experiment in this series that was intriguing for me was the experiment that opened up the next line of research and suggested that one of the reasons people choose to affiliate, to be with other people is to better evaluate how they feel. Experimentally we had created a novel, rather startling, and frightening situation for our subjects, and there was no real way for them to decide, "How do I react?" "What's the most appropriate response that I can give?" "How can I describe what I'm feeling?" I suggest in that book, and there is some support for it, that one of the reasons they choose to be with other people in that context is so that they can literally understand what they're feeling by comparing themselves with other people. They want to be with others so they can evaluate their own reactions to the situation. Those studies led into the whole line of work that I've been doing ever since. In general, since the affiliation studies, I've been concerned with the interrelationships of social, cognitive, and physiological determinants of feeling states.

Evans: It would be interesting to hear your comments on a more recent line of research that does get into affiliation. You may recall the line of bystander-apathy research that Latané and Darley (1970) have done. One of the concepts that has come from this research is the "diffusion of responsibility" idea—if you're with a lot of other people, you're less likely to help them than if you're alone. It just occurred to me that you might have something to say about that. Is there something related here in terms of anxiety affiliation behavior?

Schachter: I'm sorry, but I've never thought about the connections explicitly. I suppose, since Latané was my student, that the two bodies of work are loosely connected, but I confess that's a glib, off-the-top-of-my-head, answer.

Evans: Some research that is of interest in our society right now and that I have found valuable in interpreting various phenomena, is your work on how cues are related to the hunger drive, particularly for the person who tends to be obese, and the special nature of sensitivity to cues. I was speaking recently to a group of people who are interested in the area of oral hygiene, and they were concerned with why people cannot be taught to brush their teeth properly. I referred to your work, pointing out that when you're trying to modify an eating habit, you're plagued constantly with cues that stand out, saying eat, eat, eat, every time you pass a grocery store or listen to a commercial. But there are no cues shouting at a person about his tooth-brushing behavior. The possibility for altering that behavior might be much greater than altering the behavior that leads to obesity, and such disease-prevention behavior also may be parallel to the area of smoking. I am presently embarking on a massive study supported by the National Heart, Lung, and Blood Institute, designed to train school children to cope with pressures to smoke cigarettes, and your work opens some very interesting lines of thought about precisely how much the person is bombarded by cues. Are these interpretations too wild?

Schachter: No, very sane, very sensible. I'm fascinated to hear you make that analogy to smoking because I've been working on that for the last three years.

Evans: The big problem is taking the work of a person like yourself, a very rigorous scientist looking at these things carefully, and then extrapolating to the larger problems. We were considering your work and making generalizations that might be put into antismoking spots on television, for example.

Schachter: I now believe that these findings on external cues and eating don't generalize in smoking; but to get into the eating and obesity business, the gist of what we found on obesity is pessimistic indeed if you're in the therapy business, and helps explain why recidivism is so astonishingly high with the obese. Almost any treatment is effective in the beginning, and why shouldn't it be? All you have to do is cut down eating a little bit and you must lose weight—God says so. But the recidivism rate is an astonishing 90 percent. It seems to be the case that the obese eat in terms of environmental cues rather than in terms of satisfying any particular physiological need, and the world is full of food cues. If a cue triggers eating, then if a person is exposed to food cues, he'll eat. And with the world built as it is, it's almost impossible to avoid food cues. The behavior modifiers, as you might guess, love these findings because they imply that for the obese the stimulus world is what triggers the eating behavior, and for B. F. Skinner (Evans 1968) all that would have to follow is to extinguish the connection between the food stimulus and the eating response. Problem is, how do you extinguish a world of food cues?

Evans: This obesity work has caught the imagination of almost everyone who's obese, of course. Thinking about the problem of these findings, you seem to see this person surrounded by almost an overload of food cues. In addition to that, there is the question of why some people will and will not eat, reacting to these cues. Some of us respond more than others. Have you conceptualized something that would account for distinctions like this? Do we learn to respond to cues as a function of something going on internally or for other reasons?

Schachter: The genesis of it hasn't really been my concern, but there are two ways to look at it. Hilda Bruch (1971) thinks that you are taught to respond to the world too often by being rewarded with food. She's an analyst, and she's done extensive work with the juvenile obese. She says that all her obese patients have a mama who is the comedian's version of the Jewish mama—if the baby cries, give him a cookie; if he's cold, give him a cookie; if he comes in upset because he's had a fight with another kid, give him something to eat. The consequence, she suggests, of raising kids in this manner is a dissociation between the internal physiological state and the actual act of eating. Such people eat in response to *any* disturbing situation, rather than in response to a state of true physiological hunger.

Evans: Has the notion been supported by any of your own work, or have you approached this problem in other ways?

Schachter: I suppose Bruch's ideas are plausible enough, particularly if you're inclined to learning theory, but in my work I haven't been following up her developmental ideas. In the last work I did on obesity, I had grown intrigued by some of the remarkable resemblances between the behavior of obese human beings and the behavior of animals that have been made obese by a lesion made in that part of the hypothalamus called the ventromedial area. I don't know what the hell to make of these parallels. Is there something about the structure of the obese person, some strange muck-up in his hypothalamus that means he is particularly responsive to cues? The only evidence is the tempting kind of analogy that exists between this particular animal preparation and the obese human being, and the analogy has paid off in a fair amount of experimental work. So you have two views—the analyst's view that mama made them that way, and the physiologist's view that there are some human beings who are going to be fat because that's how God built them.

Evans: Is there anything specific in your work that a student might read that develops more fully the ideas you've briefly presented here?

Schachter: The best place for the work on the external cue determination of the behavior of the obese human is a book I wrote called *Emotion, Obesity and Crime* (1971a). The work on the parallels between the lesioned animal and the obese human is presented in a paper that I did for the *American Psychologist* (1971b) called "Some Extraordinary Facts About Obese Humans and Rats."

Evans: Moving from obesity to smoking, you said that you believe that this is not an analogous situation. It would be interestng to have you discuss more fully some of your ideas about smoking behavior and why it doesn't exactly parallel the work you did on obesity.

Schachter: The parallel doesn't hold up because one is tempted to assume casually that the heavy smoker is like the obese eater. If anything, though, the reverse is the case. One of my former students, Peter Herman, compared the effects of smoking cues, as well as of nicotine deprivation, on the smoking behavior of heavy and light smokers. It turned out that smoking cues, such as the sight of someone else lighting up, have far stronger effects on light than on heavy smokers. Heavy smokers seem to smoke largely in terms of the amount of nicotine in them. I got absorbed with some of the physiological implications of Herman's findings on heavy smokers, and that's what I'm working on now. The first thing I did was to run a study using heavy and light smokers. I gave them each a carton or two of cigarettes—one week they'd get a very low-nicotine cigarette and the next week a very high one—and then I simply asked them every day how many cigarettes they had left. We found that the heavy smokers smoked a great deal more when they were on the low-nicotine cigarettes. This is a finding that has amusing implications for the frequent suggestion that if heavy smokers are unable to give up the habit, they should at least switch to low-nicotine cigarettes. From these findings, you'd suspect that if they did so, they'd end up smoking more cigarettes, they'd get about the same amount of nicotine, and since they're smoking more, get far more of the combustion products.

Evans: Let's look more specifically at why these cues break down. One would have to hypothesize that addiction, habituation, enters in some way. Addiction or habituation can obviously be reinforced by something like nicotine, or for that matter, sugar, anything that is perceived by the person in some unusually satisfying way. Are people addicted to cigarettes in the same sense they're addicted to hard narcotics?

Schachter: It depends on what you mean by addiction. If you mean that the absence of the presumed addicting agent leads to withdrawal symptoms—that people suffer if they don't have it—and if you mean that people track the amount of the addicting agent—that is, if they have only a small amount of it in their system, they will go through hell and high water to get more—then that is the essence of the experiment I just described. The people who smoked low-nicotine cigarettes—and they didn't know that's what they were getting—smoked more cigarettes. There is something that knows how much nicotine is in the system, and when the system is deprived of the amount to which it is accustomed, there are signals that say, "Smoke, light another cigarette." I do tend to see smoking as an addiction, nicotine as an addiction, and that's why it's not in any way an easy thing to treat.

Evans: Perhaps you could describe some of the physiological effects of smoking, of nicotine, on the body, as you see it.

Schachter: Rather than do that, let me tell you what happens to nicotine when you smoke. We know that when one lights a cigarette and inhales, the nicotine is picked up by the network of blood vessels in the lungs, goes first to the brain, and then it's distributed around the body. The liver metabolizes nicotine, and the kidneys flush out the metabolites, as well as some raw, unmetabolized nicotine. That's the way the body copes with it. Nicotine is an alkaloid, and it turns out that the rate at which you get rid of nicotine depends to some degree on the pH, or the acidity, of the urine. If you have very acid urine, you simply pee out far larger quantities of unmetabolized nicotine than you do if you have an alkaline urine. Given this fact, in one of our experiments we attempted to manipulate the acidity of the urine by having the subjects take either bicarbonate of soda, which is a very effective alkalizer, or vitamin C, a safe acidifier, or a placebo. Then we kept a systematic record, over a period of weeks, of how much the subjects smoked. We did find that they smoked about 20 percent more than when they were on vitamin C. We were also able to show that this is true of other acidifying agents as well, so these results aren't due to some magical property of vitamin C but do appear to be associated with acidification. Given these facts about the metabolic rate of nicotine, let's turn back to psychology and ask why and when do smokers think they smoke? If you ask them, most smokers will tell you that they smoke more when they're tense or anxious. And it's true; in an experiment designed to test this we found that smokers smoke about 50 percent more when they're anxious than when they're calm. Now the question is why? Most psychologists tend to interpet this fact in terms of the reinforcing or anxiety-producing properties of smoking. For the analysts, for example, it's all oral dependence. Presumably it all starts at mama's teat, and anxiety reactivates the suckling impulse and so you smoke. For the learning people, smoking under stress is somehow reinforcing and anxiety-reducing. Well, maybe, but let's look at another possibility and ask, What is the effect of such presumed psychological determinants of smoking as stress on the machinery that we know controls nicotine metabolism?

Evans: That's a very interesting approach. What experiments were you able to set up to look at this problem from both a psychological and a physiological point of view?

Schachter: The first thing we did was a series of studies that examined the effect of anxiety on urinary pH. In experiment after experiment we got the same result. The urine is more acid when people are frightened than when they're calm. So now we have two facts—stress increases smoking and also increases urinary acidity; which is still a long way, of course, from proving that urinary acidity causes the increased smoking observed in stress, but at least such a hypothesis now becomes a possibility. In order to get at the causal chain we designed an experiment in which we deliberately pitted psychology against urinary acidity. We manipulated stress so that half our subjects were frightened and the other half calm. At the same time we manipulated urinary acidity by having half of the subjects take a placebo and the other half bicarbonate of soda. Bicarbonate is an alkalizing agent which stabilizes pH or the degree of acidity so that for a time nothing short of drinking a glass of vinegar will increase acidity. The results were fascinating. In the placebo conditions, frightened subjects had a more acid urine than calm subjects and they also smoked considerably more. In the bicarbonate conditions, the stress manipulation had no effect on acidity and no effect on smoking. With bicarbonate in them, frightened subjects smoke no more than calm subjects. Given this pattern of results, it's a little difficult to take purely psychological explanations of smoking very seriously.

Evans: You're research is very persuasive. I think this should be an interesting field for a student who's looking at the problems in psychophysiology. It's a very tough area, though.

Schachter: There's no such thing as a tough area. An area's tough only if you don't have an idea.

Evans: In your book, *Emotion, Obesity and Crime* (Schachter 1971a), why did you relate emotion to obesity and crime?

Schachter: It's an offshoot of some of the emotion-adrenaline experiments that we had done, which in turn came out of the affiliation studies. One of the reasons people want to be with others is so they can evaluate their own reactions and feelings in a disturbing situation. That's obviously saying there's a cognitive component in an emotion. So we embarked on a line of research in which we tried again to manipulate independently the physiological and the psychological. We used injections of adrenaline which forces the body to respond in the way it normally does when you're emotional, and then we put the subject either in a situation that was frightening, or in one that should make him euphoric. Subjects with adrenaline tend to react more emotionally than those with placebo, whether the situation is one designed to make them angry or to make them euphoric. In control conditions, if you make the situation such that they know exactly how they feel and why—that their heart is beating faster because you have given them an injection of adrenaline—then they don't react emotionally at all. The gist of the study was that these two factors—physiological and cognitive—interact in determining any emotional state at all.

Evans: You then applied these findings to several areas of study, as I recall—cheating, pain perception, and others. Is this how the "crime" part came in?

Schachter: The crime part came in when we asked what effect adrenaline—something that tends to block the endogenous activity of the sympathetic nervous system—would have on an anxiety-producing situation like cheating. By manipulating the degree of anxiety and fear by the arousal of the sympathetic nervous system, you should be able to manipulate the likelihood that a crime will or will not be committed. We blocked off the action of the autonomic nervous system, presuming that autonomic arousal is the physiologic component of fear. We found that about twice the proportions of subjects cheated when they had taken the tranquilizing and sympatholytic agent chlorpromazine as when they'd taken the placebo. This is an interesting alternative explanation for the frequent observation students make that they do much better on exams when they take a tranquilizer.

Evans: Again, the big problem is extrapolation of this to larger problems. How could this be done?

Schachter: We did it directly. We went into prisons and tried to identify criminal psychopaths, the type that, clinically, have been labeled chronically bad boys. Cleckley (1955) in his book, *The Mask of Sanity* describes them as people who are emotionally flat. They don't have any great joys or any particular fears. Cleckley hypothesizes, and David Lykken (1957) produced some data that demonstrate that this kind of person is anxiety-free. Perhaps the reason they are chronic criminals is that anxiety is one of the chief inhibitors of being a crook. We replicated some of Lykken's work on the inability of the psychopath to learn to avoid pain. When they are injected with adrenaline, however, the physiological correlates of anxiety are forced on them, and they appear to learn pain-avoidance. The data are tentative but potentially wildly intriguing.

Evans: In conclusion, Dr. Schachter, which of the many contributions that you've made do you consider to be the most important?

Schachter: The one that has the most theoretical significance is the adrenaline-emotion study I just described. But of all the work I've done, the project that I've found the most fun is this series of studies of smoking. I confess, I adore the idea of reducing apparently complicated psychological phenomena to the pH of the urine.

Evans: Are there any particular criticisms of your work that have troubled you, in the sense that you think they are basically unfair?

Schachter: I tend to get criticism from people who seem to feel that a social psychologist shouldn't get involved in physiological problems. Some of the criticism is fair; some of it is silly. Probably the silliest was an attack on the fact that I measured heart rate by putting my fingers on a subject's wrist rather than plastering him with electrodes and wiring him into a cardiotachometer.

Evans: Are you fairly optimistic about this present line of research?

Schachter: I'm immensely excited about this tie-up between smoking and the chemistry of the body as it copes with nicotine. I do like the idea of being able to reduce presumably complex phenomena to small ones.

Evans: Do you feel that these conclusions will be borne out, replicated?

Schachter: We've done so many experiments on the subject by now, that it's hard to believe that we could be seriously wrong. That's a little extreme, but we keep finding these things, and they tie together.

Evans: What I'm really trying to get at is this, that as someone moves into a line of research that is very unique and creative and in the early stages looks very positive and then five years later, someone does another piece of research and knocks it out. I want our students to share with you, as you move through these stages, what goes on in your mind. Do you maintain an optimistic mood, or do you say it might turn up to be wrong?

Schachter: Oh, on any of these I could be wrong. I sometimes think that there isn't any finding at all of psychology, my own findings, God knows, included, which *someone* won't fail to replicate. Replication is a problem that bugs me. Someday let's have a conversation about that.

Evans: It's remarkable to me that you, as a sort of neophyte, could move into this field and in a relatively short span, come up with what seems to be breakthrough constructs. The idea that this could happen is, in itself, exciting. This may illustrate the need for something other than very limited specialized training.

Schacter: It's hard to talk about some of these things without sounding pompous. But if I were forced to give advice, I'd say, get problem-oriented, follow your nose and go where problems lead you. Then if something opens up that's interesting and that requires techniques and knowledge with which you're unfamiliar, learn them.

REFERENCES

Bruch, H. 1971. Eating disorders in adolescence. In *The psychopathology of adolescence,* eds. J. Zubin and A. M. Freedman. New York: Grune and Stratton.

Cleckley, H. 1955. *The mask of sanity.* 3rd ed. St. Louis: Mosby.

Evans, R. I. 1968. *B. F. Skinner: The man and his ideas.* New York: Dutton.

Hebb, D. 1949. *The organization of behavior.* New York: Wiley.

Latané, B., and Darley, J. M. 1970. *The unresponsive bystander: Why doesn't he help?* New York: Appleton.

Lykken, D. 1957. A study of anxiety in the sociopathic personality. *J. Abnorm. Soc. Psychol.* 55: 6–10.

McClelland, D., et al. 1953. *The achievement motive.* New York: Appleton.

Murray, H., et al. 1938. *Explorations in personality.* New York: Oxford.

Schachter, S. 1959. *The psychology of affiliation.* Stanford, Calif.: Stanford University Press.

_____. 1971a. *Emotion, obesity and crime.* New York: Academic Press.

_____. 1971b. Some extraordinary facts about obese humans and rats. *Amer. Psychol.* 26: 129–44.

SELECTED READINGS

Festinger, L., Schachter, S., and Back, K. 1950. *Social pressures in informal groups.* New York: Harper & Brothers.

Schachter, S. 1959. *The psychology of affiliation.* Stanford, Calif.: Stanford University Press.

Schachter, S. 1971. *Emotion, obesity and crime.* New York: Academic Press.

Schachter, S. 1971. Some extraordinary facts about obese humans and rats. *Amer. Psychol.* 26: 129–44.

14

ALBERT BANDURA

(1925–   )

Albert Bandura graduated from the University of British Columbia in 1949 and received the Ph.D. from The State University of Iowa in 1952. As a clinical psychologist he recognized the need to examine the clinical behavior modification process more precisely. Based on Hullian learning theory, Skinnerian theory, and the concepts of modeling and imitation, his landmark research has resulted in a broader, more socially oriented approach to behavior modification which he calls social learning theory. His work on aggression illustrates the application of these concepts in a particularly clear manner. A recipient of a Guggenheim Fellowship (1972-1973) and a past president of the American Psychological Association (1974), Professor Bandura joined the faculty of Stanford University in 1953 where he is David Jordan Starr Professor of Social Science in Psychology.

Imprinted on an Experimental Model/A Better Empirical Base/More Effective Procedures//Models/Effective Tutors/Inhibitors and Disinhibitors/Cues for Action/Imitation/Identification/Modeling /Observational Learning/A Cognitive Process/Action and Consequence/An Awareness of the Relationship/Directly Observed or Self-Produced Models/The Judgmental Process//Environmental and Personal Determinism/The Reciprocal Influence Model/ Generalizing and Maintaining Change/Functional Value/Environmental Support/Self-Evaluation//Aggression/Three Views/Example/Experience/Interaction/Controlling Aggression/A Very Contemporary Example//Moral Codes and Moral Conduct/Dissociation and Self-Exonerating Mechanisms/Humanizing and Personalizing/Not a Fixed Regulator But a System//The Worth of a Theory/Translating Theory Into Practice//

As we begin our discussion, Dr. Bandura explains that he was first attracted toward a clinical program with a strong experimental em-

phasis, and tells of his early interest in developing adequately assessed methods of psychotherapy. He recalls some of the early influences that led to his conceptualization of social learning theory, and to his research in modeling and aggression. He distinguishes between modeling, imitation, and identification, and elaborates on modeling and observational learning, emphasizing the importance of cognitive processes. He then describes the complex range of consequences that affect human behavior and the interrelationship of directly experienced consequences, vicarious or observed consequences, and self-produced consequences. We discuss his reciprocal influence model of behavior control and the contingencies of that control, and he analyzes the conditions under which behavior change is effected and maintained. We then turn to his work on aggression, and after a brief review of the traditional theories, Dr. Bandura presents a concise summary of his theory of aggression, making a particularly relevant connection with the depiction of violence in the mass media. We discuss his work on the social learning view of moral codes, self-exonerating mechanisms, and self-evaluation. In conclusion, he reacts to criticisms generated by his work and emphasizes again his strong interest in converting theory to practice: "The worth of a theory is ultimately judged by the power of the change procedures it produces. Psychologists are skillful at developing theories but rather slow in translating them into practice."

Evans: Dr. Bandura, your career typifies the diversity of many of our most creative contemporary psychologists. You were trained in clinical psychology; you have demonstrated crucial innovations in the area of learning; you have looked at subtle types of motivational problems relating to aggression, and more recently, you've been looking at aggression defined in terms of morality and moral codes. To begin, what were the things that attracted you to clinical psychology?

Bandura: Well, I did my graduate work at Iowa where you get imprinted on an experimental model very effectively. I was most interested in seeing how one can begin to provide a better empirical base for clinical practice. I had a strong interest in conceptualizing clinical phenomena in ways that would make them amenable to experimental test, with the view that as practitioners, we have a responsibility for assessing the efficacy of our procedures, so that people are not subjected to treatments before we know their effects. Because there is no evidence that psychotherapy kills or maims people, it is easy to adopt a casual approach of applying methods before they have been adequately assessed. I entertained a three-stage process for the development of psychotherapeutic practices. First, we should try to understand the basic mechanisms by which change is effected; secondly, that knowledge should enable us to devise preliminary treatment methods; and only after we have some evidence of the effects of those procedures, should we apply them on a clinical level. Having that kind of model of practice, I was attracted to a program with a strong experimental emphasis oriented toward the development of more effective psychological procedures.

Evans: At Iowa, of course, you were influenced by Kenneth Spence (1956), who had worked with Clark Hull (1943, 1951, 1952) at Yale. Neal Miller, who was also influenced by Hull, attempted to conceptualize clinical constructs in more empirical, experimental terms in his work on social learning and imitation. Were you influenced by this line of thinking?

Bandura: I was very much influenced by the Miller and Dollard writings, and I was intrigued by the book, *Social Learning and Imitation* (Miller and Dollard 1941). That was a stimulus for some of my early work. I became interested in broadening the notion of vicarious experience and the range of phenomena that could be explained through a social learning approach. I distinguish between the diverse effects of exposure to models. Models function as effective tutors in transmitting new forms of behavior. They serve as inhibitors or disinhibitors in that observing the actions of models and the consequences of those actions can increase or reduce restraints in observers. Models can also serve as cues for actions—in the social-facilitation effect, the model's behavior guides the actions of others.

Evans: Miller used the term *imitation,* and Freud, *identification.* In your use of the term *modeling* you imply distinctions. Could you clarify these terms, which may be confusing to beginning students?

Bandura: Imitation, in the minds of most people, means response mimicry—the exact duplication of what the model does. The term carries a very narrow connotation. Identification usually implies a wholesale incorporation of patterns of behavior. I use the term modeling because the psychological effects of exposure to models are much broader than the simple response mimicry implied by the term imitation; and the defining characteristics of identification are too diffuse, arbitrary, and empirically questionable either to clarify issues or to aid scientific inquiry. The more interesting effect of modeling is what I call "abstract modeling." From observing examples, people, derive general rules and principles of behavior which permit them to go beyond what they see and hear.

Evans: The ethologists, Lorenz (Evans 1975) and Tinbergen, for example, have observed imitation at an animal level for many years, and find it very apparent there. The distinctions between imitation at the animal level and what you call modeling at the human level are very important, are they not?

Bandura: Modeling and observational learning involve, in large part, cognitive processes. Cognitive functions become especially important in delayed modeling, because the modeling influence is gone and you have to represent it in some way, then use that representation as a guide for action on later occasions. Most animal research is restricted to instantaneous imitation. The model serves as a direct cue for a simple response that the animal already has in its repertoire. Few animal studies involve delayed imitation. One could conduct a comparative analysis: the higher the species, the more capable it should be of delayed imitation, because whenever you have delay, there is need for symbolic representation. In humans, most observational learning occurs in the absence of performance. We observe a pattern of behavior, and have no opportunity during observation to enact it or experience its consequences. It is only later that we may exhibit what we have learned. Emphasis is placed on the human capacity for symbolization of experience because it is the representation that remains after the model is gone. The symbol serves as the guide for action. In modeling one is dealing with complex cognitive processes. I would conceptualize observational learning as essentially a cognitive process, and our theories of learnings are moving in a more cognitive direction. Operant conditioning in humans can be viewed as an instance of observational learning. You observe the consequences of your actions, and on the basis of that information, you get some idea of what behavior is appropriate in what setting. In the case of modeling, the information is derived from example. In operant conditioning, the response information is derived from the pattern of consequences to actions. Some theorists have attempted to reduce observational learning to an operant paradigm. I consider learning through response to consequences as an instance of observational learning.

Evans: B. F. Skinner (Evans 1968) took what were some of Thorndike's (1932) most fundamental ideas and expanded them in a very brilliant way, introducing this whole concept of operant conditioning. He demonstrated how it operates at the animal level in a very dramatic way, and then demonstrated that these same principles operate at the human level. One of the major criticisms leveled at Skinner is that he took principles designed and tested on lower animals and, almost literally, used them at the human level. But you're saying that in humans you cannot ignore cognition in the sense that Skinner did. Do I understand you correctly?

Bandura: Yes. The literature on human conditioning indicates that representation of the connection between action and consequence is an important determinant of whether or not a change will occur. If there is no awareness of the relationship, there is very little change effected. Cognition also plays an important role in mediating the effects of consequences where belief is pitted against actual consequences. There can be a tremendous variation in responsiveness under different beliefs, but with the same objective consequences for action. Expanding the range of consequences that affect human behavior adds complexity to the influence process.

Evans: Would you elaborate on that?

Bandura: People do not act as isolates. They operate as social beings

who see the consequences occurring to others. These observed consequences also provide a standard for judging whether the direct consequences are equitable. Depending on the schedule by which others are reinforced, your own direct experiences can be perceived as punishing, as
rewarding, or as neutral. A third source of reinforcement is the capacity
of humans for self-reaction. People adopt certain standards of conduct
and respond to their own behavior in self-approving or self-disapproving
ways, depending on whether their behavior exceeds or falls below their
standards. In the analysis of how behavior is regulated by consequences,
one must be concerned with the complex interrelationship of directly experienced consequences, vicarious or observed consequences, and self-
produced consequences.

Evans: Can you give us some examples of how these are interrelated?

Bandura: Consider the complex relationship between directly experienced consequences and self-generated consequences. You might have a
situation where a person would be generously rewarded for behavior
that produces self-condemning reactions. When one's own self-evaluation reactions outweigh the power of the externally administered ones,
the external consequences will not effect a change. If the external consequences are powerful, you get cheerless compliance. Other conflicts arise
when external punishment of behavior is a source of self-pride. The conditions under which external consequences are most likely to effect
change are when they are compatible with self-reinforcement, when the
behavior is socially approved and is a source of self-satisfaction, or when
the behavior is externally punished and is self-disapproved. In any for-
malization of theory, one would need to work on the interrelationships
of these three systems rather than focusing solely on how directly experienced consequences influence behavior.

Evans: I believe you expanded these ideas very effectively in your
book, *Principles of Behavior Modification* (Bandura 1969). It would be
interesting to hear Skinner's reactions to this. In a very basic way, you're
looking at a much broader range of reinforcers, defining consequences in
a much more subtle way. You're really challenging his notion that mental
processes are irrelevant to a science of behavior. What do you think his
reactions would be, or have you had some reactions?

Bandura: One reaction might be that these are processes that could be
externalized. If one subscribes to the view that behavior is governed by
external events, one might attempt to externalize these processes and
place them in the environment. In the case of observed reinforcement one
might characterize it, from an operant point of view, from the viewpoint
that rewards and punishments to others are discriminative stimuli for action. Externalization ignores the judgmental processes involved. I am
more interested in setting up experimental procedures to measure these
processes, to manipulate them independently, and to see how they
govern behavior. In the case of observational learning, we have studied
some of these symbolic processes in ways that are manipulated instruc-
tionally. We obtain an independent measure of their presence. It turns

out that cognitive functions do exercise a powerful control over behavior.

Evans: Perhaps the strict behavior modifiers—the so-called ''behavior modification movement''—have been too literal, more literal than Skinner ever expected, at the human level. They began to effect short-term changes, but in the long run, the modified behavior just didn't continue. For example, we are currently involved in a massive study of smoking behavior, beginning with children who have never started to smoke, rather than working with the confirmed smoker. We have what we believe is an effective behavioral measure, and we're trying to enter this idea in such a way that the permanent change we get will be the ability to cope with the pressures to smoke, so that smoking behavior is never started. Our survey of the literature indicates that behavior modification in this case has only a short-term effect; that as long as the person is under the control of the experimenter, the behavior may be controlled, but once that external control is gone, the person regresses. The issue seems to be that of shifting from external and internal control. Essentially, this seems to be a powerful challenge to behavioral science, and it would be interesting to hear how, from your system, we might attempt intervention and move from external to internal control.

Bandura: I favor a reciprocal influence model. Environmental determinism implies that behavior is governed solely by environmental conditions; therefore, if you produce a change in behavior but fail to alter the environment, the behavior will be short-lived. Personal determinism assumes that the individual is the source of all control of behavior. Both positions are extreme ones. Reciprocal determinism assumes that behavior is controlled both through personal and environmental means. One can therefore designate the conditions under which behavior change will generalize and be sustained over time, and the conditions under which it will not. If the treatment is aimed at producing functional skills, these usually persist because they have value for the individual. Procedures used to instill a pattern of behavior that is of convenience to the reinforcing agent but of no functional value to the recipient of the influence do not usually produce sustained results. I don't see that as a regrettable state of affairs. If change agents could, through brief application of reinforcement procedures, instill patterns of behavior that would persist after those procedures were removed, they could enslave people. I do not view generalization and maintenance necessarily as an unmitigated virtue.

Evans: That's a very interesting point. You're saying, in a sense, that it's better to allow a few people to be overweight, to keep smoking, to go around with neuroses, that it's better to have these checks and balances to experimental control that's too easy?

Bandura: In analyzing change processes, one must distinguish between induction of behavior change, its generalization, and its maintenance. One condition under which change is maintained is when that behavior has functional value for the person. A second maintaining condition exists when there are strong environmental supports for behavior, even though it may not have much functional value for the individual. Sometimes society decides to set up contingencies that foster behavior for the common good, even though it may be inconvenient for the individual. One's own self-evaluation also becomes an important reinforcer, particularly in those activities which we engage in for their own sake. Originally, such activities did not hold much interest. For example, blowing a tuba is not intrinsically reinforcing for most people, but to a tuba artist, a skillful tuba performance could be a tremendous source of reinforcement. To develop this kind of reinforcement requires skill acquisition, adoption of standards of excellence of performance, and investment of the activity with self-evaluative significance. Signs of progress then serve as sources of personal satisfaction. Performances that fall short of the standard motivate performance until improvement is achieved. Self-reinforcement for that activity is self-provided. Under such conditions, a self-reinforcement for that activity is self-provided. Under such conditions, a self-reinforcement system can sustain a tremendous amount of tuba blowing in the absence of any external reinforcement. So self-reinforcement is another maintenance system. In the more difficult areas where a pattern of behavior is immediately rewarding with delayed detrimental consequences, such as overeating, smoking, etc., one is involved in the difficult task of helping people acquire some capacity to control their own behavior. The research on self-control provides the most promising approach to self-management of detrimental behavior.

Evans: As a social psychologist, some questions have always bothered me, and your work in some of these areas has been particularly fascinating. What about the social influences that are involved in destructive behavior, not only suicide and war, but in the progressive self-destructive behavior that's involved in ignoring cardiovascular and cancer risk factors in such behavior as smoking, etc., and in alcoholism, which is becoming an increasing problem among our youth? I'm sure you're familiar with all these areas, and others, and I'm wondering if there is some tie-in here to the whole area of aggressive behavior. Was it this kind of thinking that led you into your work on aggression, or was it a logical outgrowth of some of the other things you had been doing?

Bandura: I originally began studying aggression in children. Dick Walters and I conducted field studies on the familial antecedent of aggression, and we found that the best predictors were not the frustration determinants, but the life styles that the families exemplified and reinforced. The behavior that the parents modeled and the attitudes they exhibited toward the expression of aggression, both in the home and outside it, emerged as important determinants.

These studies suggested that modeling influences and reinforcement patterns were critical determinants in extreme forms of aggression. This led to laboratory studies and the development of modeling paradigms to examine systematically the effects of exposure to aggressive models on children's behavior. In the course of this research, I became more interested in the general issue of observational learning and modeling, but I'm in the habit of working on several different things at the same time—I find that more interesting and challenging than working only in one area.

Evans: That's obvious!

Bandura: I became fascinated with issues of observational learning and the processes and mechanisms by which this occurs. But I never gave up my interest in trying to formulate an alternative view of aggression. There are, essentially, three views. The instinct theory contends that man is innately endowed with aggressive energy.

Evans: The view Konrad Lorenz took in his controversial book *On Aggression* (1966) when he described man as a dangerous aggressor. In our discussion (Evans 1975) he emphasized this point again, and also talked about his dream of seeing these aggressive forces directed toward socially useful, creative ways. And of course, Freud had a tremendous interest in this area.

Bandura: Freud, of course. The second view is the reactive drive theory, in which the aggressive drive is instigated by frustrating environmental conditions. Frustration is ever-present; man is burdened by aggressive drives which he must discharge, hopefully in ways that are not interpersonally injurious. The frustration-aggression theory (Dollard, et al. 1939) is still very popular, even though it does not fit well with the cumulative evidence. We know that frustration has diverse effects on behavior. You don't need frustration to aggress. Much human aggression is based on anticipated benefits of the aggression rather than the push of distress. And the term frustration has been stretched to the point where it no longer has any particular meaning. The approach that interests me looks at aggression as a style of behavior that is acquired through observation, through direct experience, and is, to some extent, influenced by structural biological factors. A theory of aggression must explain three things: How is the behavior acquired? What instigates aggressive action? What sustains the behavior over time? In my conceptualization, aggressive behavior is acquired through example, through direct experience, and through interaction with structural factors. People are instigated to aggression by modeling influences, by seeing others aggress. They are instigated through aversive experiences—personal insults, physical assaults, thwarting of goal-directed behavior, adverse reductions in the quality of life. Then there is obedient aggression; people are trained to obey orders, and they are willing to aggress when legitimate authorities who possess coercive power instruct them to aggress. Some aggression, of course, is provoked by bizarre beliefs.

Then there are the regulators of aggressive behavior. Aggression is maintained by many different factors. First it's maintained by external consequences—material rewards, social and status rewards. Some people are reinforced by signs of injury in the victim. Aggression is also reinforced when people alleviate punitive treatment by defensive recourse. Performance of aggression is affected by observed rewards or punishment—vicarious reinforcement. One must also consider the role of punishment in the regulation of behavior. The reason that deterrent procedures often do not work well is because when people have limited options, and the benefits of successful aggression are high, people don't discard aggression under risk of punishment. They simply refine the behavior to increase its chances of success. Self-reinforcement likewise serves as a regulator because aggressors have to contend with themselves as well as with others. This is where the role of moral codes comes in. From the social learning point of view, the origin, instigation, and regulation of aggression is a complex process.

Evans: Let's discuss, for a moment, the effect of models of aggression—obviously a great concern of society. There are differing points of view, for example, about the effect of aggressive behavior, or violence, as it is depicted in the mass media. One point of view suggests that watching professional football games or violent drama on television allows persons to extinguish aggression vicariously. Another group argues that such viewing tends to instigate aggressive acts. From your rather sophisticated analysis, it seems that such conclusions are too simplistic. It's just not that simple, is it?

Bandura: The evidence indicates that in general, exposure to aggression tends to increase, rather than to reduce, aggression, but since aggression is controlled by so many different factors, predictions about the effects of modeling must consider all these different determinants. It involves a qualified judgment.

Evans: You've looked at this problem as intricately as anyone in contemporary psychology, and your book on aggression (Bandura 1973) is rapidly becoming a classic. Suppose you were asked by a government agency, for example, about the advisability of some form of control in depicting violence in the mass media. All things being equal, would you recommend such control?

Bandura: In the aggression book, I outline four different strategies for trying to reduce commercial modeling of violence on television. The first is congressional control. Congress doesn't have that authority, and to avoid government censorship, few of us would want to grant it that authority. If you go the congressional route, every three or four years a hearing is scheduled. These are like television re-runs—same characters, same plots, same outcomes. The researchers present evidence and the network researchers negate the evidence, and nothing much changes. You have a re-run every few years. Restrictive control is a negative approach. If there is any general principle of behavior change that's well established, it is that change is achieved more effectively through a better alternative than by prohibiting what is disvalued.

Evans: There has been some attempt at industry self-control. How do you see that?

Bandura: That's the second approach, industry self-control. That's largely a joke. Television is used to deliver audiences for marketing purposes, and commercial considerations are very powerful. People have been led to believe that viewers are attracted to violent content. If you examine the ratings, the violent program are usually absent from the top ten. The reason they are so prevalent on television is because the action-adventure format is economical. For a western, all you need is a transient evil-doer, a superhero, a makeshift saloon, and the open range. It's a very attractive proposition economically. Another approach is the development of a system for monitoring the level of violence; the presence of a violence index might reduce excesses. Here you face the tremendous diffusion of responsibility. No one feels personally responsible for what is shown on television. The approach I favor is the development of alternate programming outside the commercial medium, and then using that as a means for influencing commercial television. One improves the quality of programming by providing people with more interesting alternatives, and then influencing commercial television by the tastes developed on noncommercial broadcasting systems.

Evans: Public broadcasting, by and large, has not received the support that would make such programming possible, but ideally, I think what you're describing makes excellent sense. Moving to another area, now, we have a tremendous amount of evidence that we are, somehow, going to be cruel and aggressive toward our fellow man; that we are involved in a duplicity of roles where in one setting we can be cruel and destructive and in another setting kind and considerate. I'm particularly thinking of the studies of Latané and Darley (1970) on bystander apathy, Milgram's (1974) obedience to authority work, Zimbardo, Haney, and Banks (1973) and the prison-simulation study, and others that seem to emphasize this impersonal, cruel, or vicious side of man. I was very pleased to see that you have moved into this question of moral codes, ethics, the morality of aggression.

Bandura: I think the issue raises the fundamental question of the relationship between people's moral codes and principles and their moral conduct. Our traditional theories of morality assume that one adopts a set of moral principles and that these serve as built-in regulators of conduct. If we could only instill the proper moral codes, our society would not be burdened with injurious behavior. From a social learning point of view, moral codes and self-evaluative actions do regulate behavior, but under certain conditions, one can dissociate reprehensible actions from self-sanctions. In fact, through self-exonerating mechanisms one can produce radical shifts in behavior at different times and in different settings without altering moral principles. I have been interested in the methods by which this disengagement process operates. One method is to assign high moral purpose to the activities; through appropriate moral justifications, one can transform aggressive behavior into an honorable activity. Much human cruelty has been perpetrated in the name of religious principles and righteous ideologies. Another method is the palliative comparison process. By comparing one's actions against more heinous deeds, the actions take on a benevolent quality. Moral justification and palliative comparison are especially powerful ways to neutralize moral self-reactions because they convert injurious behavior into positive behavior through cognitive restructuring. Another mechanism is the displacement of responsibility, which was studied by Milgram. As long as authorities are willing to assume responsibility for the consequences of culpable behavior, people feel they are not personally responsible. And then, you can dehumanize the victim. If those who are objects of attack are treated as subhumans, one is less likely to generate moral self-reactions. You can't engage morality if the consequences of your actions are distorted or not assessed. You can also attribute blame to the victim. All of these are mechanisms that enable one to behave injuriously with the same moral principles. We have studied in some detail how self-sanctions are acquired. The disengagement of internal control, which has considerable theoretical and social import, is a more intriguing issue. Our current research is directed at that very question. How does one produce marked variations in moral conduct with the same moral principles?

Evans: You've done research that attempts to move away from the dehumanization that leads to aggression to the opposite end of the spectrum, in the sense that increased humanization would lead to less punishment and aggression. Could you tell us something about that?

Bandura: Many of our social conditions are especially conducive to dehumanization—bureaucratization, automation, urbanization, mobility and social practices that separate people into in-groups and out-groups—all of these produce estrangement and depersonalization. One of the instructive findings in the experiments we have been conducting is that it is difficult to aggress toward people who are humanized and personalized without eliciting self-condemning consequences for such actions.

Evans: The old trick of catching the other driver's eye, when you want to cut in, driving in heavy traffic!

Bandura: I know exactly what you mean. There is another point that I would emphasize here. We tend to use examples from military and political violence. These same mechanisms operate where people are trapped in activities and occupations requiring them to produce products for profit that have dehumanizing effects. The study of these processes in common practices is important because they affect our everyday life, whereas political and military violence are episodic.

Evans: You mentioned earlier conditions under which moral codes are and are not activated. Could you describe an example of this?

Bandura: The most dramatic example would be a general consensus in a country about the morality of war. Given adequate moral justification, people are willing to kill without having to undergo personality transformations. When they are discharged from the military, they are not put through a resocialization process. After they return to civilian life, their internal control system is reengaged. Self-sanctions do not operate as fixed, internal regulators of conduct. Many external factors exercise control over their activation.

Evans: The implications of that for such things as prison reform could be extremely interesting, too. Now, Dr. Bandura, in conclusion, certainly your work must have precipitated some criticism. Which of those criticisms have bothered you, if any?

Bandura: In the early research on aggression, I was criticized for using nonhuman targets for measuring the acquisition of aggressive behavior. Different methodologies are required to assess whether aggressive patterns have been learned and whether these skills will be used for injurious purposes. One does not use live targets to study learning effects. To assess the learning of bombardier skills, one does not bomb New York City. People subscribing to the operant view object to the introduction of cognitive operations into behavioral process. And in the area of aggression, my view differs from the traditional ones. So there's a lot of room for controversy there.

Evans: Yes. I think you've made that clear. Now, what do you have planned for the future?

Bandura: I would like to move in at least four directions—I will continue to examine the processes underlying observational learning; because I believe that it is a fundamental mechanism by which human beings learn, I will pursue my research on component process in self-regulation; I plan to continue the study of aggression, especially the processes by which internal control is selectively activated and disengaged. I am involved in research design to develop the power of modeling for therapeutic purposes. The worth of a theory is ultimately judged by the power of the change procedures it produces. Psychologists are skillful at developing theories, but rather slow in translating them into practice, so I maintain an interest in translating theory and principles into practice.

REFERENCES

Bandura, A., Ross, D., and Ross, S. 1961. Transmission of aggression through imitation of aggressive models. *J. Abnorm. Soc. Psychol.* 63: 575–82.

_____. 1969a. *Principles of behavior modification.* New York: Holt.

_____. 1969b. Social learning of moral judgments. *J. Pers. Soc. Psychol.* 11: 275–79.

_____. 1971. Psychotherapy based upon modeling principles. In *Handbook of psychotherapy and behavior change,* eds. A. Bergin and S. Garfield, pp. 653–708. New York: Wiley.

_____. 1971. *Social learning theory.* New York: General Learning Press.

_____. 1973. *Aggression: A social learning analysis.* Englewood Cliffs, N.J.: Prentice-Hall.

_____. 1973. Institutionally sanctioned violence. *J. Clin. Child Psychol.* 83: 301–03.

Dollard, J., et al. 1939. *Frustration and aggression.* New Haven: Yale University Press.

Evans, R. 1968. *B. F. Skinner: The man and his ideas.* New York: Dutton.

_____. 1975, *Konrad Lorenz: The man and his ideas.* New York: Harcourt.

Hull, C. 1943. *Principles of behavior.* New York: Appleton.

_____. 1951. *Essentials of behavior.* New Haven: Yale University Press.

_____. 1952. A behavior system: an introduction to behavior theory concerning the individual organism. New Haven: Yale University Press.

Latané, B., and Darley, J. 1970. *The unresponsive bystander: Why doesn't he help?* New York: Appleton.

Lorenz, K. 1966. *On aggression.* New York: Harcourt.

Milgram, S. 1974. *Obedience to authority.* New York: Harper.

Miller, N., and Dollard, J. 1941. *Social learning and imitation.* New Haven: Yale University Press.

Spence, K. 1956. *Behavior theory and conditioning.* New Haven: Yale University Press.

Thorndike, E. 1932. *The fundamentals of learning.* New York: Teachers College.

Zimbardo, P., Haney, G., and Banks, C. 1973. Interpersonal dynamics in a simulated prison. *Int. J. Criminol. Penol.* 1: 69–97.

SELECTED READINGS

Bandura, A. 1962. Social learning through imitation. In *Nebraska Symposium on Motivation: 1962,* ed. M. R. Jones. Lincoln: University of Nebraska Press.

Bandura, A. 1969. *Principles of behavior modification.* New York: Holt.

Bandura, A. 1971. *Social learning theory.* New York: General Learning Press.

Bandura, A. (Ed.) 1971. *Psychological modeling.* Chicago: Aldine-Atherton.

Bandura, A. 1973. *Aggression: A social learning analysis.* Englewood Cliffs, N.J.: Prentice-Hall.

Bandura, A., and Walters, R. H. 1963. *Social learning and personality development.* New York: Holt.

15

WILLIAM MCGUIRE

(1925–   )

William McGuire completed his undergraduate work in philosophy and psychology at Fordham College and spent a year studying at the Louvain University in Belgium as a Fullbright Scholar in Philosophy before earning his doctorate in psychology at Yale University in 1954. His probabilogical theory of cognitive structure has formed the basis for much of his important work on resistance to persuasion and attitude change. His work includes contributions in the areas of verbal learning, personality and persuasibility, consumer choice, and self-concept. Dr. McGuire received the Annual Socio-Psychological Award in 1963 from the American Association for the Advancement of Science, and was president of the Division of Personality and Social Psychology of the American Psychological Association in 1973. He has held positions at the University of Minnesota, Columbia University, the University of California at San Diego, and Yale University, where he has been professor of psychology since 1970.

Early Work in Experimental Psychology//Hull/Graduate Research on Verbal Learning//Interest in Epistemological Issues//Cognitive Structure//Post-Doctoral Fellowship with Leon Festinger//The Probabilogic Model/Changes in Beliefs/Socratic Method of Changing Beliefs//Irrationality in People's Thinking/Postulates of a Less Rational Nature//Hedonic Consistency//Alogical Inertia/ Distortions/Varieties of Logic/Inoculation Against Persuasion//The Biological Analogy//Subsequent Developments in Advertising//A Theory about Individual Differences in Persuasibility//Cognitive Psychology//Matrix of Persuasion Model/How Is Intelligence Related to Persuasibility//Stressing a Rational View of the Person/The Prevalent Neglect of the Coherent Aspect of the Person//Laboratory-Oriented Psychology//Stage Managers/Finders/Reporting Circumstances That Both Support and Refute the Hypothesis//Interactionalism//Any Given Hypothesis Is of Limited Validity//

171

We begin our discussion as Dr. McGuire describes his early work in experimental psychology, which, combined with his interests in philosophy and epistemology, led him to social psychology. He outlines the early development of his probabilogical theory of cognitive structure, which he created to describe how one idea leads to another. According to this theory, the person behaves as if he were a logician and probability theorist who maintains a consistency among the subjectively perceived probabilities of his beliefs about the world. Acknowledging that many "irrationalities" enter into our belief systems, he defines his additional postulates of "hedonic consistency" and "alogical inertia." Dr. McGuire and I then discuss the relationship of his cognitive theory to changes in beliefs. He describes research which shows that inducing change in one belief will alter a related belief to restore consistency among subjectively contingent probabilities. McGuire and I then discuss his theory of cognitive inoculation against persuasion, which he based on an analogy to biological inoculation against disease. "I predicted that pre-exposing the believer to a weakened form of the attacking material would stimulate his or her defenses before the massive attack comes." He then responds to my questions about individual differences in persuasibility and he relates this to his input/output matrix of communication. Some of the differences in persuasibility occur because of differences at various levels of communication: attention, comprehension, retention, and yielding. Dr. McGuire concludes by offering his views on research in social psychology. Although he feels that the move from laboratory to more field research has been beneficial, he states, "Any hypothesis is of limited validity. I am proposing that we recognize this limitation and . . . endeavor to discover through empirical research the circumstances under which a given hypothesis is right and under which it is wrong."

Evans: Bill, in looking over your work, it's evident that your very early work was not in the field of social psychology but would best be described as experimental psychology or perhaps learning psychology. What were some of the things that you were doing at that time?

McGuire: Well, I came from a background in philosophy and when I did switch to psychology in graduate school, the behavioral theory approach to learning fascinated me. I became interested in Clark Hull's beautiful theory, with its postulates and corollaries. The idea of applying symbolic logic to psychological theory, I think, was what attracted me into psychology from philosophy. You remember an old book by Hull

(1940) and his colleagues called *Mathematico-Deductive Theory of Rote Learning*. In it they deduced from a few common-sense postulates some nonobvious relationships in memory, like the serial position effect, the reminiscence phenomena, etc. This work got me to apply for the doctoral program of the Yale Psychology Department. The faculty there must have been amused to read in my application that I wanted to work with Hull on applying symbolic logic to the psychology of memory, since Hull had stopped working in this area years before. I am not the last student to have gone to the right place for the wrong reason. My M.A., Ph.D., and other graduate-student research were all on verbal learning. Some of these studies were on practical issues, such as the effects of camera angle, slow motion, etc., on the viewer's learning of motor skills from a filmed model; and some were among the earliest studies on vicarious reinforcement, modeling, and social learning theory. We showed an actor in the film being reinforced or punished, and tested whether this had a hedonic or informational effect on the viewer through vicarious participation (McGuire 1961).

Evans: So your early work came out of your interest in Hullian stimulus-response reinforcement theory. How did this develop into your work in social psychology?

McGuire: A basic interest in epistemological issues lies behind my being attracted to philosophy and then successively to learning and to social psychology. I'm fascinated by questions like why do we notice some things and not others. For example, until this instant I did not notice what color your tie is, even though I've been looking at you for a good while. Why was I registering some of the things I was seeing in you but not others? Answering this "selective perception" question gets one into both basic and social psychology; so does the "cognitive structure" question of how one idea leads to another. I got into this cognitive structure area when as a graduate student I took a course in physiological psychology with Frank Beach. We studied the technique of tracing nerve tracts through the spinal cord by making a lesion and tracing how the neural path deteriorates over time, allowing one to map the spinal cord pathways. This strategy suggested to me an analogous way in which to study how the mind is organized. Why not put a whopping change somewhere in a person's belief system and then trace how this change subsequently spreads to related beliefs? During my third year in graduate school I developed a theory of how the mind works, using logic and probability theory, and used that analogous technique to test the theory and map cognitive structures by introducing a change in the target belief, technically a problem that lies in the "attitude change" area of social psychology. Which explains how I got to be a social psychologist.

Evans: As you moved into social psychology, there was a very important group of social psychologists at Yale led by Carl Hovland. What led you to move over to work with that group, whose research was to become a major thrust of communication theory in psychology?

McGuire: It was a productive group. I can say that without immodesty because I really wasn't a member of it. Though Carl sponsored my learning theory dissertation, I was hardly aware of this communication and attitudes group. My only social course was a tutorial with Leonard Doob that got me interested in group dynamics, so I got a post-doctoral fellowship at the University of Minnesota with Leon Festinger to apply learning theory to group dynamics. Once again, as with Hull, my chosen mentor's interests had moved elsewhere by the time I caught up with him. At Minnesota, Festinger had become interested in dissonance theory. When he heard the term "group dynamics" his eyes would glaze. So I went back to work on my probabilogical theory of cognitive structure. That 1953–1955 work later appeared in my 1960 paper (McGuire 1960). I've just written a chapter (McGuire 1979) reviewing the subsequent work on that probabilogical model by myself, Bob Wyer, and others.

Evans: Now, could you summarize rather briefly the major ideas that you were presenting in this sequence of research, and the model that you developed?

McGuire: Okay. I started with the assumption that when one thinks, one functions as if one were a logician and probability theorist (the probabilogic model per se) with some add-on tendencies like wishful thinking. The logic part says that whether I expect something to happen depends on whether I expect that antecedents which would lead to it will happen. Or to put it in the logic jargon, if I believe in the antecedent, I'll believe in the consequent that follows from it.

Evans: That's the "logic" part. Now what about the probability part of the probabilogical model?

McGuire: The usual systems of logic use a two-value belief scale, true versus false (or 1 versus 0, to put it in numerical terms). But my theory recognizes that people do not simply believe or disbelieve propositions absolutely. If you ask someone if gasoline will cost two dollars a gallon by 1982, the person doesn't say "true" or "false" but, more likely, something like, "It could happen." So in our probabilogical model we ask people to express their belief about such propositions in probability terms. We ask, "What is the probability that gasoline will cost two dollars a gallon by 1982?" If a person thinks this unlikely, he can rate it as .10 or .20 or whatever; if he thinks it rather likely, he can rate its probability as .70 or .80 or whatever.

Evans: How do you use this probabilogical model? Could you give an example of this?

McGuire: Let me use the example I just mentioned to illustrate its use in predicting the person's belief system at any point in time. Suppose I ask the person to rate the probability that she will be doing much less driving in 1982 and also to rate the probability that if gas cost as much as two dollars per gallon she will cut her driving drastically, and also the probability that gas will be costing two dollars per gallon in 1982. The person might express her belief in each of these propositions by rating their probabilities as, say, .10, .60, and .50, respectively. But note that the three propositions form a "syllogistic" argument. That is, the first-mentioned one—cutting one's driving—follows logically from the other two (the price of gas's going up and one's driving being dependent on the price of gas). Let's call the proposition that one will cut one's driving c (as in "conclusion"), and the other two propositions, the premises from which c follows, we'll call a and b. The person's beliefs regarding the three propositions would then be p(c), p(a), and p(b), which represents the subjective probability that each proposition has for the person. Then we need only apply the axioms of probability theory and logic and we can specify that if the person is to be cognitively consistent, these three beliefs must be in the following relationship to one another:

$$p(c) = (a) \, p(b) + (p \, c/ \, (a \, b) \, p \, (a \, b)$$

It may look complicated, but it is easy to derive from probability theory and easy to test by measuring the person's probabilistic beliefs regarding the propositions.

Evans: That describes how you use your probabilogical model to identify inconsistencies in a person's belief system at one point in time. But the more interesting question involves changes in beliefs. Could you explain how your probabilogical model applies to changes in belief systems as, for example, when attitude change is produced by some kind of propaganda or persuasive communication?

McGuire: It applies just as much to attitude change situations as it does to the initial state of the belief systems that we've just been discussing. In fact, before we get to the effect of persuasive messages, let me mention our "Socratic method" of changing beliefs simply by asking questions. The idea here is that the person does have a need for cognitive consistency in her/his belief system but often neglects to think about the related beliefs all at one time, so they get out of line with one another.

Evans: Like in the two dollar gasoline example you just mentioned?

McGuire: That illustrates the situation exactly. In the example, we conjectured that the person reports a low .10 probability that she will be driving substantially less in 1982. And yet she sees a .60 probability of two dollar per gallon gas by then and a .50 probability that two dollar per gallon gas would substantially reduce her driving. The lengthy p(c) equation of the probabilogical model that we've just given shows that her belief system is logically inconsistent: if p(a) and p(b) are .50 and .60, then her p(c) would have to be at least .30 to be logically consistent with p(a) and p(b), since p(a) $\times$ p(b) = .60 $\times$ .50 = .30. Hence, within her own belief system her p(c) value of .10 is much underestimating the .30 value that she would logically have for believing that she would be drastically reducing her driving by 1982. This is exactly the situation where we can use the "Socratic method" of changing opinions simply by asking questions. By asking the person to report on one occasion her beliefs on interrelated propositions like a, b, and c, we find that when we come back the next time and ask for these three beliefs again, the person's probabilistic expectations are closer to that required by the probabilogical model. We have changed the person's beliefs, not by giving her any new information from an outside source but simply from within, by asking questions that direct the person's attention to inconsistencies within her own belief systems. Empirical research confirms the probabilogical model prediction that on the next occasion when we ask this person her belief that she will be driving much less in 1982, we find that her p(c) has been increased somewhat, from .10 to a more consistent .15.

Evans: And besides this "Socratic method" of changing beliefs from within, the probabilogical model also deals with changing beliefs by presenting communications from an outside source, does it not?

McGuire: Yes, it has equal relevance to the persuasive communication, attitude change situation. Suppose we present the person with a message giving various arguments as to why the price of gasoline is going to rise drastically in the next few years (declining U.S. domestic petroleum production, increasing dependence on imports at prices set by the OPEC cartel, increasing demands by other developed and developing nations, etc.). In the usual attitude change research, we would then test how this persuasive message affects the explicit target belief, p(a), the probability that a gallon of gas will cost two dollars by 1982. If p(a) = .60 before the attitude change communication, the argument in the message might increase p(a) to .75 or .80. But in our cognitive consistency approach, we ask a further question: How does this persuasive message explicitly aimed at raising p(a) have additional logical ramifications on p(c) (the person's expectation that she will be driving less), even though this latter issue was never mentioned in the communication.

Evans: And using the axioms of probability theory and logic once again, I assume that your probabilogical model can predict how much of a logical ramification on the conclusion should be produced by the persuasive message.

McGuire: Right. Let's grant that the persuasive communication has some measurable impact on the explicit target premise (that gas will cost two dollars a gallon by 1982), perhaps raising its subjective probability from the initial .60 to a post-communication level of .80 or so. From the probabilogical model we can derive an equation, just a bit more complicated than the one above, that allows us to derive how much the belief in the unmentioned conclusion (about reduced driving) should go up as a result of this communication-induced rise from .60 to .80 in belief in the explicit premise. For example, the probabilogical equation would predict that belief in the driving-less conclusion will rise from its initial .10 level to .15 due to the Socratic effect, even without any persuasive message, and then further to .25 due to the communication-induced change in the explicit premise. Empirical research (McGuire 1979) pretty much supports these probabilogical predictions.

Evans: In a sense, the operations you're describing are not unlike the kind of model out of which Piaget works (Evans 1971). You assume that there's a logical substratum underlying the person's thinking processes.

McGuire: Oh yes, I don't mind being associated with Piaget. I suppose I would in this respect be classified with the structuralists.

Evans: Now, how do you account for what appears to be irrationality in people's thinking, which is stressed in so much of social psychology? A lot of the research shows that there's very little correlation between the strength of our beliefs and the amount of information we have. How do you account for these apparent inconsistencies?

McGuire: Well, like in court, by pleading guilty with an explanation. The probabilogical model per se postulates extreme rationality, but our total theory (McGuire 1960, 1979) includes a number of add-on postulates of a less rational nature. For example, I also added a hedonic consistency assumption, that people like to keep their expectation of a conclusion (like having to cut one's driving drastically by 1982) in line with their desire about that conclusion (as well as in line with their expectations on premises that lead to the conclusion, as assumed by the probabilogical model). I also postulated inertial phenomena such that while the person's belief on the conclusion is chained to beliefs about the premises, the chain isn't pulled taut. Hence, a persuasive message of whatever has got to pull the premise belief a little distance before it begins to exert a pull on the conclusions that follow from it. These add-on assumptions, like wishful thinking and cognitive inertia, help account for the nonrationalities that sometimes appear in people's belief systems.

However, the empirical research has actually left me somewhat embarrassed by the success of the probabilogical part of the theory. The additional assumptions about alogical inertia, etc., have improved predictive power a little, but so little that they hardly seem worth adding. Research on this theory has shown that people's belief systems behave remarkably logically. At least this is so when one analyzes grouped data. Perhaps we all think weirdly, but each of us has a different weirdness so that one person's alogicality cancels out another person's opposite alogicality. If so, the strong appearance of logicality may be a group outcome of compensating individual quirks.

Evans: Let's be more concrete. Let's take racial prejudice in the United States. One reason for prejudice might be that there is some selective social reinforcement for it. People who think that blacks are unintelligent may encounter some unintelligent blacks or they may read Jensen's (e.g., Evans 1976) work and perceive what they think is empirical support for it. But when confronted repeatedly with blacks who are intelligent, many people with negative attitudes toward blacks still continue to maintain this negative attitude. How, when confronted with information that is (as Festinger calls it) "dissonant" with one's existing beliefs, the process of resolving dissonance has nothing to do with facts; it's just a way of trying to make ourselves feel more comfortable. There is considerable evidence that this kind of irrationality prevails. Are you saying that to handle such conflicts the person with negative attitudes toward blacks tries to construct a rational system to justify it?

McGuire: Yes, indeed. The "irrationalities" that you have pointed out are among the things that our theory is trying to account for. Our hedonic consistency (or "wishful thinking") assumption predicts that one adjusts one's expectations and one's desires on an issue so that they agree with one another. And even our cognitive consistency, or "probabilogical" assumptions, accounts for distortions: it predicts that one tends toward consistency either by adjusting one's beliefs to conform to the evidence or by adjusting one's perception of the evidence to conform with one's beliefs.

Evans: In fact, did not Freud use the word "rationalization" to describe a person seeking a good excuse rather than the real reason for his or her behavior?

McGuire: Right. Rational doesn't necessarily mean right, and cognitive consistency doesn't necessarily mean reality oriented. I'm even willing to accept that there are varieties of logic.

Evans: Let's turn to another line of your research. You became noted for provocative research dealing with inoculation against persuasion. Put very simply, your approach seemed to say something like this: If an individual is about to be exposed to some information that might be surreptitiously designed to change his attitude or beliefs, there are ways to forearm the individual so that he would be more resistant to the devious persuasive material.

McGuire: Yes, that puts it well. I would caution that the theory applies not to all beliefs but especially to "truisms"; that is, beliefs that are generally accepted without question within one's culture. With respect to these truisms, people are like somebody brought up in a germ-free environment, and thus appear to be very healthy but typically prove to be very vulnerable when exposed to a massive dose of attacking viruses. The biological strategy is to inoculate such overprotected persons in advance, pre-exposing them to a weakened dose of the attacking material to stimulate the development of resistance-promoting antibodies before the massive attack comes.

Evans: In other words, you're using the biological analogy to suggest that one has to stimulate the production of resistant cognitions to protect people against devious efforts to persuade them. In this case, the attacking material is destructive propaganda rather than a virus of some sort.

McGuire: Yes. I felt that people are vulnerable because one tends to be brought up in an ideologically germ-free environment that overprotects one against hearing things that attack culturally shared beliefs. This leaves the person very vulnerable to propaganda. I drew upon the analogy to biological immunization to develop ways of inducing resistance to persuasion by pre-exposing people to weakened forms of the attacking arguments that would stimulate, without overwhelming, their defenses prior to their being exposed to the massive persuasion campaign. We carried out many experiments using this approach (McGuire 1964).

Evans: How about citing one study of the many that you did in this area to illustrate this inoculation model in an experimental situation?

McGuire: We were testing ways of making people more resistant to massive attacks on beliefs that they take for granted; for example, the belief that penicillin is a good thing. It turns out that almost everyone expresses complete acceptance of such cultural truisms when you initially measure their opinions, but these beliefs prove highly vulnerable when someone makes a reasonable-sounding attack on them, just the picture you would expect for an overprotected belief. How can we prepare people to resist attacks on such cultural truisms? Using the biological analogy we were just talking about, I predicted that pre-exposing the believer to a weakened form of attacking argument would stimulate his or her defenses before the massive attack comes.

Our research shows that a defense-stimulating, slightly threatening pre-exposure to a weakened form of attacking argument is more effective in producing resistance to subsequent massive attacks than is the alternative of attempting to bolster beliefs by giving the person supportive arguments in advance; that is, giving a lot of favorable information about penicillin. We have tried both ways. If you give the supportive defense in advance, it seems superficially to make the belief even stronger, but this is a paper tiger effect. When the strong attack comes, the people who had this supportive belief-bolstering defense cave in as much as those who had received no defense at all. But those who are given the more threatening defense that pre-exposes them to weakly belief-threatening arguments show sizable resistance to the massive attack when it comes. The resistance is especially strong if a couple of days are allowed to intervene between the pre-exposure and the massive attack. It is like getting your smallpox inoculation a couple of days in advance to make sure that the resistance has built up by the time you might get exposed to the strong dose of attacking material.

Evans: Your work stimulated many other investigators to look into this area. How do you feel about that today? Do you feel that this inoculation model is still a valuable one worth pursuing further?

McGuire: I think that its empirical validity has held up pretty nicely as other people have replicated and extended our studies. The theory tends to generalize well from truisms to controversial issues. That it works for controversial issues also is a bit embarrassing. Theoretically, the findings shouldn't generalize to these controversial issues to which the biological analogy doesn't really pertain.

One testimonial to the success of our immunization research is the amount of practical application it has received. Actually, I don't feel so good about this practical applicability for two reasons. I must confess that I felt like Mr. Clean when I started this immunization work because while everybody else was studying how to manipulate people, I was studying how to keep them from being manipulated. But now I appreciate more that the person has to be open to outside influence: if one had to learn everything from one's own direct experience, one probably wouldn't survive. One has to have some basic trust as well as some basic mistrust, as Erikson points out in your interview of him (Evans 1969). In principle, one could make anybody resistant by turning him into a catatonic schizophrenic so that he becomes completely oblivious to outside influence. Immunizing somebody against change isn't always very healthy for the reason that people do have to be open to outside influence.

I am also uneasy because subsequent developments in advertising show that our immunization research can be used for questionable purposes. I remember a call I got from an advertising agency bigwig just after this research was publicized. He said, "Very interesting, Professor: I was really delighted to read about it." Somewhat righteously I replied, "Very nice of you to say that, Mr. Bigwig, but I'm really on the other side. You're trying to persuade people, and I'm trying to make them more resistant." "Oh, don't underrate yourself, Professor," he said. "What you're doing will be very helpful to us in reducing the effectiveness of our competitors." And so it has turned out. Before our immunization research, advertisements always ignored the opposition as if it didn't exist. But now mentioning the other brands and deflating their claims is becoming almost standard in the advertising of many product classes. Our immunization research has brought home to the ad agencies that with audiences likely to be exposed to strong ads for competing brands, it is more efficacious to mention the opposition claims in advance, but in weakened form that builds up resistance to them.

Evans: That's right. Now Coca-Cola mentions Pepsi and the margarine ads mention the "high-priced spread."

McGuire: Right. Embarrassing!

Evans: Another area of research in which you have worked is individual differences in persuasibility. There is a history of this type of research that started with hypnosis and suggestibility, when questions were asked as to whether passive people, or if males or females, differed in susceptibility to hypnosis. It involved the idea that perhaps certain individuals and certain groups are more persuasible than others. In fact, the study of individual differences is one of the oldest, but still one of the most perplexing problems in psychology. Could you tell us a little bit about your thinking as you got into this field and how you feel about that field today?

McGuire: I think my getting involved in this susceptibility work, as well as the immunization work we just discussed, may have derived in part from the notoriety of the "brainwashing" episodes during the Korean War and in the show trials in the Socialist countries. Many of us wondered if there was some way of making people more resistant to propaganda and whether one could predict which individuals were likely to be most susceptible to it. Work on this latter issue gets us into the area of individual differences, which is, as you say, one of psychology's oldest and most persisting areas of interest. Paradoxically, the two great discoveries of psychology are: first, that basically everybody is the same; and second, that everybody is fundamentally different. We are all persuadable, but some of us are more persuadable than others. I developed a theory (McGuire 1968) with six basic postulates and two corollaries to answer questions about individual differences in persuasibility, such as, how intelligence (or self-esteem or anxiety) relates to persuasibility. Our theory is a complicated one, but it is formulated to account for a complex set of results. If you're trying to explain a pretzel-shaped universe, you may need a pretzel-shaped theory.

Evans: So you can't deal with the problem in quite the simplistic way as the post-Korean War United States Army did. They supplied each American solider with a ready-made set of beliefs to protect them from the pressures of communist "brainwashing."

McGuire: No. We find that frequently relationships between individual difference variables and persuasibility are nonmonotonic (first showing a positive and then a negative relationship). And often how an individual difference variable relates to persuasibility reverse, depending on other factors in the situation (that is, the relationships are in the form of interaction effects).

Evans: As you know, in recent years in American psychology there has been a revitalization of interest in "cognitive psychology." Already the field of communication has developed and applied some very interesting information-processing models, including your "matrix of persuasion" model of persuasive communication. This matrix is an input/output model in which the communication input is divided into sets of independent variables (source, message, channel, etc.) and the output persuasive impact is divided into successive dependent variable steps of attention, comprehension, yielding, etc. This model can serve as a primer for the analysis of verbal interchange. Since it enters into your personality-persuasibility theory, would you describe your communication/persuasion matrix here?

McGuire: Well, this input/output model is a common description of the communication process. While not startling, it does serve to organize and integrate economically most of what has been learned from attitude change research, and it suggests new hypotheses yet to be tested. I've recently published (McGuire 1978) an elaborated version of this input/output matrix in which I divided the communication input factors into dozens of classes and subclasses of independent variables; and the output, persuasive effect, side into twelve steps, each with numerous subheadings. Then I indexed seven thousand studies on persuasion in terms of the variables in this expanded input/output matrix.

Evans: A basic implication of your communication/persuasion matrix is that any communication input factor—for example, a personality characteristic of the target person—will affect the persuasive output according to that personality trait's impact on each of the mediating output steps, like attention, comprehension, yielding, etc. Could you give us an example of how this works?

McGuire: All right. Consider the question, "How is intelligence related to persuasibility?" The thoughtful lay person tends to answer that the two variables are probably negatively related; that is, the more intelligent one is, the less susceptible one is to being persuaded. Ask why, and this thoughtful lay person might say that the more intelligent one is, the more information one has, the more critical ability one has, the more one is willing to maintain a deviant opinion, and so on, all of which tend to make one more resistant to persuasion by lessening one's tendency to yield to the arguments that one receives. This analysis is probably cor-

rect as far as it goes, but it focuses only on the yielding mediator and ignores other mediators of being influenced, like how much the person at-
tends to the message, understands its contents, retains them in memory,
etc. These reception mediators also affect persuasive impact. When we
consider these reception mediators, being intelligent makes one more susceptible to persuasion by making one a better attender, understander,
retainer, etc. of the persuasive arguments. Hence, being more intelligent
makes one both more vulnerable to persuasion via these reception
mediators and less vulnerable to persuasion via the yielding mediator.
What the bottom line will be, whether those with more intelligence will
be higher or lower in persuasibility, depends on the interacting situational factors. For example, in situations where the message is complicated so
that there is a lot of variance in the reception mediators, persuasibility
goes up with intelligence. On the other hand, as situations become more
suspicious and controversial, so that there is more variance in yielding,
susceptibility will be negatively related to intelligence.

Evans: Could you give an example of how this works in a practical
situation?

McGuire: A good example would be the results of the *Why We Fight*
indoctrination program, to which the U.S. Army personnel were exposed in World War II. It included Frank Capra's films, such as *The
Battle of Britain, Our Russian Ally,* etc., designed to convince the U.S.
soldiers, among other things, that Allied countries were doing their
share. Research has shown (Hovland, Lumsdaine, and Sheffield 1949)
that the more educated the soldier was, the more he was influenced by
these propaganda films. This finding is opposite to the lay person's com-
mon-sensical expectation that intelligence, education, and other cognitive abilities will make one less persuadable. Such common-sense analysis focuses too much on the yielding mediator and overlooks the role of
the attention, comprehension, etc., mediators in making the intelligent
person more susceptible to persuasion.

Evans: In this theory of individual differences in persuasibility, just
like in your cognitive consistency work that we discussed earlier, it seems
that you were stressing a rational view of the person even before cognitive psychology once again became fashionable. Since your work has
often gone against the fashions, it must have been subjected to some criticism. To you, which of these criticisms were the most important?

McGuire: Your question puts the finger on the major criticism of my
approaches, both in the cognitive structure work and again here in the
personality and persuasibility work. Critics have complained (with some
justification) that I overstress intellectualizing by the person. The criticism is that my theoretical analyses often assume that the person is
more deliberative, more intellectually analytical, than people really are.
It is indeed the case that I take as a working hypothesis that people are
cognitively coherent to a rather high degree. In part, this overstress is
adopted as a corrective to the prevalent neglect by most theorists of this
coherent aspect of the person. It also represents the unfortunate necessity

in research of focusing on the partial aspects of the person whom one is investigating, often to the neglect of other important aspects. But while there is an overstress on the rationality of the person in my theorizing, it should be recognized that I have not been implying that this rationality occurs on the conscious level. Rather, it is an "as if" rationality. I assume that the person operates "as if" he or she were a logical and subjective probability theorist. But I rather assume that his or her tendencies occur in the deep structure and not on the conscious level.

Evans: You just mentioned your views on the nature of research. Turning to these philosophy of science considerations, how do you feel now about the plea you made in papers a few years ago (McGuire 1969, 1973) that social psychologists should move out of the laboratory to real-life settings in the field?

McGuire: I now feel that this prescription will treat only the symptoms and not the underlying malaise. I feel that a more basic philosophical reorientation is needed, a strategic change rather than the mere change of tactics in switching from laboratory to field. I still criticize our laboratory-oriented doctoral programs in psychology for training students to be stage managers rather than theory developers. That is, we are training our students to be skilled not so much in testing hypotheses as in staging laboratory experiments to bear out those hypotheses. In our "experimental social psychology" doctoral programs, the student is taught, in effect, to think up some hypothesis that is obviously true under certain conditions and then to try to create in the laboratory circumstances that bear out the hypothesis. In practice, the student learns that if one's initial laboratory test does not come out right, one then decides that one didn't set up the right circumstances and one fiddles around with the experimental conditions until it works. One might decide that the experimenter should look older and wear a white coat, or perhaps that one should use a more controversial issue, or switch from volunteer to paid subjects, etc. The skillful and admired experimental social psychologist is one who has a creative knack for setting things up "right" in the laboratory. I had hoped that a switch to field research, using the real world to test our hypotheses, would result in some ecological validity in contrast to the bizarre or abstruse situations created by the stage managing adepts in the laboratory.

Evans: Are you implying that you no longer think that we should have more field research?

McGuire: Oh, I still think that more field research would be a desirable corrective to the overemphasis on laboratory studies. While field experiments are more difficult, they are obviously more reality oriented. What I have realized with disappointment is that in training students to be field researchers, we may not turn out stage managers but instead develop what in real estate are called "finders." So a clever and admired field researcher is one with a creative knack for finding those special places in the natural world where the same kind of hypothesis (one that is obviously true given the right circumstances) will come out right. Rather than demanding skills in using empirical observation to develop our theories, these finders develop intuitive sensitivity to real life situations that enables them to recognize the right testing circumstances, those implicit in the thinking that gave rise to the hypothesis.

Evans: What is your current view of the problem and the solution?

McGuire: I think we must change our conception of both the hypothesis-generating and the hypothesis-testing aspect of research. We should recognize that all of our hypotheses tend to be true under certain circumstances. To stress the paradoxical, let me say that not only are all plausible hypotheses true but so also are the opposites of each of these hypotheses, once again given the right circumstances. For example, it is a reasonable hypothesis that I like best those who are most like me, and under certain circumstances this is undoubtedly the case. But it is also plausible to assert the opposite hypothesis, that under certain circumstances I would more like people who are unlike me. For example, in playing tennis I may prefer a partner of the same gender as myself, while in marriage I may prefer a spouse of the opposite gender.

Evans: Are you saying that all hypotheses are equally true, or that there is no need for empirical research to test hypotheses?

McGuire: Not quite the first (although I do agree with Blake that "everything possible of being believed is an image of truth") and definitely not the second. I think that empirical research is a vital part of the discovery process. But I take its function to be not in testing whether or not our hypothesis is true but rather in clarifying what our hypothesis means. One should carry out research to discover the circumstances under which the hypothesis is true and those under which it does not obtain. I think that the most useful information for advancing our knowledge is in those pre-studies exposing when the hypothesis does and does not work. What I am urging is that lab and field researchers design their studies and their reports to capitalize on this discovery process, seeking and reporting circumstances that both support and refute the hypothesis. I call this approach "interactionalism" (McGuire 1980).

Evans: Does interactionalism propose that we change in any basic way our view of what we are doing or the way we do it?

McGuire: Yes. Researchers and editors who serve as gatekeepers on what gets published and study-section members who determine what research proposals get funded should promote research designed and reported in this programmatic way, which recognizes that any given hypothesis is of limited validity and that experimentation should be designed to show the circumstances in which it does not obtain as well as the circumstances in which it does. Any hypothesis or theory, indeed any item of knowledge, is a very partial view of what it is describing. I am proposing that we recognize this limitation and, instead of trying to determine which hypothesis is right, we endeavor to discover through empirical research the circumstances under which a given hypothesis is right and those under which it is wrong, thereby enhancing our grasp of the theoretical housing in which the hypothesis fits.

REFERENCES

Evans, R. I. 1969. *Dialogue with Erik Erikson*. New York: Dutton.
_____. 1973. *Jean Piaget: The man and his ideas*. New York: Dutton.
_____. 1976. *The making of social psychology*. New York: Knopf.
Festinger, L. 1957. *A theory of cognitive dissonance*. Evanston, Ill.: Row, Peterson.
Hovland, C. I., Lumsdaine, A. A., and Sheffield, F. D. 1949. *Experiments on mass communications*. Princeton: Princeton University Press.
Hull, C. L., Hovland, C. I., Ross, R. T., Hall, M., Perkins, D. T., and Fitch, F. B. 1940. *Mathematico-deductive theory of rote learning*. New Haven: Yale University Press.
McGuire, W. J. 1960. A syllogistic analysis of cognitive relationships. In *Attitude organization and change*, eds. C. I. Hovland and M. J. Rosenberg. New Haven: Yale University Press.
_____. 1961. Effects of serial position and proximity to "reward" within a demonstration film. In *Student response in programmed instruction*, ed. A. A. Lumsdaine. Washington, D.C.: National Research Council.
_____. 1964. Inducing resistance to persuasion. In *Advances in experimental social psychology*, Vol. 1, ed. L. Berkowitz. New York: Academic Press.
_____. 1968. Personality and susceptibility to social influence. In *Handbook of personality theory and research*, eds. E. F. Borgatta and W. W. Lanbert. Chicago: Rand McNally.
_____. 1969. Theory-oriented research in natural settings. In *Interdisciplinary relationships in the social sciences*, eds. M. Sherif and C. W. Sherif. Chicago: Aldine.
_____. 1973. The yin and yang of progress in social psychology. *J. Pers. Soc. Psychol.* 26: 446–56.
_____. 1978. The communication/persuasion matrix. In *Evaluating advertising*, eds. B. Lipstein and W. J. McGuire. New York: Advertising Research Foundation.
_____. 1979. The probabilogical model of cognitive structure and attitude change. In *Cognitive responses in persuasion*, eds. T. Brock, T. Ostrom, and R. Petty. Hillsdale, N.J.: Earlbaum.
_____. 1980 (in press). The development of theory in social psychology. In *The development of social psychology*, eds. R. Gilmour and S. Duck. London: Academic Press.

SELECTED READINGS

McGuire, W. J. 1960. A syllogistic analysis of cognitive relationships. In *Attitude organization and change*, eds. C. I. Hovland and M. J. Rosenberg. New Haven: Yale University Press.
McGuire, W. J. 1964. Inducing resistance to persuasion. In *Advances in experi-*

mental social psychology, Vol. 1, ed. L. Berkowitz. New York: Academic Press.

McGuire, W. J. 1968. Personality and susceptibility to social influence. In *Handbook of personality theory and research,* eds. E. F. Borgatta and W. W. Lanbert. Chicago: Rand McNally.

McGuire, W. J. 1969. Theory-oriented research in natural settings. In *Interdisciplinary relationships in the social sciences,* eds. M. Sherif and C. W. Sherif. Chicago: Aldine.

McGuire, W. J. 1973. The yin and yang of progress in social psychology. *J. Pers. Soc. Psychol.* 26: 446–56.

McGuire, W. J. 1979. The probabilogical model of cognitive structure and attitude change. In *Cognitive responses in persuasion,* eds. R. Petty, T. Brock and T. Ostrom. Hillsdale, N.J.: Earlbaum.

16

STANLEY MILGRAM
(1933–   )

Stanley Milgram completed his work for the Ph.D. at Harvard University in 1960 and became an assistant professor of psychology at Yale University for several years before returning to Harvard where in the department of social relations he joined the faculty in experimental social psychology. Since 1967 he has directed doctoral studies in social psychology at the Graduate Center of the City University of New York. Dr. Milgram began to explore conformity pressures and the effects of authoritarianism, a study which led to his highly controversial demonstration of blind obedience to authority. His research has consistently evolved out of creative approaches to such social problems as the effects of life in large cities, and the American Association for the Advancement of Science awarded him its Prize for Research in Social Psychology in 1964. His innovative approaches have included an award-winning film, The City and the Self.

Just How Far Will a Person Go?/Obedience to Authority//Better/Worse// The Same as Me/Conformity or Obedience with Some Social Implications//You Don't Know There Will Be Stress/Ethics in Psychological Research//The Experience of Living in Cities//

Dr. Milgram and I begin our talk with the widely discussed experiment on obedience to authority. He describes the development of this study and the way in which it was carried out, and he reacts to some of the criticisms that have been directed toward it. "I'm convinced much of the criticism," he states, "whether people know it or not, stems from the results of the experiment. If everyone had broken off at slight shock or even moderate shock, this would be a very reassuring finding and who would protest?" He distinguishes between the concepts of conformity and obedi-

*ence and points out their significance for society. We discuss
the problem of ethics in psychological research, and particularly
the issues raised by the obedience-to-authority study and Philip
Zimbardo's Stanford prison simulation. Dr. Milgram then moves
to his research involving the experience of living in the city and
why he thinks this work is so important. In conclusion, he describes the studies that have been most meaningful to him, and
some of his plans for the future.*

Evans: Dr. Milgram, in looking over your very interesting career in
social psychology, one can't help but be impressed by the apparently
high regard that you had for the eminent, innovative, social psychologist
Solomon Asch, how he influenced you, and how, in fact, his work on
conformity to group pressure (Asch 1958) obviously had a marked efect
on some of your work. One of your experiments has received particularly wide attention. It was a kind of outgrowth of the group-pressure
study, testing just exactly what people will do under pressure from an experimenter, a scientist in a kind of laboratory setting. How did you happen to begin thinking in terms of this type of experiment? Maybe you
would describe it briefly for us.

Milgram: Very often, when there's an idea, there are several points of
origin to it. It doesn't necessarily develop in linear fashion from what one
has been working on previously. I was working for Asch in Princeton,
New Jersey, in 1959 and 1960. I was thinking about his group-pressure
experiment. One of the criticisms that has been made of his experiments
is that they lack a surface significance, because after all, an experiment
with people making judgments of lines has a manifestly trivial content.
So the question I asked myself is, How can this be made into a more hu-
manly significant experiment? And it seemed to me that if, instead of
having a group exerting pressure on judgments about lines, the group
could somehow induce something more significant from the person, then
that might be a step in giving a greater face significance to the behavior
induced by the group. Could a group, I asked myself, induce a person to
act with severity against another person? And since my natural inclination is to get right to the bottom line of things, I envisioned a situation
very much like Asch's experiment in which there would be a number of
confederates and one naive subject, and instead of confronting the lines
on a card, each one of them would have a shock generator. In other
words, I transformed Asch's experiment into one in which the group
would administer increasingly higher levels of shock to a person, and the
question would be to what degree an individual would follow along with
the group. That's not yet the obedience experiment, but it's a mental step

in that direction. Then I wondered how one would actually set it up. What would constitute the experimental control in this situation? In Asch's experiment, there is a control—the proportion of correct judgments the person makes in the absence of group pressure. So I said to myself, Well, I guess I would have to study a person in this situation in the absence of any group pressure. But then how would one get the person to increase the shocks? I mean, what would be the force that would get him to increase the shocks? And then the thought occurred that the experimenter would have to tell him to give higher and higher shocks. Just how far will a person go when an experimenter instructs him to give increasingly severe shocks? Immediately I knew that that was the problem I would investigate. It was a very excited moment for me, because I realized that although it was a very simple question, it would admit itself to measurement, precise investigation. One could see the variables to be studied, with dependent measure being how far a person would go in administering shocks.

Evans: Well, let's be a little bit more specific. We could talk about authority in the form of the experimenter, or we could talk about group pressure, acquiescence to the group. There's a very interesting distinction here.

Milgram: There are both features in common and features that are different. What we have in common is, in both instances, the abdication of individual judgment in the face of some external social pressure. But there are also factors that are quite different. I would like to call what happens to Asch's subjects "conformity," and I would like to call what happens in my experiment "obedience." In conformity, as illustrated by Asch's experiment, there is no explicit requirement on the part of the group members for a person to go along with them. Indeed, the presence of an explicit requirement might even eliminate the person's yielding. The individual members of Asch's group give their judgments; there's pressure to comply with them, but there's no explicit demand to do so. In the obedience situation, the experimenter explicitly prescribes certain behavior. That's one difference. A second very important difference is that in conformity, as illustrated in Asch's experiment, you're dealing basically with a process in which the end product is the homogenization of behavior. The pressure is not that you be better than me or worse than me, but that you be the same as me. Obedience arises out of differentiation of social structure. You don't start from the assumption that we are the same; one person starts with a higher status. You don't repeat his action; you execute his order. And it doesn't lead to homogenization of behavior, but rather to some kind of division of labor. There's another distinction that's quite important psychologically. After subjects have been in Asch's experiment and they are questioned by the experimenter, they almost invariably deny that they gave in to the group. Even if errors in judgment are pointed out, they will tend to ascribe them to their own deficiencies. But in the obedience experiment, the result is the opposite. The subjects disclaim any responsibility for their action. So I think there are factors in common, certainly. We're dealing in both cases with what I would call the abdication of individual initiative in the face of some external social pressure. But there are also these distinguishing aspects to it. And in a broader philosophic way they're quite different also. I would say that conformity—I say it about 175 years after de Tocqueville said it—conformity is a natural source of social control in democracy because it leads to this homogenization. But obedience in its extreme forms is the natural expression of fascistic systems because it starts with the assumption of differences in the rights of people. It's no accident that in Nazi Germany, the virtues of obedience were extolled and at the same time an inherent part of the philosophy was the idea of inferior and superior groups; I mean, the two go together.

Evans: As an example, let me just take a current piece of research that we are involved in dealing with a very fascinating phenomenon in our culture—smoking. Now we have some pretty good evidence, and this is one of the things we're going to be looking at, that perhaps smoking begins as a reaction to peer pressure. On the other hand, we have the very interesting fact that authorities stress that this type of behavior is going to lead to cardiovascular disease, cancer, etc. Here you have at once peer and authority pressure. In terms of this distinction you made, how could you resolve this type of situation?

Milgram: I'll try. First, the word authority is used in many different ways. When we talk about a medical authority, we're talking about someone with expertise. That's not quite the same as the kind of authority I was studying, which is someone perceived to have the right to control one's behavior. When a teenager hears an authority on television saying he shouldn't smoke, he doesn't accept the fact that that person has the right to control behavior. Secondly, you still have these conflicts between peer pressure and authority pressure. In one of the experiments I carried out, it was shown that when peers in my experimental situation rebelled against the experimenter, they tremendously undercut his power. I think the same thing is operating here; you have pressures from an authority, but you have pressures from peers that sometimes neutralize this. It's only when you have, as you have in my experiment, an authority who operates in a free field without countervailing pressures other than the victim's protests that you get the purest response to authority. In real life, of course, you're confronted with a great many countervailing pressures that cancel each other out.

Evans: One of the things, of course, that you're acutely aware of is that, partly because of congressional pressure, partly because of some—what would we say—some second looks at our consciences in the behavioral sciences, we are beginning to get increasingly concerned now about the whole matter of what rights we have with respect to our subjects. When you were doing that earlier obedience-to-authority study, it's very clear that you were operating completely within the ethical framework of psychologists in those days. You debriefed the subjects, and there was really no harm done to the victims and so on. However, in the present utilization of subjects, we are very hung up on the phrase, "informed consent," and this raises a very tough problem for the investigator. For example, do you think you could have done that experiment if you followed the present ethical standards of "informed consent"? Let's say that you were about to engage in an experiment where the subjects were going to be exposed to a certain amount of stress. One type of stress might be the fact that you're going to be ordering somebody to get shocked.

Milgram: Well first of all, before you do the experiment, you don't know there will be stress.

Evans: All right, that's a good point.

Milgram: The subject must make a decision, but we don't know if it's going to be accompanied by stress. Many of the most interesting things we find out in experimentation you don't learn until you carry it out. So to talk about "informed consent" presumes that you know the fundamental consequences of your experiment, and that just isn't the case for my investigations. That's one aspect of the problem; it's not the entire problem, however. There is the fact that misinformation is used in these experiments, that illusions are used. For example, in my obedience experiment the victim does not actually get the shocks, although the subject is told that the victim is getting the shocks. Furthermore, it's an experiment on obedience in which the subject is the focus of the experiment, rather than the other person, but a cover story attempts to deflect attention from that. Now could the experiment be run if we told people beforehand that this was going to be the case? Not in its particulars. It is possible that one could develop a system whereby people are told generally that they're asked to be in a psychology experiment, and that in psychology experiments illusions are sometimes used. Sometimes stress arises. Perhaps a subject pool of such persons who are not necessarily used immediately could be created. They would then be invited to an experiment, having been given the general instruction that these things may, but don't necessarily, happen in psychology experimentation. That would be one way of handling the problem.

Evans: Well, if I may get a bit personal here, since we are talking about the whole area of ethics in psychological research, at the last American Psychological Association meeting, I chaired a symposium in which Philip Zimbardo participated. He took this opportunity to present his Stanford prison experiment (Zimbardo, et al. 1973). He talked in great detail, including slides, and presented the entire picture of what happened to the "guard" students as they increasingly began to assume roles of authority. In fact, this role playing soon led to surprising reality. The persons playing prisoners began to feel this. A reporter from *Newsweek* was there and asked me afterwards how it was that of the hundreds of psychologists sitting there in the audience very few were protesting the horrible things that were happening to the subjects. Now, as a matter of fact Dr. Zimbardo's experiments, and yours, have been singled out in terms of having particularly, shall we say, captured the imagination of those who are concerned about violating the rights of human subjects. So it's only fair, in this total context, to hear you react a little bit to Zimbardo's experiment and whether or not it's fair to group his and yours together. Perhaps neither one of them should be, as you see it, the object of this concern.

Milgram: Well, it's hard to know whether to call the Zimbardo prison study an experiment. An experiment ordinarily calls for many trials; this was a one-shot run through. It was a reenactment of sorts. Many psychologists have said recently that role playing, simulation, is the answer to the ethical problems of deception. Some psychologists, for example, have suggested that my kind of work could be done without any ethical problem through simulation.

Evans: For example, Herbert Kellman at Harvard.

Milgram: Exactly. Well, now we have Zimbardo who does the simulation. After all, he's simulating a prison situation, and what we get is a reaction against that effort. People ought to put these two facts together —that on the one hand, they've been calling for simulation, and on the other, Zimbardo has done a simulation and he now becomes the focus of criticism. One of the points worth making, therefore, is that simulation doesn't seem to be the answer psychologists have sought. The fact of the matter is that in the degree to which the simulation approaches reality, it gives one the psychological substance one wants to deal with. In the degree to which it's a pallid imitation of reality, it becomes ethically unobjectionable, but it also removes you from the phenomenon you want to study. There's one essential detail in Zimbardo's experiment that I don't know about, and that is under what circumstances could the person involved leave prison. Could you tell me that?

Evans: Yes, as I understand it, they really had the option to get out any time they wanted to.

Milgram: Well, I would say that that's a very serious scientific difficulty in the study, because the essence of being a prisoner is precisely that you cannot get out when you want to. Now, there's another question. Didn't Zimbardo give them a fairly detailed account of the experiment beforehand?

Evans: Yes, yes he did.

Milgram: So he also met the requirement of informed consent. Now, is it simply going to be the case that whenever there's something exciting and real in psychology it evokes ethical criticism? He seems to have met two of the requirements that psychologists have called for: informed consent and simulation.

Evans: Of course one of the points that has been made about informed consent is that we're often dealing with a purely phenomenological situation. How can you give informed consent in advance as a human subject in an experiment when the total mass of feelings and experiences and sensitivites, even pain, cannot really be verbalized?

Milgram: Well, I think to some extent that's true, added to the fact that one is very often ignorant of what will happen before an experiment.

Reactions to such situations can be diverse. Ninety percent of the subjects can react in a perfectly calm way; others can become agitated. But then we must know whether psychology is excluding stress and agitation from its domain of study. Do we really want to say that any of these aversive emotions are to be excluded from psychological inquiry? I think that's a question that's yet to be resolved, but my personal vote is "no." I don't want to be put in the position of saying that I'm *for* any kind of experimentation.

Evans: Were you surprised by the reaction to your obedience experiment?

Milgram: I must say that I was totally astonished by the criticism that my experiment engendered. I thought that what I was doing was posing a very legitimate question: How far would people proceed if they were asked to give increasingly severe shocks to another person? I thought that the decision rested with the subject. Perhaps that was too naive an assumption from which to start an investigation. It is true that technical illusions were used in the experiment. I would not call them deceptions because that already implies some base motivation. After all, the major illusion used was that the person did not receive shocks. One might have imitated the investigators who have done studies in traumatic-avoidance conditioning, where human beings are, in fact, shocked to near-tetanizing levels. I chose not to. I thought that the illusion was used for a benign purpose. I'm convinced that much of the criticism, whether people know it or not, stems from the results of the experiment. If everyone had broken off at slight shock or moderate shock, this would be a very reassuring finding and who would protest? Indeed, I would say that there's a tendency these days to make inferences about the experimenter's motives on the basis of the results of his investigations, and I think that's a very pernicious tendency. Personally and even professionally I would have been very pleased if people had broken off at mild shock.

Evans: Were you surprised that they went so far?

Milgram: I was, but even if they had not been so obedient, it would not have prevented my research program. I would simply have studied the variables leading to an increase or diminution in the amount of obedience. And in fact, one could say that the results that I got threw a wrench into the program in that many variables were wished out because too many people obeyed. One didn't have that distribution of responses— that bell-shaped distribution—that would have been most convenient for studying the effect of specific variables.

Evans: There have been statements made by people about both the work of Zimbardo and yourself that I think it's only fair to hear you react to. Some people have suggested, some journalists particularly, that both you and Dr. Zimbardo got involved in experiments that were exciting, interesting, unique, and that because of the uproar about the ethics, you have begun to rationalize by trying to extrapolate from your findings something relating to a bigger picture. For example, in the case of Zimbardo, he has now become a strong advocate for prison reform, arguing that this little experiment will teach mankind how horrible prisons are. In your case, you have, more or less, extrapolated the whole question of the dangers of authoritarian rule in American culture. In your book *On Obedience to Authority* (Milgram 1974a) you go into this. Now, Dr. Zimbardo is not here to speak for himself, but what about your reaction to this?

Milgram: The very first article that I wrote on obedience, "Behavioral Study of Obedience" (Milgram 1963), before anyone had really reacted to the experiments, discussed the societal problem. So it's not true that trying to find the larger application of the issue is motivated by ethical criticism. Beyond that, what disturbs me somewhat is the absence of any assumption of good will and good faith. I believe that a certain amount of good will is necessary on the part of society for the conduct of any enterprise. Criticisms of that sort seem to me to start from some assumption of bad faith on the part of the investigators, which I don't believe has anything to do with the truth, in my case or in Zimbardo's case.

Evans: Were there any criticisms of this particular effort that have troubled you that perhaps we haven't mentioned?

Milgram: Well, I think the question of the limits of experimentation is a real one. I believe that there are many experiments that should not be carried out. I don't oppose criticism becaue I think there's a societal function served by it. The investigator wants to study things. Society, in the form of certain critics, will establish limits. I think the net outcome will be a kind of equilibrium between scientific values and other values, but I don't believe that most investigators, certainly myself, are limited to scientific values. There are thousands of experiments that could be very useful from the standpoint of increasing knowledge that one would never carry out because in one's own estimation they would violate strong moral principles. It doesn't mean that one doesn't think of them. For example, an experiment in which neonates are deposited onto a deserted island and their development watched over three generations, assuming they survived, would be stupendously informative but grossly immoral.

Evans: Well now, moving to another area of your work that is extremely intriguing, we have the research dealing with the experience of living in cities. While in your earlier experiment you were studying obedience to authority and the resulting cruelty, at the same time, beginning to become noticeable were cases like the famous Kitty Genovese case, where we had another kind of, shall we say, horrendous reaction to a fellow man. But in this case, rather than the administering of shock under experimental conditions, the apathy was what was cruel. The work of Latané and Darley (1970) and a great deal of subsequent work has very carefully gone into trying to understand something about the nature of bystander apathy, and also asks: Is there any real altruism in man? The findings of this line of research suggest that there's some cause for optimism. It seems to me that in your analysis of living in the cities (Milgram 1970a, 1970b), in a very broad and fascinating way, you extend some of these interpretations, and so, it might be interesting to hear what led you in this particular direction.

Milgram: May I, before doing that, try to draw some connections between the bystander work and the work on authority?

Evans: Oh yes, certainly.

Milgram: To some extent, a lot of bystander work shows that when society becomes complicated, there are specialized organizations set up, such as the police, which have authority in particular domains, and then people abdicate responsibility to them. After all, in the Genovese case, people thought it was not their responsibility; it was the responsibility of those in authority—that is, the police—to do something about this matter. The particular tragedy in the Genovese case was that no one even notified the police. There's another thing that comes out in some of the other Latane and Darley studies—I'm thinking particularly of the smoke experiment; they showed that a group of people is less likely to respond to an emergency than a single individual. That really shows how ineffectively people function in the absence of authority. When there's no group structure, when there's no predesigned leadership, it can lead to enormous inefficiency. You see, none of these issues is really one-sided. Under certain circumstances, authority is very useful. It wouldn't exist in human society, I assure you, if it did not perform important adaptive functions.

Evans: You might be a little bit more specific about the experience of living in cities.

Milgram: I guess my underlying view is that people are adaptive creatures. To some extent I accept the tone and insight of the Darwinian interpretation. Now I don't want to apply it with a naive directness to the issues I study, but in a general way, I see people as very adaptive. If you live in a town with two hundred people, you can say hello to every one of them as you're walking along a country road. If you live in a town with five million people, you find that it's simply not possible to do that, and so certain standards of behavior develop in response to these demographic realities. Think what it would mean to walk up Fifth Avenue and nod your head, smiling, and saying hello to every one of the people you pass in the course of a half hour; there might be five thousand people. You would be reduced to a robotlike creature who would immediately be shipped off to the nearest mental institution. I think people adapt to realities, and that norms, standards of behavior, in some way reflect these adaptations. I think this is a thought that underlines any explanation of both obedience to authority and the response to the city. Why do we have authority? It must be that it performs some useful function. An organized group of people can deal more effectively with the input from the environment than those who are planless, without direction. Some people think I am implying that there's something wrong in the city, and life is much better elsewhere—say in the small town—but that's not what I'm saying. I'm saying that given any set of demographic realities, there's a certain optimal level of adaptation that has its advantages and disadvantages. In the city, you have the possibility of choice, the possibility of much greater communication than you have in small towns. On the other hand, you can't have the pleasure of saying hello to everyone you meet on a road. In a small town, the possibilities for choice are more limited. On the other hand, there's a closer feeling of community and solidarity. Every set of demographic facts will give rise to an optimal social adaptation. That is all one is speaking about when he's talking about adapting to these realities. But this then comes to create the characteristic feeling and tone of city life. It's true that I can walk up the street and not see anybody I know in New York City, and that's one of the characteristics of the city. It's true that there are norms against intrusion on people, so that if you see two people arguing, it's very unlikely that you will intrude in the situation. But that seems almost to be a requirement of living in the midst of millions of other people.

Evans: In many of your experiments, illustrated by your film "The City and the Self" (Milgram 1974), where you are on location, say, in a subway, you are really studying life on the city streets. But actually, life in the city is, well, we're living in the city right now, sitting here in your office talking. Life in the city is in your home, at a party. Perhaps what happens to be happening on the streets is not even very important. Even as a stranger, I could find social climates in many places in this city that are entirely different from what I would find out here on Forty-second Street.

Milgram: I think you're quite right, but I am dealing with the public life. I think it is important. It's the only aspect of the city to which the traveler has access. It has an importance in itself because it reflects something about the city, and the public lives of different places are enormously different. You're quite right, though, that almost all the work I've done deals with the atmosphere, the street ambience, I notice enormous differences in the ambience of different public settings when going through different cities and towns. You can sense differences in the friendliness, unfriendliness, hostility, suspicion, liveliness, and I thought that these were worthy of investigation. Sometimes psychology becomes so academic and removed from the ordinary nature of things that it has to be balanced by turning attention to them.

Evans: It would be interesting at this point to hear what you consider to be your most important contributions to psychology. You're a relatively young man; you've already become very well known.

Milgram: Well, I'll list some papers that I personally like the best. One would be "Some Conditions to Obedience and Disobedience to Authority" (Milgram 1965), which I think tells the authority story quite well. Another is "The Small World Problem," (Milgram 1967; Travers and Milgram 1969; Korte and Milgram 1970) which social psychologists are not very much aware of, but in certain ways, it was a very exciting study—the idea you could take two people in any part of the country out of two hundred million and you could find an acquaintance network linking the two. It seemed to me a problem with potentially vast technical difficulties that were surmounted by rather simple means. And then I think I would choose "The Experience of Living in Cities." (Milgram 1970). One article that I think expresses my methodological viewpoint very well is not known at all. It's called "Interpreting Obedience" (Milgram 1972), and it's a response to a criticism by Martin Orne. It appeared in Arthur Miller's book, *The Social Psychology of Psychological Research*.

Evans: What are you working on now, Dr. Milgram?

Milgram: I spent last year in France trying to study the mental maps of Paris held by the residents of that city. I interviewed over two hundred Parisians coming from all parts of the city and was interested in the parts of the city they knew and those they didn't. As you know, the mental map may not correspond to the geographic reality, as Kevin Lynch showed in his seminal book *The Image of the City* (Lynch 1960). I want to know what kind of emotional overlay there is on the city of Paris. Are there parts that attract, parts that repel? That is my current area of interest.

REFERENCES

Asch, S. 1958. Effects of group pressure upon modification and distortion of judgments. In *Readings in social psychology*, 3rd ed., eds. E. E. Maccoby, T. M. Newcomb, and E. L. Hartley. New York: Holt.

Korte, C., and Milgram, S. 1970. Acquaintance networks between racial groups: aplication of the small world method. *J. Pers. Soc. Psychol.* 15: (2) 101–8.

Latané B., and Darley, J. 1970. *The unresponsive bystander: Why doesn't he help?* New York: Appleton.

Lynch, K. 1960. *The image of the city.* Cambridge, Mass.: M.I.T. Press and Harvard University Press.

Milgram, S. 1963. Behavioral study of obedience. *J. Abnorm. Soc. Psychol.* 67: 371–78.

———. 1965. Some conditions to obedience and disobedience to authority. *Hum. Rel.* 18: (1) 57–76.

———. 1967. The small world problem. *Psychol. Today* 1: (1) 60–67.

———. 1970a. The experience of living in cities. *Science* 167: 1461–68.

———. 1970b. The experience of living in cities: A psychological analysis. In *Psychology and the problems of society*, eds. F. F. Korten, S. W. Cook, and J. I. Lacey. Washington, D. C.: American Psychological Association.

———. 1972. Interpreting obedience. In *The social psychology of psychological research*, ed. A. Miller. New York: Free Press.

———. 1974a. *Obedience to authority.* New York: Harper.

———. 1974b. The city and the self. Time-Life Films: Time-Life Building, Rockefeller Center, New York, N.Y. 10020.

Travers, J., and Milgram, S. 1969. An experimental study of the small world problem. *Sociometry* 32: (4) 425–43.

Zimbardo, P., et al. 1973. The mind is a formidable jailer: A Pirandellian prison. *The New York Times*, p. 38, April 8, 1973.

SELECTED READINGS

Milgram, S. 1963. Behavioral study of obedience. *J. Abnorm. Soc. Psychol.* 67: 371–78.

Milgram, S. 1965. Some conditions to obedience and disobedience to authority. *Hum. Rel.* 18: 57–76.

Milgram, S. 1967. The small world problem. *Psychol. Today* 1: (1) 60–67.

Milgram, S. 1970. The experience of living in cities. *Science* 167: 1461–68.

Milgram, S. 1972. Interpreting obedience. In *The social psychology of psychological research,* ed. A. Miller. New York: Free Press.

Milgram, S. 1974. *Obedience to authority.* New York: Harper.

17

PHILIP ZIMBARDO

(1933-   )

Philip Zimbardo received his B.A. from Brooklyn College in 1954 and his M.S. and Ph.D. from Yale University in 1959. He held positions at Yale University and New York University before moving to Stanford University in 1968. Dr. Zimbardo has examined the effects of authoritarianism including the relation of authoritarian social systems to the individual and his role in society. To demonstrate in an impressive manner some of his conceptualizations, he simulated prison conditions for a group of volunteer student subjects with far-reaching consequences and significant results. He has generalized the effects of this study to a number of other authoritarian systems. His current research involves a diversified range of ideas, including studies on the effects of shyness on the individual and a model of madness.

Full Circle Back/Moving from Experimental to Social Behavior/Transcending the Limits of Biology and Environment/Cognitive Control of Motivation/ Some Practical Examples/Becoming an Active Controlling Agent/The Individual and the Social Institution/In Order to Change Society You Have to Change Both //Broader Classes of Variables/Time Perspective/ The Single Most Important Determinant/The Implications for Society/ Some Very Obvious Examples//The Dynamics of Human Choice/Individuation/Deindividuation/The Ultimate Deindividuating Circumstance/ Simulating the Experience/The Stanford Prison Simulation/The Relationship Between Research and Social Change /Knowledge and Political Activity//The Process of Becoming Mad/Discontinuities/A Model of Madness//

As we begin our discussion, Dr. Zimbardo describes how his career has come full circle. He entered Yale with the intention of studying social psychology, became intrigued by the behavioristic model

199

then prevalent, and gradually, through research based on Festinger's cognitive dissonance theory, moved into social psychology. He tells about his research in the cognitive control of motivation, its implications and practical applications. We discuss the individual and the effects of the psychotherapeutic model, and he contrasts individual and social pathology, concluding that the most effective means of change can come through approaching problems on a societal basis. Dr. Zimbardo presents his very interesting view of time perspective and tells why he thinks it may be the most important single determinant of human behavior. A discussion of his ideas about individuation and deindividuation leads to a description of his well-known Stanford prison simulation, which he believes made a compelling point because it focused attention on a particular problem. "My feeling is," he explains, "that if you believe in your research and in your discipline, then you have gone beyond being a researcher and a theorist; you actually have to go out and bring your results to the people in question because they don't read our journals." In conclusion, Dr. Zimbardo elaborates on his recent work in developing a model of madness and speculates on its implications.

Evans: Dr. Zimbardo, in your work you demonstrate an interesting pattern. You seem to have moved from what we would call fairly hard, experimental training into broader problems dealing with society and the individual. Does that analysis make any sense to you?

Zimbardo: I think, Dick, that in one sense, I've come full circle back to where I was before I got my training as a graduate student at Yale. That training was very rigorous and, I think, very sound, not only in research methodology, but in a kind of Hullian, rational behaviorism. But having grown up in a lower-class, southeast Bronx ghetto, a neighborhood of changing minority groups—Italian, black, Puerto Rican, Jewish—I have always been interested in intergroup relations. I went to Yale with the intention of studying social psychology, particularly race relations. However, when I got there, I was told to begin training rats. I worked with Professor K. C. Montgomery (Montgomery and Zimbardo 1957) for the next several years on research in exploratory behavior in the male albino rat. And after a while, I began to think of doing that as "my thing"—being a laboratory psychologist, running rats, doing rigorous research. Then two things happened that changed my orientation. The first occurred when my mother came up to Yale for a weekend. I proudly brought her into this rat lab where I had several hundred rats I had bred, housed, watered, and nourished from infancy to maturity.

Aghast, she said, "What are you doing?" And I told her that we were teaching them all these wonderful responses, to which she replied, "You're not supposed to be making them smart; you're supposed to be exterminating them!" Suddenly I realized that for a person from a ghetto neighborhood, rats are the enemy, not the Hullian prophylaxis against anthropomorphic subjectivism. The other thing that I think moved me out of that orientation more toward what could be called a social humanism is my contact with the late Professor Arthur R. Cohen. He pointed out to me that here were all these people in the world who were complex and interesting, who often acted in mysterious ways, who had conflicts and problems, and didn't I think that would be more interesting, spending my life trying to understand, and perhaps even help them, rather than just building a better mouse cage and Y-maze? Ultimately, I saw the light in his wisdom.

Evans: And so you really began to move into the kinds of inquiries that led to your career as a social psychologist. You wrote a very provocative book dealing with the cognitive control of motivation (Zimbardo 1969a). As I understand it, you had been looking at the area of dissonance theory, and that led to some thoughts about the way people may be cognitively rationalizing their behavior, or cognitively rationalizing ambiguities and inconsistencies and discrepancies. I wonder if you'd tell us how you viewed this field, and the direction you took in your own research.

Zimbardo: I guess one of the most interesting and important events that occurred early in my career was meeting Leon Festinger just before the theory of cognitive dissonance was published (Festinger 1957). Festinger came to Yale to give a colloquium, and one of the basic, new aspects of his approach was his consideration of the ways in which behavior affected thinking, attitudes, and values. Until that time my whole training in a behavioristic approach assumed that behavior was the end product, and we looked at all the things that influenced behavior. But he opened up a whole new realm of speculation by turning the causal relationship around. Over time, as I began to do research in that area, I began to see that there was a whole other dimension of significance inherent in the dissonance theory approach. Traditional models of human behavior were models that subjugated the integrity of human beings to the demands of external stimulus conditions and dictates of internal biological conditions. My work on extending dissonance theory into the realm of cognitive control of motivation was important in making me realize that it is through our cognitive intervention that human beings transcend the limits of their biology and the confines of their environment. And so I saw in the implications of the cognitive control of motivation a very different kind of humanism than the humanistic therapists were talking about at the time. I began to see that the way the individual defines reality may be the most important dimension of reality; that is, the cognitive, social reality may in fact determine not only how people perceive the world, but whether or not they are physiologically aroused, whether or not a given event is seen as a reward or a bribe, whether they are motivated to approach or withdraw, and whether a stimulant is painful or irrelevant.

Evans: I believe you put a lot of this together in your book, which I mentioned earlier, *The Cognitive Control of Motivation* (Zimbardo 1969a).

Zimbardo: What it was, essentially, was an edited book of experiments. The experiments themselves are largely rigorous laboratory experiments stimulated by Jack Brehm's original research. The experiment I'm most personally pleased about is the one in which we show the extent to which there can be cognitive control over pain. The methodology is sound and the results powerful. We used paradigms borrowed from the behavioristic approach to show that when people have to justify a commitment to a certain kind of decision, they will come to control the impact that a painful stimulus has on them. They can do so to the same extent as occurs when a pain stimulus electric shock, is physically lowered by twenty-five volts. The power of perceived environmental control has not yet been fully appreciated by psychologists, teachers, and parents.

Evans: Let's take a practical example of the control of pain. Suppose someone goes to the dentist.

Zimbardo: Well, all of my early experiences with dentists were very painful, but each time I went back, I always told myself that it wouldn't hurt so much this time, and it turned out it hurt as much or more. Once I began dealing with cognitive control of motivation, I also got interested in hypnosis, because for me, hypnosis is little more than cognitive control of behavior. Hypnosis uses techniques that enable you to believe in yourself; you come to believe that when you say, "It will not hurt as much," you believe in the reality of that statement. When I now go back to the dentists, I believe in what I tell myself, that it won't hurt me so much, and it doesn't. What has really changed is my belief that *I can* control the pain. I may not be able to cut it off altogether, but I can minimize it, and I can do it in a variety of ways. I can distract myself, or I can reconceptualize the experience. I think for a variety of reasons each of us is programmed (at home, at school, and other training sites) not to believe in ourselves. What applying cognitive control would involve is specific training from the time we're very young to believe in the control we have over our physiology and stimulus inputs. This involves thinking of ourselves, not as pawns of fate, not as passive information processors where stimuli come in and responses go out, but as active, controlling agents. We also need to develop confidence so that when we say positive things about ourselves, we believe them.

Evans: How far removed from this is Julian Rotter's (1962) concept of the internal and external locus of control? For example, Rotter argues that the person who is internal sees himself as actually being master of his own destiny, and the person who is external feels like a feather in the wind, a victim of environmental determinants.

Zimbardo: I think to some extent those ideas are overlapping. I see in Rotter's work more of a description of existing differences between people, and what has been coming out of my work is more prescription, that is, ways to improve the quality of an individual's life. In my current work, I'm also moving into an analysis of the social institutions and in our basic socialization training, so that we can come to have a greater sense of control over our own lives. That is not to disparage or make light of the effects of the economic, political, or social forces. My feeling is that all levels exert significant influences; in order to change society, you have to change the psychology of the individual as well as the broader situational forces that exist in any given society.

Evans: Let's look, for example, at the kind of therapeutic process described by Carl Rogers (Evans 1975) and to some degree by Victor Frankl (1962) and others as well. They would also say that what they're trying to do is shift responsibility to the self. Starting from an experimental base, how are you really approaching this problem differently than, say, the self-actualizing humanistic kinds of therapists?

Zimbardo: The therapeutic model, whether it's the humanistic model of self-actualization or a more traditional model, has a basic flaw from my orientation, and that is that it is too individualistic. It deals only with a limited number of people who recognize "their problem" to begin with, and even if any therapy were 100 percent effective, if every single person who went to see Carl Rogers were "cured" and left feeling actualized, it would still have a minimal effect on changing society. What we have to do is to look not at individual pathology, but at social pathology, where we now have "epidemics" of violence, alienation, helplessness, shyness, free-floating paranoia, and the like. Whether it is being promoted by religion, by certain socialization practices, by things happening in school, or business, we must approach the problem as a social problem, not an individual one.

Evans: Kurt Lewin was very interested in what he called time perspective—the idea that a person can be preoccupied with the past, the present, or the future—and even argued that the time perspective would have a lot to do with survival in certain situations. Lewin's ideas were pretty well supported by the work of both Bruno Bettelheim (1943) and Victor Frankl (1962) that discussed concentration camps, where they demonstrated that those who survived had to keep thinking of the future. In your experiments you pursue a similar idea in a very interesting way. I wonder if you could expand on this.

Zimbardo: In my own intellectual development, I've been looking at broader and broader classes of psychological variables, those that, if they do make a difference, will make a big difference. As you move toward concerns like time perspective, you're moving away from problems that are tightly prescribed, that can be approached with rigorous methodology. You begin to move into the area of philosophical speculation, basic values, and political change. For myself, I am beginning to feel comfortable doing that. The thinking I've been doing about time, very briefly, begins with the assumption that time perspective is the single most important determinant of human behavior, and that it is one of the major aspects of the socialization process, perhaps second only to learning our native language or maybe it is equally important. For me, the concepts of past and future are logical human constructs, not empirical ones, that are invented and promoted by society in a variety of ways; it is upon the conceptions that all mechanisms of the social control of human behavior rely. For example, the young child has only one reality, the immediate and present. Such a child is at the mercy of the immediate stimulus situation.

Evans: The child is incapable of delay of gratification.

Zimbardo: There is no concept of "delay" for the young child who has no sense of the future. The concept of delay requires knowing that if I don't delay, I will be punished; if I do delay, I'll get a reward. But you first have to learn the concepts of future and past. We've been so imbued with belief in the reality of past and future that for many of us the least important part of our life is the present moment. We're insensitive to the fact that time perspective is an independent variable that influences our thinking, our feelings, and much of our daily behavior. For example, you could not have meaningful concepts of guilt, fear, incentive, deterrence, of commitment, liability, responsibility, obligation, unless you had the foundation of past and future. Therefore it is incumbent on society to program into us concepts of referring present behavior to future consequences as well as to past contracts. What I've been doing in my research, with Christine Maslach, is using hypnosis as a technique for altering time perspective. You take college students who have been programmed to be very future oriented, to delay gratification, and put them in an expanded-present orientation, and they switch from being reflective and analytical to being reactive, impulsive, emotional, spontaneous, and sensual. They get totally involved in action for its own sake; they're not concerned with consequences or products, only process and belief.

Evans: Won't certain drugs do this?

Zimbardo: I think one of the attractions of not only mind-expanding drugs, but a lot of the tranquilizers, as well as alcohol, is that they perform a similar kind of function for us. They stop you from being concerned about past and future, and your behavior becomes "uninhibited," that is, liberated from time-bound controls.

Evans: Aren't anxiety, fear, depression, most of the "ills" of our times, wrapped up in this concept?

Zimbardo: Precisely. Now in any technologically oriented, productive society, people have to plan ahead; they have to delay gratification, "save for a rainy day," and we couldn't have stronger people attacking weaker people just because they felt like it at any given moment. So we have to have some mechanisms of social control.

Evans: This is the idea with the prisoners "doing time."

Zimbardo: I was just going to raise that point, in fact. Think of the effect of the concept of deterrence on a criminal. Middle-class people make the laws and enforce them. They say that they wouldn't commit a certain crime because it would get them fired or get them five years in jail. They may act on this knowledge but those laws are most likely to be really applied to lower-class people. Even so, they are not as likely to be deterred by a future-time perspective as the middle class. This argument goes on to suggest that lower-class people have a vague or nonfunctional sense of the future. To have a sense of the future, you have to have faith in the future—that is, when you plan ahead, the rewards will be waiting—and further, you have to have a relatively stable environment. Lower-class people learn to cope with an environment that is neither stable nor benign, one that discourages faith. Consider the classic studies done by Mischel (1958, 1962) and others on delay of gratification. You tell a young child that he can have a candy bar immediately, but if he waits ten minutes, he can have two. At a very young age, when the experimenter leaves the room, the kid will eat the candy bar immediately. He hasn't learned the concept of "future" so the temptation of now wins out over the promise of later. At some older age, the middle-class child will wait and reap the reward of the two candy bars. Now think of the same experiment done in the ghetto. The experimenter tells a lower-class nine-year-old, "You can have one candy bar now, but if you wait ten minutes, I'll give you two." The kid waits ten minutes, and the experimenter says, "Sorry, but they were stolen from me (or I lost my job, etc.) so I can't give you any." You continue this type of training in faith-violation until at some point the kid will behave in a way that looks totally irrational to an observer when he says, "I want the little slice now. I'm not going to wait for pie-in-the-sky." His belief that the future will pay off has been extinguished. What happens then is that you get this terrible negative feedback cycle. One of the reasons your're poor, or in a ghetto, is that you have not learned to delay gratification; you have not learned to plan ahead, to sacrifice pleasure for progress. Unless you do, you can't break out.

Evans: So you have been looking at time perspective as a not frequently enough observed factor that contributes to making a person a victim. And being a victim deindividuates a person; he loses his individuality. You set up one of the most intriguing and controversial social psychological experiments in the last forty or fifty years, when you took some of these ideas into a simulation, I emphasize *simulation* because I think that's one of the areas of misunderstanding about your "prison experiment."

Zimbardo: Actually, there are two threads of thought that merged to become this Stanford prison simulation—one purely theoretical, the other social and pragmatic. In an anticle called "The Human Choice" (Zimbardo 1969b), I speculated quite freely about the dynamics of human choice. We are each aware of our individuality, of our mortality, of our degree of social fit, of our concern for what others think about us. Those are the forces of individuation, reason, and order; we see ourselves as consistent over time and situation. We are constantly evaluating our own behavior so that behavior is under the control of our past and our future conceptions, under the control of rules, of laws, of norms, of social expectations. On the other hand, there is in each us, I believe, the deindividual self, the child who takes what he or she wants. There is not the concern for past and future, but concern for the present, enjoying life to the fullest right at this very moment. It's what you experience when you get drunk or when you get stoned. In a sense, it's "stepping out of yourself." Your behavior is totally responsive to the forces in the immediate physical and social environment, so you can become part of a lynch mob or part of a sexual orgy with equal facility. From thinking like this, I began speculating on what the constraints on human behavior are, and what kinds of things liberate behavior from these typical constraints. So I began doing research on deindividuation, and one aspect of deindividuation is anonymity. If no one knows who you are, or no one cares, then one of the main constraining influences on doing what is "good," "proper," "appropriate" is eliminated. We began doing research on the effects of anonymity on aggression, and we demonstrated in laboratory and field studies that conditions that make people feel anonymous facilitate antisocial behavior.

Evans: What kinds of antisocial behavior specifically?

Zimbardo: Cheating, lying, cursing, physical and verbal aggression, and vandalism, all are shown to be facilitated by conditions of perceived anonymity. In this deindividuated state, as it relates to time, there's also a sense of expanded present; behavior is not as much controlled by the past and future. You get this deindividuation where social responsibility is diffused in a group, where you're in an altered state of consciousness, where you're physically involved in an action, a process, and not in pro- ducing a product. This kind of research led me to wonder what happens when the social environment makes everyone anonymous. Well, I then began thinking about prison as the ultimate deindividuating circum- stance. I decided that it was important to me to understand more about prison experience. I tried to gain access to some of the local prisons, but was denied for various reasons. So we decided to simulate a prison en- vironment, maximizing the deindividuating properties of it—taking away people's names and identities, giving them numbers, substituting role and function for identity and human values, and putting people in an environment where we took away their sense of time and their liberty to avoid or escape one another.

Evans: So this was a functional simulation of a prison?

Zimbardo: We did not try to create a literal translation of a prison. We had some of the mundane realities of a prison; there were bars on the doors, there were guards with billy clubs and prisoners in uniforms, as well as visiting hours from parents and friends. The important thing was that we had previously done a social-psychological analysis of the nature of imprisonment, and we tried to recreate that cognitive aspect, that phe- nomenology in our subjects. For example, we had learned through talk- ing to a number of prisoners and guards and reading much of the avail- able literature that one of the things that a prison environment does is try to emasculate male prisoners. To be masculine and antisocial means to be very dangerous, because then you are aggressive, assertive, independent. By emasculating you in a variety of ways—by promoting homosexuality, by making you dependent, by making you behave in regressive ways, by giving you no control over any aspects of your life—it's easier to run a prison. So we put our prisoners in smocks, with no underclothes. In real prisons they don't do that, but by doing this we immediately created a psychological set in which young, virile males felt more like a woman than a man.

Evans: Now, what kind of people populated your prison?

Zimbardo: We put an ad in both the student newspaper and the city newspaper that simply said, "Wanted: Volunteers for an experiment on prison life—$15 a day. The experiment will last two weeks." We got about one hundred callers. We screened about twenty-five over the phone; we didn't want anybody with prior prison experience. Craig Haney and Curt Banks personally interviewed each of the remaining seventy-five in a long clinical interview and gave them a battery of a dozen psychological tests. Then we picked out twenty-four of the applicants, who, on all dimensions, we felt were most average, most normal, most representative of middle-class, intelligent youth. We randomly assigned half of them to be guards and half of them to be prisoners—and they knew the basis of choice in that assignment. None of them were there because they wanted to experience what it meant to be a prisoner—they were there simply to make the fifteen dollars a day. We didn't tell the prisoners they were going to be prisoners; we simply told them to wait at home, and we'd call them when the study was going to begin. However, we made arrangements with the Palo Alto Police Department to arrest them. And so, each one was picked up on a Sunday morning, brought to the police station in a police car, handcuffed, and put through a very formal, very realistic booking. The purpose of that was to deprive them abruptly of their freedom, which is a critical element in becoming a prisoner. The guards were called earlier to come down and help set up the prison.

Evans: Did you give either group any training for their roles?

Zimbardo: No, and once the experiment began, we, as experimenters, had very little input into the guard-prisoner interaction. At that point, we were simply videotaping and observing the drama unfold. We had intended it to last for two weeks, but the pathology we observed was so extreme, we ended the study after only six days. By "pathology" I mean that half the students who were prisoners had emotional breakdowns in less than five days. On the other hand, the guards behaved brutally, sadistically; the only difference among them was their frequency of brutal, sadistic, dehumanizing behavior. But they all did it to some degree. What we had done was put good people in an evil situation, and the situation won. My feeling is that the evil situation will always win unless we begin to train people in our society to very different ways than we now do. My argument is that *society* did the training of our subjects to be guards or prisoners, just as society trained

Milgram's (1974) subjects to be obedient to authority.

Evans: Of course, you're referring to Stanley Milgram's study on blind obedience to authority, where people thought they were shocking other people and were willing to give higher and higher voltage on instruction of the experimenter, despite the cruelty.

Zimbardo: The argument that I'm making is that in both Milgram's study and our study, the training took place not in the experiment, but in society. In school and at home, they learned the meaning of power and blind obedience to authority and witnessed guard-prisoner roles in their various forms (teacher-student, parent-child, doctor-patient).

Evans: Currently, there is great concern in the behavioral sciences over the problem of ethics. One of the most difficult issues has been that of "informed consent." Now, as I understand it, both you and Milgram got, in effect, what amounted to signed contracts from subjects that involved obtaining their informal consent to participate in these studies.

Zimbardo: In fact, it's even more extreme than that. The informed-consent contracts I had drawn up by the legal staff of Stanford University had a statement that said, in effect, "If you are a prisoner, you can expect to have some of your civil rights violated, loss of freedom, harassment, and for this you will get fifteen dollars a day, a minimally adequate diet, and health care." There were no deceptions during the experiment. We told them it was going to be a prison, and in fact it was, but before doing it, we had no idea how extreme it could be. There is no question that people suffered in this. But we and the legal staff and the subjects all made the same assumption, namely, how bad could it be, if we all know it's an experiment, if we all know it's role playing, and obviously they could leave at any time. What happened is that we all were insensitive to the power of social situational forces, and too certain of dispositional power, thus, within a very short time, identify was totally overwhelmed by role. In terms of the ethics, I'm very much concerned because people did suffer, even with "informed consent" contracts.

Evans: You're studying means of trying to alleviate human suffering and here you're causing some of it. For a humanistic person such as yourself, it must have been pretty traumatic.

Zimbardo: Well, it was traumatic. You could argue why not end the experiment after a prisoner broke down. But we kept assuming they were faking. We began to have long discussions about whether our personality tests didn't really pick out the pathology that was there; we kept blaming it on the person, not the situation. I should mention something else that people are unaware of: parents of those kids came down and saw them in that situation, so did friends, a Catholic priest, who was a former prison chaplain, a public defender. Twenty or thirty psychologists and some of their wives came down and looked in through our observation screens. Not one of these people said we ought to end the experiment because they, too, were playing roles. They came down as my "guests," and were in a guest-host relationship, and in a sense, they were more bound by that role relationship than by, say, their filial relationship with their child, or their social relationship with people suffering.

Evans: And in the informed-consent contract, they were given the option of withdrawing at any time. Is that correct?

Zimbardo: Yes, they could have withdrawn at any time; instead of doing so, they asked for a doctor, a lawyer, a priest, etc., and we accommodated these requests. We had a parole board meeting, and the first question we asked was, "Are you willing to forfeit the fifteen dollars a day you've earned for your prison labor if we parole you?" And most of the prisoners said, "Yes." So we said, "O.K. Go back to your cell and we'll think about it." And every one of them did. It wasn't until two days later that we wondered why. When they had reached the point at which they said, "We don't want your money," they should have just gotten up and walked out. I mean there were no guns. We were still playing the game—not consciously—to keep them in, but that was the verbal reality that began to govern all our relationships.

Evans: On the subject of informed consent, you can't really project what subjects are going to experience, can you?

Zimbardo: I would think that what is important in overseeing research on human beings is that there is foremost a concern for any possible danger to the subjects. Informed consent helps minimize that, but especially where it's a new area, you can never be certain in advance. I think where an experiment is judged to be of social significance—there are clear benefits to be gained, but there are also clear risks—approval should be provisional, the human subjects research committee should put a detached, dispassionate monitor onto the study. That person would observe the experiment in progress and have the authority to terminate it at any time.

Evans: You have paid a personal price for this experiment in terms of some of the reactions of the public and of follow psychologists. On the other hand, you have done something that may have a tremendously important social significance. I know for a fact that you have been invited to testify before Senate and House committees. You've been called in to various prisons as a consultant to share your views. Would you say that your work has been more important in persuading individuals to favor prison reform than efforts that have come out of first-hand reports by participant observers in actual prisons?

Zimbardo: I think that for me that is the most critical question of all. It's really a question of relationship between research and social change, and it gets into the whole question of where research ends and advocacy begins. In one sense, we didn't discover anything new from this experiment. But we've used the fundamental characteristics of the scientific method to produce a truth which is compelling. By preselecting subjects who had normal personalities, who had never behaved antisocially, we picked people who were similar to the lawmakers, criminal justice people, and law enforcement personnel. Then by randomly assigning the prisoner and guard roles, we eliminated all of the so-called dispositional explanations of prison pathology, namely, antisocial prisoners and psychopathic guards. We peopled our prison with middle-class people who had never committed crimes nor abused power and found that such an institution has within itself powerful forces that will overwhelm years of socialization, personality traits, and deeply ingrained values. And on the basis of that message, we have been able to get prison officials, as well as legislators, and judges, and lawyers, looking more closely at conditions in their prisons. My feeling is that if you really believe in your research and in your discipline then you have to go beyond being a researcher and a theorist; you actually have to go out and bring your results to the people in question because they don't read our journals. Social change never comes merely from knowledge; it comes from the political activity that knowledge of injustice generates.

Evans: Recently you have been doing research in the area of madness. It would seem that "madness" has been looked at in so many ways— what else is new? How are you approaching it?

Zimbardo: I think I have interesting perspectives in trying to understand the process by which normal people become mad. The basic approach I've been taking is that the process of going mad is essentially a very normal, rational search for explanation for an experience an individual has which is anomalous, some perceived discontinuity. For me, the basic process begins with awareness of source of discontinuity. For example, you suddenly notice that your heart is pounding; there's a sinking feeling in your stomach; you're perspiring; your head is aching; that's a discontinuity because you weren't feeling that a few moments ago. There are other types. One is in your performance. Perhaps one day a man can't get an erection in a situation where he normally does, making love to a woman he cares for. That's a discontinuity from previous performance although there seems to be nothing in the environment that has changed. There are also discontinuities in the natural environment, like an eclipse of the sun or a drought. Life is filled with discontinuities— birth, sickness, failure, death—and for each one that seems significant, human beings come up with an explanation. My research focuses upon the many things that make the search for these explanations into a *biased* search, so that we end up with explanations that other people in society define as "crazy" or "mad." Often, the society provides an explanation or a pseudoexplanation for us, like telling a child he has had a "nightmare" when at some point in his life he is suddenly being chased by lions and tigers, and he wakes up screaming. Where there is no apparent explanation, or no one provides you with one, you are already socially isolated in some way. Sometimes we don't want to acknowledge the "true" cause of a discontinuity, especially if it is a chronic, apparently nonmodifiable state, such as being "ugly," "stupid," "incompetent," "unloved," etc. Then we generate motivational explanations that appear to be more modifiable, such as being impotent or frigid, distracted, hostile, and so on. When the cause occurs infrequently or randomly, or is transient, then any explanation is an "effective" one. The ultimate test of such explanations is whether others with more social power than the person in question accept it as "rational." Because in the final analysis, madness is always an attribution of social inappropriateness of one person by others in his or her society. Some explanations that we come up with are in terms of unseen causes. Explaining observed discontinuities, such as eclipses, lightning, famine, and so on, by saying God, or the gods, were the cause, was probably the way religion started. Now, when you say, "I'm having headaches because there are cosmic forces from outer space causing them," that explanation is not approved in our society, and you would be judged as crazy. But if you say, "God is making me suffer for my sins," there is a large class of people who would accept that explanation as reasonable.

Evans: How are you going about testing this?

Zimbardo: We've been using hypnosis to create states of unexplained arousal to create the experience of discontinuity. A person, under hypnosis, is told that later when he sees a certain object he will experience a sinking feeling in his stomach, his heart will pound, he will have difficulty breathing, and he won't know why. Then we have also told him that it's important for him to find out why, and we've programmed in classes of explanations. My feeling is that different societies and different subgroups in a society give higher priority to certain classes of explanations than others. So to some subjects we will say, "The explanation will have something to do with your physical health." To others, we say the the explanation will have something to do with other people. A third explanation is to search the physical environment. And also, we tell others the explanation may be in their past experience. What we think we've done is produce analogs or models for different kinds of pathology. Thus, a paranoid person is one who sees people as central to the explanation or a series of discontinuous events. For the phobic person, anxiety is channelled into explanations that point to external stimuli in the physical environment. Hypochondriacal persons center explanations for their discontinuities on physical health issues. People who search for explanations in the past, I think, are people who become depressed, who stimulate in themselves guilt and feelings of helplessness. After this posthypnotic suggestion, we run through a standard interview, and what we've been able to show is that normal people come up with explanations that are limited or biased by the categories we gave them. Many of the explanations are very reasonable and rational, but some of them turn out, in fact, to be made—"mad" judged by logical standards. It is the explanation that becomes the symptom, and the symptom is the madness.

Evans: The experience, then, has got to be discontinuous; no one else in the group has it, and they can find no social confirmation for it?

Zimbardo: Well, suppose you experience a discontinuity, and you search for some explanation of it, but nobody else present is reacting the way you are. One of the things you can do is actually proselytize, getting other people to believe in your explanation. If you can convince two people to believe in your madness, then nobody judges you mad because it's the start of a social movement. Other people can think you're crazy, but nobody's going to hospitalize you because you have "followers," "true believers." So I guess my model says: At an individual level, if the person does not have the power of the social resources to get at least two other converts, then he or she is more likely to be judged by other people as mad, and possibly institutionalized. But that same process of trying to explain a perceived discontinuity, I think, is the process that starts social movements and gives rise to intellectual, "disciplined" searches for discontinuities in physics, astronomy, history, medicine, religion, and psychology. Once again, I believe, it is essential for psychologists to deal with such phenomena on both the personal and societal levels if we want to understand the dynamics of human behavior and also to improve the quality of human life.

REFERENCES

Bettelheim, B. 1943. Individual and mass behavior in extreme situations. *J. Abnorm. Soc. Psychol.* 38: 417-52.

Evans, R. I. 1975. *Carl Rogers: The man and his ideas.* New York: Dutton.

Festinger, L. 1957. *A theory of cognitive dissonance.* Stanford, Calif.: Stanford University Press.

Frankl, V. 1962. *Man's search for meaning.* Boston: Beacon.

Milgram, S. 1974. *Obedience to authority.* New York: Harper.

Mischel, W. 1958. Preference for delayed reinforcement: An experimental study of a cultural observation. *J. Abnorm. Soc. Psychol.* 56: 57-61.

———, and Metzner, R. 1962. Preference for delayed reward as a function of age, intelligence, and length of delay interval. *J. Abnorm. Soc. Psychol.* 64: 425-31.

Montgomery, K. C., and Zimbardo, P. G. 1957. The effects of sensory and behavioral deprivation of exploratory behavior. *J. Percept. Motor Skills* 7: 223-29.

Rotter, J. 1962. An analysis of Adlerian psychology from a research orientation. *J. Indiv. Psychol.* 18: 3-11.

Zimbardo, P. G. 1969a. The cognitive control of motivation: The consequences of choice and dissonance. Glenview, Ill.: Scott, Foresman.

———. 1969b The human choice: Individuation, reason and order versus deindividuation, impulse, and chaos. In *Nebraska Symposium on Motivation,* eds. W. J. Arnold and D. Levine. Lincoln, Neb.: University of Nebraska Press.

———, et al. 1973. The mind is a formidable jailer: A Pirandellian prison. *The New York Times,* p. 38, April 8, 1973.

———, Marshall, G., and Maslach, C. 1971. Liberating behavior from time-bound control: Expanding the present through hypnosis. *J. Appl. Soc. Psychol.* 4: 305-23.

SELECTED READINGS

Zimbardo, P. G. 1969. *The cognitive control of motivation.* Glenview, Ill.: Scott, Foresman.

Zimbardo, P. G. 1969. The human choice: Individuation, reason, and order versus deindividuation, impulse, and chaos. In *Nebraska Symposium on Motivation*, eds. W. J. Arnold and D. Levine. Lincoln Neb.: University of Nebraska Press.

Zimbardo, P. G. 1978. *Shyness.* New York: Harcourt.

Zimbardo, P. G., and Formica, R. 1963. Emotional comparison and self-esteem as determinants of affiliation. *J. Pers.* 31: 141–62.

Zimbardo, P. G., Haney, C., Bands, W. C., and Jaffe, D. 1973. The mind is a formidable jailer: A Pirandellian prison. *The New York Times*, p. 38, April 8, 1973.

Zimbardo, P. G., Weisenberg, M., Firestone, I., and Levy B. 1965. Communicator effectiveness in producing public conformity and private attitude change. *J. Pers.* 33: 233–55.

18

JOHN MCCANNON DARLEY
(1938–   )

John McCannon Darley is the youngest contributor included in this
volume. He received his undergraduate degree at Swarthmore
College, his master's in 1962, and his doctorate in 1965 at Harvard University. Influenced by many of the founders of social
psychology, including some in this volume, he represents a
newer generation of social psychologists. His provocative line
of research on bystander apathy with Bibb Latané stands as a
model of the application of experimental social psychological
approaches to significant real life social phenomena. Their
book, The Unresponsive Bystander: Why Doesn't He Help?
earned for them the American Association for the Advancement
of Science Socio-Psychological Award and the Appleton-Century-Crofts Monograph Prize. Dr. Darley taught at New York University before moving in 1968 to Princeton University, where he
is now professor of psychology.

Man Is a Creature that Lives His Life in Groups///"Homo Urbanis," the
City Dweller//Emergencies Don't Come Wearing Signs/ Diffusion
of Responsibility/ Staged Emergencies in Laboratory Settings/
The Strength of Experimental Studies//Ethics of Our Research//
How People Define Ambiguous Events//The Generalizability of
the Effect//Elegant Study by Abraham Ross// Solomon Asch/ Conformity and Deviation//Haight-Ashbury/ A Kind of "Conformity
of Deviance"//Moral Judgment//Functions for Criticism//A Social
Psychological Theory of Personality//

As we begin our discussion, Dr. Darley describes his early contact with
important figures in social psychology at the University of Minnesota, where his father was chairman of the psychology department. He early became committed to the premise that "man

214

*is a creature who lives his life in groups," and he sees his later
work as an elaboration of that assumption. He describes the famous Kitty Genovese murder, when thirty-eight onlookers failed
to intervene in behalf of the victim. Rejecting the idea that a new
type of unfeeling, uncaring man, "homo urbanis" had been
spawned, Dr. Darley describes the genesis of his series of studies
with Bibb Latané in which two factors, the social determinants
of the definition of an ambiguous situation and the diffusion of
responsibility in group situations, emerged as more plausible explanations of the behavior of the so-called unresponsive bystander. Next, we discuss his work on conformity and deviance,
which derived from the work by one of his teachers, Solomon
Asch. Dr. Darley describes a study in which he and his collaborators demonstrated that a subject who behaved as an "independent" in one study could be led to behave as a "conformer"
in a following experiment. This study suggested that the use of
socially acquired information about our environment was more
or less universal, and that "informity" was more descriptive of
the process. In concluding, Dr. Darley discusses his plans for
future work on the social psychology of moral judgment and a
social psychological theory of personality: "I will take the idea
about man's life being intrinsically led in groups and see what
other corners it will lead me to illuminate."*

Evans: Many of the significant contributors to social psychology included in this volume have indicated that there was a historical context
that has influenced their thinking. Looking at your career, and perhaps
even at your earlier experiences at the University of Minnesota, where
your father was chairman of the psychology department, do you remember some of the important figures in psychology with whom you had
contact who influenced the development of your thinking in social psychology?

Darley: Yes, I do. When I was growing up, some of the Lewin Group
Dynamics Laboratory had moved from Michigan to Minnesota, and
Leon Festinger, Stan Schachter, Riecken, and Kelly were all there. I remember listening to their discussions in our living room. I think I gained
from them, and later from Solomon Asch, a real belief in the unclear but
central notion that man is a creature that lives his life in groups and is influenced by the groups around him. Much of what I do simply explores
the ramifications of that and comes directly from those teachers.

Evans: A prevailing cynical statement about our society is that we're
losing touch with our fellow human beings. We are not willing to really

be concerned about the other person, because the final payoff is our survival as individuals. There was a series of events that occurred in various large urban areas that called dramatic attention to our apparent unwillingness to help individuals who are in trouble. Probably the most famous of these instances was the Kitty Genovese case, in which a group of bystanders was unwilling to render aid to a young woman who was being literally stabbed right in front of them. You and your colleague, Bibb Latané, responded to this cynicism about this lack of concern for our fellow human beings with your theoretical and empirical investigations of this problem (e.g., Darley and Latané 1968). Would you tell us a little bit about how you happened to get into the area of bystander apathy? I think this is a historic example of a response by social psychological researchers to a very disturbing social problem.

Darley: Let me see if I can explain it to you in a way that gets lost in formal written presentations, so you can see how we began. As you said, a young lady, Kitty Genovese, had been stabbed to death late one night on her way home to her apartment building. It was later determined that a good many bystanders, thirty-eight, had watched this event. None had intervened. Sadly, none had even taken the safer step of calling the police. This seemed to prove some of the statements you were making that people were becoming terribly indifferent to one another, particularly in the cities. A great many articles were written on the dehumanization of man, and there was the suggestion that we needed to think about a new kind of man, "homo urbanis," the city dweller, who cared only for himself. There was a focus on speculating on the personality flaws of people who could stand and watch while others died. It was almost as if we were reverting to the kinds of explanations used in the sixteenth century, that people were possessed by devils to do such cruel things.

Latané and I, shocked as anybody else, met over dinner a few days after this terrible incident had occurred and began to analyze this process in social psychological terms. Since this research is a case study of a social psychological attack on a problem, let me make a few comments about that approach. First, social psychologists ask not how are people different or why are the people who failed to respond monsters, but how are all people the same and how might anybody in that situation be influenced not to respond. Second, we asked: What influences reach the person from the group? We argued for a several-step model in which a person first had to define the situation. Emergencies don't come wearing signs saying "I am an emergency." In defining an event as an emergency, one looks at other people to see their reactions to the situation and interpret the meaning that lies behind their actions. Third, when multiple people are present, the responsibility to intervene does not focus clearly on any one person. For example, consider yourself driving a car, and up ahead you see a stalled car by the side of the road, perhaps in difficulty. If you're driving and you're the only other car in sight, you're very likely to stop and say, "Hey, do you need help, can I take you to the gas station?" But if there are twenty other cars passing by, then naturally you say,

"Why me? Somebody else could stop." You feel a diffusion of responsibility in that situation and you're less likely yourself to take responsibility. We argued that these two processes, definition and diffusion, working together, might well account for a good deal of what happened.

Evans: So although these people seem to be acting in a selfish and indifferent way, actually there may be a rational information processing going on that would potentially influence even a concerned person in the same situation not to help the victim.

Darley: Yes, it's a very normal, human problem-solving process. People are trying to interpet what's going on and what they ought to do. We may find ourselves reacting the same way; not with apathy, but with conflict, confusion, and concern, without necessarily understanding what actions should follow from our concern.

Evans: Could this be an example of when simply observing a behavior may lead to some misleading conclusions about that behavior?

Darley: Indeed it can. It seems so clear that failing to help somebody is apathetic and monstrous behavior that we don't consider the possibility that there might be quite different causes of the inaction of the people who failed to help. What Latané and I argued, and what the research tended to support, is that we need to consider a very different interpretation of what is going on in the so-called bystander apathy phenomenon (Latané and Darley 1970).

Evans: As you approached this question of bystander apathy, did you begin with the intention of launching some basic experimental studies, or did you feel that this was a problem that had to be explored primarily under actual field conditions?

Darley: When Latané and I finished our analysis over dinner, several things were clear to us. First, that we were talking about a cascading phenomenon in which two or three specific processes were fitting together to lead to a very counter-intuitive result: no one helping. Second, we were both trained as experimental social psychologists and we wanted to conduct experiments in order to isolate each process and demonstrate its function in relative independence of the other. At the same time, we felt that it was important to preserve the emergency character of the situation, so we staged emergencies in laboratory settings that were perceived by the subjects as signaling that there genuinely was a person in trouble or signaling an ambiguous event that was very important for the subject to interpret.

In the first experiment, the most difficult task we faced experimentally was to arrange that the emergency would be plausible to the subject, and that he would know that other people heard or saw it as well. That's critical to the diffusion-of-responsibility idea. It was also important to us that they didn't know how the other people reacted because that was our second process, to be dealt with in the second study on definition of the situation. In the first experiment, we arranged for people to be communicating over an intercommunications network. The victim simulated a fit or seizure and preempted the communication channel, which meant there was no possible way for the subject to know what any other by-stander was doing.

Experiments are sometimes criticized for their artificiality, but I think this demonstrates the reasons why experiments are often useful. We were attempting to show that a single process is going on while ruling out the other process. Of course, that could have been demonstrated in field experiments if you created disasters out in the real world and watched the reactions of the people. I think it's important to notice we didn't do that for ethical reasons. One needs to be very careful about the feelings of the subjects who react to these situations, and having the subject in the laboratory setting, where debriefing is possible, is greatly to be preferred to staging emergencies in the real world. And, if we had done field observational studies (not field experiments), we could not have separated the processes.

Evans: This shows the advantage of experimental studies in the exercising of controls as contrasted with field observational studies, which limit such controls. By creating plausible, staged situations, you were hoping to get the best of both worlds. Is that what it boils down to?

Darley: Exactly.

Evans: As you know, in social psychology there has been an increasing concern with the ethics of such research. One of the ethical questions that could be raised concerns the emotional effect of an emergency situation on a "victim" or "bystander" who is not aware that an event is being staged. Can you carry out such a study if you are bound by constraints of receiving the informed consent of the subjects who participate in the study?

Darley: That was very much a concern shared by Latané and myself. There did seem to be a great deal of social value in the research, and yet there also did seem to be some stresses produced for the participants. We dealt with that by informing the subjects generally that stresses were to be expected in the process of this research, and attempted to give some indication that the magnitude of those stresses might be high. I think we need to be terribly concerned about the ethics of our research to avoid an unreflective willingness to do almost anything to our subjects.

Evans: A whole group of studies, including yours, Stan Milgram's (1974) study of obedience to authority, and Phil Zimbardo's (1973) simulated prison study, are examples of those that have generated interest not only of psychologists but of the public at large.

Darley: They are all studies about evil, and that's an age-old human problem. Man has been concerned with the problem of evil and where it comes from for a long period of time, and it's no surprise that social psychology is concerned with it as well. The studies that capture the popular imagination are frequently those that analyze the conditions for the doing of evil actions.

Evans: Your systematic approach to this problem appears to be a model of sound research strategy. You did not do a single experiment, but examined bystander apathy from several different points of view and completed various experiments. You already mentioned the diffusion of responsibility study, but other studies preceded this one, did they not?

Darley: Yes. We did a logically prior study, concerning the definition of the situation and group influences on how people define ambiguous events. The argument is that at least some emergencies don't come wearing signs saying "I am an emergency." It's necessary that the person define what's going on. When we come to an ambiguous situation, such as an oddly parked car on the side of the road, what we seem to do is look at this until we figure out what's going on. We don't react, we think. And we maintain a rather poker face in our Anglo-Saxon influenced culture.

If I come up on a not very well dressed man slumped over in a doorway by the side of the street there are a good many explanations for what might be going on. He might be drunk, or he might be having some sort of medical emergency. All those things are possible, and before one reacts, before one helps, it's necessary to figure out which is the case. But, let's assume that I stop and look at the person, and try to figure out what's going on. The next person comes up and stops also. For the next person, because I was there first, my reactions need to be considered. One interpretation of my reactions is that I don't know any more than he does. But a second very natural interpretation is that I was there first and perhaps I saw something he doesn't see, or perhaps I know something he doesn't know, and that explains my inaction. Maybe I know information that shows it is not an emergency. Thus he interpets my inaction as giving clues about the event, and decides it is not an emergency. That's the process that we wanted to demonstrate. The ambiguous event we designed was that of smoke leaking into a room of a building (not necessarily wood smoke, just acrid white smoke jetting through a vent in a wall). A person who had come to the building for an interview on urban environments confronted this ambiguous situation.

One interpretation of this situation was that emergency action was required. Subjects confronting this alone behaved sensibly. They didn't panic or run out screaming, "Fire! Fire!" They left the room, found somebody who looked to be an authority, like a secretary, and said, "I don't know if there's anything wrong, but we may have a fire," or "There's smoke leaking in, come see it."

Now what about people in groups? We argued that the presence of other people who were not responding would signal a very different definition of the situation. So initially we wanted to "create" other people who didn't respond. We trained people to act in a nonresponsive fashion, so when a subject confronted the smoke stimulus, he or she was surrounded by two other people who were, in fact, actors. All the subjects were filling out questionnaires and the actors were trained to notice the smoke, make sure the subject saw them noticing it, and then return to the task of filling out their questionnaires. Smoke continued to blow into the room, and they continued to fill out the questionnaires.

This had the effect of pretty well freezing the subject. The response rate here dropped toward 10 percent. In other words, almost everybody

was frozen in place by the presence of two other unresponsive bystanders. There are several ways to interpret this. One is to interpret this as
essentially a stupid act on the part of the naive subject. Our interviews
with the subjects led us to a different interpretation. Many of them had
ideas about what the smoke might be: a chemistry lab next door, or an
air-conditioning leak; but they had ruled out the possibility that it was an
emergency. Under the influence of the other people, they had defined the
situation in a particular way and eliminated certain definitions.

Evans: So in this situation you controlled the responses of all participants but the subject, to see how a person might react to an emergency
situation when those around him are completely unresponsive.

Darley: Yes, and it did occur to us that we might have stacked the
cards in our favor. That is, we had shown that in the unnatural circum-
stance, when two people in the room out of three are working for the experimenter,you get a definition of the situation effect. But it's rather difficult to generalize that to real world events. So we brought together
three ordinary uninformed people and presented the same ambiguous
event. And we discovered the same effect. The people, on observing the
smoke, kept a poker face and didn't immediately respond, and this
caused most groups not to respond to the situation.

Evans: So even without the collaborators, you got the same response.

Darley: Indeed, and it strengthened the generalizability of the effect.

Evans: Let me make a distinction between internal and external validity. As you know, of course, in experimental social psychology, when
we're dealing with well-controlled but artificial situations, an investigation can have a fairly high degree of internal vaidity but may not generalize to real life or even to other experimental situations. For example,
your results may not generalize to other populations or to emergencies
other than those involving a possible fire, and so on.

Darley: Yes, and here other researchers have strengthened our confidence in the generalizability of the effect. Bibb Latané with Judy Roden
(1969) did a study in which the ambiguous situation involved a person
falling down in the next room and perhaps being hurt, and demonstrated
that again the presence of another person made you less likely to respond, because you defined the situation as less of an emergency if the
other person was less responsive.

Evans: What do you do when people ask you to convert this very important type of finding into developing strategies for actually saving lives
in emergencies? This may be the ultimate question of external validity.

Darley: This question is often asked, and Latané and I have discussed
it frequently. We don't have answers that will give us Utopia. We can't
say how to turn everybody in every situation into an appropriate re-
sponder. One may scientifically understand the process and still have no
particular ways of intervening in the process. But in this case there are
some things we can say. First, if we can make people aware of the way
they are influenced in defining events, that process can be overcome. If
you realize that other person is standing there not because it's no emer-

gency but because the other person is just as confused as you are, you may make a more intelligent decision about the situation. One of the things that we found in our studies is that if the other person were not a stranger, but a friend, then you are much more likely to initiate contact and to say, "Hey, am I thinking what you're thinking? We better go check." So one thing to do is to understand the processes at issue. The same thing can be said about the diffusion process. One can simply shift one's thinking and realize that it would not necessarily be bad if two or three people helped. We can cease to punish people for reporting what turn out to be false alarms. We can teach the police how to respond in an appropriate way rather than in a way that seems to punish the reporter.

Evans: What are some of the other studies generated by your work that you think are particularly important in this area of bystander apathy and reacting to emergencies?

Darley: There's a particularly elegant study by Abraham Ross (1973) that takes the notion of definition of a situation and shows that people use it with some subtlety. The notion is that you pick up a definition of what's going on by observing the reactions of other people. Ross created two potential emergencies. One was signaled auditorially, by a loud noise, and the other was signaled visually. He put the naive subject in the presence of a person who the subject believed was blind (unsighted), and he showed that the subject was affected by the inaction of the blind person only if the ambiguous event was an auditory one, not if it was visual. In other words, the subject reasoned, "Gee, that other person heard it, but he isn't doing anything, so there must be nothing wrong," but was unaffected by the actions of the blind person if the emergency was visually signaled because he inferred that the blind person didn't see the signal. This is quite a subtle demonstration of the way one uses complex reasoning in picking up knowledge from other people.

Evans: Another area of your work may reflect on a topic that Solomon Asch and I discussed about a year ago.* We were talking about his work and its implications and he said that a lot of people misinterpreted his work on conformity (Asch 1952, 1956) and missed the point that he was really not interested in damning the conformist but in trying to study independence, individuality, and maybe even deviance. Knowing that you studied with him at Swarthmore, I wonder what observations you would make on Asch's point, and what your own work has been in this area.

Darley: Conformity and deviation has always been a favorite area of mine. I think it's quite clear from Asch's research that he was trying to maintain that the conformer was doing something reasonable (e.g., Asch 1956). But the paradigm has been taken to show that the conformer is a

*Much to my regret, we were unable to complete an interview with Solomon Asch in time for this volume. He has promised to consider doing it sometime in the future.

weak-willed individual. There are perhaps hundreds of studies taking personality tests and showing that the conformers are more likely to be the ones at the bad end of the scale.

I once did a study with Susan Darley, Tom Moriarty, and Ellen Berscheid (1974) in which we attempted to argue that the person labeled as an "independent" in the Asch experiment was as much influenced by the experiment as the "conformer" had been, but the ordinary way of doing the Asch experiment didn't show it. Now, recall: If you surround people with conformity pressure, but provide one other individual who gives the same answer that they do, then the naive subject tends not to conform. All right, so that person in that situation stays independent. But what we then did was run a second half of the experiment, and in this half of the experiment we sent the "independent" naive subject and the person who previously gave him social support off by themselves. We had the social supporter now put conformity pressure on the subject, and the conformity rate of the subject was now very high. In the process of getting social support from the other person in the first place, which gave him the strength to stand against the entire group, he had been strongly bonded to the social supporter. The bonding showed up in the increased conformity with the social supporter on new topics in the second half of our experiment.

Evans: One of the things that was observed in the San Francisco Haight-Ashbury area in the 1960s was that the "hippy nonconformists" were in fact very wedded to a kind of "conformity of deviance." They appeared to be quite intractable in their conformity with the mores of their "deviant" social groups in terms of dress, appearance, and various elements of their lifestyle.

Darley: And it's sadly relevant to this particular age to point out that part of the phenomenon involved in cults is that they regard themselves as being out-groups surrounded by a hostile majority so that they must, for their own survival, conform within their own group.

Evans: As a matter of fact, the conformity pressure within those groups tends to be more powerful than that we find in the so-called majority.

Darley: Yes, people really have a great difficulty living without social support for their opinions. Having no social support for your opinion is a pretty good definition of being insane. There's a terribly high value placed on social support, and therefore the source of social support can put great conformity pressures on you.

Evans: Moving to another area, John, looking back, what criticisms of your work have bothered you the most?

Darley: I think on human terms any criticism bothers us, but there are well-known functions for criticisms within the scientific community. I guess I also see a role for argument. The things I have said that have been less carefully stated, and therefore more validly criticizable, have also been useful. For instance, Latané and I wrote a paper (Latané and Darley 1968), concerning the role of norms in helping behavior, that we recognized at the time was considerably overstated. Essentially we argued that the concept of norm was not a useful explanatory construct. That argument has pushed people into a dialectical process to clarify what's meant by norms and how they might work. It seems to have advanced thinking about norms in a very useful way. I don't want to say that one ought to put out wrong statements, but reasonably clear statements of strong positions seem to be useful in advancing science in a dialectical way.

Evans: What would you consider to be the most important aspect of your work so far?

Darley: There's a consistency in the research I've done. The origins of that consistency are in the notion I mentioned earlier of man's existence being necessarily and essentially lived in groups, and man being a symbolizing individual making sense of the world around him, which is very often a very interpersonal world. At various times, I felt it important to point that out in different specific areas. Certainly the most well known is the work with Latané, in which we pointed out the application of that principle to one set of problems that were being analyzed very differently. The deviance research also was saying that the influence of other people is a very normal process, one that we're all involved in. At the moment I'm concerned with moral judgment and how people go about making moral judgments.

Evans: Would you approach this as an outgrowth of your work on altruism and bystander apathy, or is your work going in the direction of building a model of moral development, like Piaget (1948) or Kohlberg (1969)?

Darley: I'm concerned with specifying the rules by which people— adults and children—make moral judgments. I'm concerned with the content of the rules so that I want to be able to say when we will excuse a child for hurting another child as opposed to saying, "He should have known better." I want to say what the rules are by which ordinary people make those decisions. I think there are rules and I think they are quite elaborate and complicated rules. This emphasis has some similarities with Piaget's program and fewer similarities with Kohlberg's program. Kohlberg concerns himself with the formal properties of the rules. He has not been as concerned with the decisions they come to. One can come to any decision in a case in Kohlberg's system from any stage perspective. I'm less concerned with stages of development and want to suggest that the rules are present in quite a sophisticated way even in quite young children. I think Piaget's insight that rules arise out of social interactions is a very important one and needs to be taken further.

Evans: You are a young man in the field, and you have already attained a lot of visibility. What are you hoping to do in the future in this field?

Darley: I will take the idea about man's life being intrisically led in groups and see what other corners it will lead me to illuminate. Coming up on the horizon is some work on a social psychological theory of personality. Instead of talking about people possessing traits, we need to begin to create a theory that's consistent with what we've learned in the last twenty years in social psychology about how people define themselves in actions and how one defines oneself as a social entity.

REFERENCES

Asch, S. E. 1952. *Social psychology*. Englewood Cliffs, New Jersey: Prentice-Hall.

————. 1956. Studies of independence and conformity: I. A minority of one against a unanimous majority. *Psychol. Monogr.* 70: No. 9.

Darley, J. M., and Latané, B. 1968. Bystander intervention in emergencies: Diffusion of responsibilities. *J. Pers. Soc. Psychol.* 8: 377–83.

————, Moriarty, T., Darley, S., and Berscheid, E. 1974. Increased conformity to a fellow deviant as a function of prior deviation. *J. Exper. Soc. Psychol.* 10: 211–23.

Kohlberg, L. 1969. Stage and sequence: The cognitive-developmental approach to socialization. In *Handbook of socialization theory and research*, ed. D. A. Goslin. Chicago: Rand McNally.

Latané, B., and Darley, J. M. 1968. Group inhibition of bystander intervention. *J. Pers. Soc. Psychol.* 10: 215–21.

————, and Darley, J. M. 1970. *The unresponsive bystander: Why doesn't he help?* New York: Appleton-Century-Crofts.

————, and Rodin, J. 1969. A lady in distress: Inhibiting effects of friends and strangers on bystander intervention. *J. Exper. Soc. Psychol.* 5: 189–202.

Milgram, S. 1974. *Obedience to authority*. New York: Harper & Row.

Piaget, J. 1948. *The moral judgment of the child*. Glencoe, Illinois: Free Press.

Ross, A. S. 1973. Effect of increased responsibility on bystander intervention: II. The cue value of a blind person. *J. Pers. Soc. Psychol.* 25: 254–58.

Zimbardo, P. G., Haney, C., Banks, W. C., and Jaffe, D. The mind is a formidable jailer: A Pirandellian prison. *The New York Times*, p. 38, April 8, 1973.

SELECTED READINGS

Darley, J. M., and Batson, C. D. 1973. "From Jerusalem to Jericho": A study of situational and dispositional variables in helping behavior. *J. Pers. Soc. Psychol.* 27: 100–108.

Darley, J. M., and Latané, B. 1968. Bystander intervention in emergencies: Diffusion of responsibilities. *J. Pers. Soc. Psychol.* 8: 377–83.

Darley, J. M., Moriarty, T., Darley, S., and Berscheid, E. 1974. Increased conformity to a fellow deviant as a function of prior deviation. *J. Exper. Soc. Psychol.* 10: 211–23.

Latané, B., and Darley, J. M. 1968. Group inhibition of bystander intervention. *J. Pers. Soc. Psychol.* 10: 215–21.

Latané, B., and Darley, J. M. 1970. *The unresponsive bystander: Why doesn't he help?* New York: Appleton-Century-Crofts.

INDEX

227